# Sales Management:
# A Global Perspective

As sales managers are encouraged to manage increasingly global territories, the art of selling is more complicated than ever and the rules of negotiation more diverse. This book considers the many facets of cross-cultural sales management, to provide salespeople and managers with a guide to making the most of the global sales force. Topics covered include:

- Cross-cultural negotiations
- Hiring, training, motivating and evaluating the international sales force
- Customer retention
- Sales territory design and management

Included in the book are ten case studies, featuring companies from the US, Europe, New Zealand and Asia, all designed to give sales students, salespeople and their managers an explanation of what diverse cultures entail, and the dilemmas, situations and problems which arise when selling across borders. The authors have international experience of both the theory and practice of selling, and have brought together the most up-to-date information to guide salespeople through the global marketplace.

*Sales Management: A Global Perspective* differentiates itself from existing sales books in that it clearly addresses the global marketplace, a subject neglected by most other texts. While still tackling sales from a managerial perspective, the cross-cultural approach of this volume makes it essential reading for sales management students, and sales managers seeking to succeed in global sales.

**Earl D. Honeycutt** is Professor of Business Administration at Elon University, Elon, North Carolina. **John B. Ford** is Professor of Marketing and International Business at Old Dominion University, Norfolk, Virginia. **Antonis C. Simintiras** is Professor of Marketing and Director of the European Business Management School at the University of Wales, Swansea.

## ABOUT THE AUTHORS

**Earl D. Honeycutt** is Professor of Business Administration at Elon University, North Carolina. He earned the Ph.D. in Business Administration at the University of Georgia and worked in industrial sales and marketing for a division of TRW, Inc. Dr. Honeycutt has previously served on the faculties of the University of North Carolina – Wilmington and Old Dominion University. He publishes constantly in multiple outlets that include the *Journal of Personal Selling and Sales Management* and *Industrial Marketing Management*. Dr. Honeycutt's credits total more than 120 articles in national and international journals and conferences, plus a book: *Business-to-Business Marketing* (2001). He holds an undergraduate degree in history/Asian Studies and is an annual traveler to Asia and Europe.

**John B. Ford**, Ph.D. (University of Georgia), is Professor of Marketing and International Business at Old Dominion University in Norfolk, Virginia. He specializes in cross-cultural/international strategic issues in marketing management. His research has been published in such outlets as *Journal of the Academy of Marketing Science*, *Journal of Advertising*, *Journal of Advertising Research*, *Journal of International Marketing*, *International Marketing Review*, *Journal of World Business*, *Industrial Marketing Management*, *Journal of Personal Selling and Sales Management*, and *Business Horizons*, to name a few. Prior to his academic career, he worked in industry as an international sales manager, management consultant and executive recruiter, and as a stockbroker and bank trust administrator.

**Antonis C. Simintiras**, Ph.D., is Professor of Marketing and Director of the European Business Management School at the University of Wales, Swansea. He has had many years of work experience in industry and holds visiting professorial appointments at various Universities in Europe and the United States. His research interests are in the areas of personal selling and sales management, research methodology and industrial marketing. He has published over fifty refereed articles, and part of his work has appeared in *Industrial Marketing Management*, *Management Decision*, *Journal of Marketing Management*, *Journal of Managerial Psychology*, *European Journal of Marketing* and *International Marketing Review*.

# Sales Management: A Global Perspective

Earl D. Honeycutt, John B. Ford and Antonis C. Simintiras

Routledge
Taylor & Francis Group

LONDON AND NEW YORK

First published 2003
by Routledge
11 New Fetter Lane, London EC4P 4EE

Simultaneously published in the USA and Canada
by Routledge
29 West 35th Street, New York, NY 10001

*Routledge is an imprint of the Taylor & Francis Group*

© 2003 Earl D. Honeycutt, John B. Ford, Antonis C. Simintiras

Typeset in Perpetua and Bell Gothic by Florence Production Ltd, Stoodleigh, Devon
Printed and bound in Great Britain by TJ International Ltd, Padstow, Cornwall

*British Library Cataloguing in Publication Data*
A catalogue record for this book is available from the British Library

*Library of Congress Cataloging in Publication Data*

A catalog record for this book has been requested

ISBN 0–415–30043–6 (hbk)
ISBN 0–415–30044–4 (pbk)

To Laura, Travis, and Cole
To Sarah, Lisa, Kim, John, Jamie and Ainsley
To Mary and Constantinos

# Contents

# Figures

# Tables

# Exhibits

# Foreword

Most texts on the subject of selling tend to relate the subject from a domestic standpoint and do not take into account the broader global perspective. This text examines in detail those more complicated relationships that tend to dominate international selling and explains why people behave differently. It looks at the nature of culture in this context and explains how this can affect the task of selling, so a more 'scientific' approach is adopted in this respect rather than simply through the provision of anecdotal advice.

Guidance is then provided in both the text, and the many international cases that form part of it, as to how, by understanding these relationships, sales management can be successful. This is especially poignant in these modern times, when markets throughout the world are becoming more closely integrated through GATT accords that seek to take away restrictions to world trade and the expansion of trading blocks (e.g., the European Union has just set about its next phase of expansion as this foreword was being written). One of the guiding principles of this book has been 'to bridge the gap between theory and practice' and in this respect it has been outstandingly successful.

The book is useful for both students and practitioners alike and in this respect it is eminently "readable," but at an intelligent level. The three authors are well known authoritative sources on the subject of selling in an international context and each has published, practiced and written widely in this area. The book is well organized and each chapter indicates a number of learning objectives. Practical vignettes permeate the text to demonstrate the relevance of material that has been presented. Chapter summaries assist in terms of providing an effective *aide memoire* as do the discussion questions that can be used in a practical manner for individual or group work. The case studies at the end allow the reader to understand the significance of ideas that have been presented throughout the text.

In terms of its logic, the book contains fifteen chapters that start from a general cultural perspective and then go on to show how these are applicable in the framework of personal selling. It then adopts a more global approach relation to aspects of negotiation and the actual selling process including the contemporary area of building relationships. A more macro approach is then adopted as aspects of building a global sales force are examined. The practical aspects of how this can be attained are explained in terms of selection, training, motivation, compensation and management of a global sales force. Forecasting and its implications for sales force planning is then examined along with strategic issues in a Global marketplace. The text concludes very appropriately with a detailed practical and theoretical examination of a contemporary area of sales practice that relates to Customer Relationship Management.

This is a very well written and presented book that is a valuable addition to literature in the area of global selling and sales management and it has my fullest endorsement.

Professor Geoff Lancaster

*Professor of Marketing, London Metropolitan University, Chief Examiner,*
*Institute of Sales and Marketing Management and Chairman,*
*Durham Associates Group Limited,*
*Castle Eden, Co. Durham, UK*
*(corporate communications consultants).*

# A guide for the reader

The goal of this book is to bring a truly global perspective to the teaching of sales management. This is accomplished by infusing each chapter with theory that is supplemented by practical examples and implications that prepare sales managers for the wide array of contingencies they will encounter. This note is written so the reader can maximize the material presented and enhance their knowledge of the subject matter.

## Guiding principles

There are four guiding principles that provide value to both students and sales managers:

- It is essential to bridge the gap between theory and practice with illustrative examples that enable the reader to clearly understand practical applications of the concepts presented.
- Sales managers must understand the nature of culture and how it affects interpersonal relationships; therefore, cultural basing is integrated throughout the text to enhance the sales manager's understanding of diverse situations.
- World markets are becoming more integrated, and population shifts are occurring in the United States, Europe, and Asia. Successful sales managers must understand these trends and how they impact the real-world practice of sales management.
- Managing a global sales force is a complex undertaking. This book breaks down complex relationships and explains why circumstances happen as they do, why people behave distinctly, and how the sales manager can succeed by understanding these situations.

## Aims of the book

This book is intended to be a core textbook for business classes that focus on sales management at either the graduate (MBA) level or at the undergraduate (BSBA) level. The book can also be used as a selected resource text for a course in international marketing management at the Master's level. The authors have blended their prior work experience in the Triad nations, with their knowledge of the sales management literature, to present a practical and relevant manual for today's sales managers.

## Pedagogic features of the text

- An *overview of the content* presented in each chapter that allows the reader to quickly identify special areas of interest.
- A series of *learning objectives* stated at the beginning of each chapter demonstrates what the reader should accomplish after studying the material contained in that chapter.
- A *case vignette* is provided early in each chapter to set the contextual stage and clearly illustrate the relevance of the material covered in that section.
- A *chapter summary* is provided at the end of each chapter that establishes a mechanism for the efficient review of important material.
- *Discussion questions* are included at the end of every chapter so the reader can test their knowledge of essential concepts and applications. These questions aid in preparing for class discussions and as a review for exams.
- A series of *case studies* are presented in the appendix which require the reader to integrate important concepts and understand their practical relevance. These cases can also serve as a basis for effective group or individual projects.

## Teaching and learning resources

The text *Sales Management: A Global Perspective* web site can be viewed at: http://www.routledge.com/textbooks/

# Acknowledgments

As with any undertaking of this scope, in addition to the authors, numerous people contributed to the success of the project. In particular, the authors would like to thank Francesca Poynter and Rachel Crookes at Routledge for their confidence, assistance, and for keeping us on schedule. My sincere thanks to Shawn Thelen (Hofstra University), a great doctoral assistant who provided invaluable assistance in compiling tables and figures for this book. Others who edited chapters, provided advice, or offered encouragement during the process include: Greg Marshall (Oklahoma State University – Tulsa), Sandra Mottner (Western Washington University), Jerry Xu (Stryker Industries), Angela Pimentel (Astra Zeneca), Leila Borders (University of New Orleans), Ashraf Attia (SUNY at Oswego), Araceli Suzara (Old Dominion University), Wilfred Vanhonaker (UST – Hong Kong), Asri Jantan (SUNY College at Brockport), Peter LaPlaca (Rensselaer Polytechnic Institute), Lew Kurtzman (Growth Resources Associates) and Laurence Jacobs (University of Hawaii – Manoa). Reference librarians at the University of Hawaii – Manoa and Hawaii Pacific University also provided noteworthy assistance in locating Asian reference materials.

Earl D. Honeycutt
John B. Ford
Antonis C. Simintiras

# Part I

# Introduction and culture

## Chapter 1

# An introduction to managing the global sales force

This first chapter is an introduction to managing the global sales force. It provides new, as well as experienced, students of sales management with key and basic concepts that can be carried with them throughout the remainder of this book.

### LEARNING OBJECTIVES

*After reading this chapter, you will be able to:*

- Appreciate the importance of a global sales perspective for all firms, whether or not their firm is currently pursuing global business.
- Identify forces in the global environment that are moving markets toward greater levels of trade and business.
- List and discuss the three technological forces that are impacting sales force management practices.
- Discuss demographic trends that are impacting the marketplace and, based upon these trends, how customer relationship management must be managed.
- Explain why firms are adopting a relationship management approach with their best customers.
- Understand the importance of economic trends, in various parts of the world, and their impact on the global sales manager.
- Discuss legal and ethical variations that exist in the global economy and their influence on how and where global sales activities are formed.

**KEY TERMS**

- Globalization.
- Customer relationship management.
- Relationship marketing.
- Foreign Corrupt Practices Act (FCPA).

Managing a sales force today is an extremely complex undertaking. In fact, individuals who become sales managers are expected to bridge gaps that exist between the firm producing or selling the product/service and the customer/client that purchases the product/service. To achieve success, the sales manager engages in the traditional management tasks of planning, implementing, and controlling activities to accomplish organizational goals. Within this complex relationship, the sales manager hires, trains, assigns, motivates, compensates, evaluates, coaches, and leads the sales force. Finally, the sales manager's chief responsibility is to insure that sales force actions produce satisfied customers that will continue to partner with the sales firm and purchase future goods. It should be apparent that the sales manager's responsibilities must be performed well and, to perform these duties successfully, the sales manager must work long and full days. This is why sales professionals are among the most sought-after employees.[1]

Given these myriad duties and responsibilities, the sales manager of the new millennium must also be concerned about an even larger force. That is, today's sales managers must be able to manage and lead a sales force in the global marketplace! There are very few economic markets that are not currently impacted by global forces. Even when firms do not pursue customers in the global marketplace they must be prepared to compete against global competitors in home markets. In fact, consumers and industrial firms may not know where a product is made, who owns the parent company, or what role the partner plays that represents the brand in local markets. Therefore, the role of the sales manager is significantly more complex and difficult in today's marketplace (see Exhibit 1.1).

As one *Wall Street Journal* article cautioned about managing in a global market, "[T]o be successful, you will have to deal with nationally and culturally eclectic staffs and teams, understand foreign competitors, and devote more time to studying the culture, politics, and operating styles of world markets."[2]

## SALES MANAGEMENT IN THE GLOBAL ENVIRONMENT

The global marketplace offers numerous benefits and unique opportunities for sales managers. In many parts of the world, and especially in the areas designated as "The Triad," global marketing has become the norm.[3] Research confirms that the majority of world trade either originates or is purchased in: (1) North America (NAFTA); (2) Western Europe; and (3) Japan and the Pacific Rim – hence the name Triad or three major commercial areas of

## EXHIBIT 1.1 MANAGING AN INTERNATIONAL SALES FORCE

Imagine being a salesperson employed by a Korean firm that had just sold 50 percent of the business to a Western firm. At first, two rumors circulated: (1) that Korean workers would be dismissed to lower the cost of conducting business and (2) that Western managers would not respect former lifetime employment policies. When the foreign managers arrived in Seoul, it was difficult for the Korean sales force to make formal presentations in English and to speak openly with their supervisors. The Western supervisors were less interested in the firm's hierarchy, seniority, and unswerving loyalty to the boss than their former managers. The Western managers also insisted that Korean salespersons speak openly when asked and to work by well defined rules to achieve clear objectives. These sharp diversions, from the former cultural rules, were at first difficult for the Korean force to practice.

Korean salespersons were surprised to learn that the Western managers had their own fears. Managers tried to determine how they could get workers to talk openly about ways to improve the business. One solution that worked was having a Korean manager facilitate discussions at formal meetings. Another concern arose when a ceiling was set on credit sales to customers. This new policy resulted in complaints from customers, and the sales force claimed the policy prevented them from responding to changing market conditions. Finally, after accepting that this was the way business was conducted in Korea, the policy was revised.

Subsequently the Western firm purchased a competitor in order to gain market share. This resulted in workers of the purchased firm going on strike and 40 percent of the customer base being lost. To regain the lost customers once the strike was settled, the Western manager placed a sign in the sales manager's office that read: "War Room." Salespersons promised former customers special deals, free beer glasses, and other gifts to return to their former supplier. This strategy worked and nearly all customers reopened their accounts.

Blending workers from the East and West is difficult for all concerned. However, in this case the merger worked well and sales and profits are higher than before the merger. It appears that a large number of Korean workers retained their jobs and may actually prosper because of the merger.

*Source.* Michael Schuman, "How Interbrew blended Disparate Ingredients in Korean Beer Venture," *Wall Street Journal*, July 24, 2000, A1, A6.

---

the world. To conduct business successfully in the Triad, sales managers must be aware of and conversant with such diverse subjects as geography, culture, technology, and legal systems, while concurrently understanding mundane topics like currency exchange, international travel expenses, and changing time zones. To be successful, twenty-first-century sales managers must also be fully familiar with the following fast-paced and interrelated forces that are occurring around the globe.

CASE VIGNETTE **COMPUSTAT AND PACIFIC MARKETING**

Compustat, a manufacturer of computer software based in Great Britain, wants to expand sales to the United States. Senior management at Compustat is considering two options: hiring its own sales force that will be comprised of experienced computer salespersons with knowledge of the US marketplace and a successful record of sales accomplishments. A second option would be to find a US partner, with a non-competing product line, to represent its products. Senior management must gather all relevant information about these options, before making a decision about how to best expand its operations.

Jerry Jones, sales manager for Pacific Marketing, must hire a replacement for a retiring salesperson. While most of the sales representatives for Pacific are white males, Jones has seen a significant change in the types of customers and engineers the firm calls upon. A larger portion of purchasing agents and managers are Asian, female, and recent immigrants who possess needed technical expertise. The question that arises is whether the new salesperson should be reflective of the changing customer base? Jones has scheduled diversity training for the sales force and now the question is whether or not to seek out a more diverse sales force for Pacific Marketing.

## Globalization

The level of globalization, or interlinking of the world economy through commerce, increases each year. Some firms are threatened by globalization, particularly those companies that are heavy users of labor or that believe they cannot compete directly against larger, better organized, and financed competitors. Conversely firms that are organized to sell their products worldwide embrace globalization. When goods are "world class" global companies can standardize the manufacturing process, increase quality, and drive down total product cost. This means that a global firm could manufacture its product offering(s) in the Philippines, Mexico, and Ireland, sites that are geographically part of Triad customer markets. The firm's engineering and design work might be conducted in southern California and India to take advantage of creative engineers found in those areas. Operations oversight would occur at headquarters in London. Marketing activities would be the responsibility of local Triad partners. However, it is quite likely that marketing partners in one area of the global economy would be competitors in other markets.

One apparent concern raised by globalization critics is that no one fully understands or controls globalization. Since no one country or organization controls the force of globalization, this suggests that the economic forces at work are free of interference found in other marketplaces. But actions such as outsourcing, moving manufacturing among lower wage countries, and competing on the basis of price and quality, are scary for both less skilled workers in developed nations and for small firms in emerging nations. In response, domestic businesses seek protection from their government in order to reduce global competitors. True globalization, where companies take advantage of efficiencies found around the globe, is an extension of free trade. No matter your perspective on globalization, a number of things appear certain. One

## EXHIBIT 1.2 WHAT GLOBALISM IS (AND ISN'T!)

"Globalism" has almost as many meanings as the number of people who use the term. In examining the way firms and countries use the term, we find a great deal of confusion about what globalism means. For example, companies operating in two countries like Mexico and Brazil may call themselves "global," when in fact they are "hemispheric." Also, a consumer goods firm like the San Miguel Corporation may describe globalization as expanding its operations in the Philippines and Hong Kong, to Singapore, Indonesia, and Malaysia. In reality this appears to be a regional focus. Global strategies are important, since trade and technology now link most nations of the world. However, few people, including managers, really understand globalization. Listed below are five "misperceptions" often associated with globalism.

- That offices, factories, or representatives are found in other countries.
- That the product or process is standardized in every country.
- That the firm becomes a stateless entity.
- That country images and values are abandoned.
- That sales operations occur in another country.

So what is "globalism"? According to Harvard Business Professor Rosabeth Moss Kanter, globalism means a firm should be "holistic" in its business approach. That is, a truly global firm takes an integrated approach to all aspects of business, to include suppliers, markets, production locations, and competitors. Every product marketed by the firm is evaluated in regard to domestic and global standards. The needs of global customers are designed into the product, not added as an afterthought. This leads to the firm producing and marketing world-class products both at home and abroad. In the process, managers must acquire a deep and accurate understanding of cultures – both at home and abroad – if they are to become global. The global firm focuses on excellence in the face of a multitude of possible global scenarios, assesses the synergies available across markets and partners, and is aware of the important cultural differences that exist. In effect, global thinking is more important than global selling, because the thought process increases market opportunities for the global firm.

*Source.* Adapted from Rosabeth Moss Kanter, "Getting a Grip on Globalism," *Sales and Marketing Management*, August 1997, 34, 39.

is that globalization will continue at a rapid pace and firms can either take advantage of globalization or continually react to the force. Second, given the pervasiveness of globalization, sales managers must plan and strategize from a global viewpoint. Finally, a firm's success, wealth, and its workers' standard of living are affected by the firm's ability to compete in the global marketplace. If a firm is unable – or unwilling – to satisfy global customers, then competitors that are both capable and willing to undertake this responsibility will reap the economic rewards of meeting customer needs.

## Technological innovations

Technology is changing the way people live, work, and think. While technology is impacting manufacturing processes and medical services at a rapid pace, other technological forces – the Internet, communications, and customer relationship management – are modifying global sales force management. The Internet, or worldwide web (www), has revolution-ized the way firms communicate with one another and their customers. Likewise, firms can construct web sites on the worldwide web to provide their publics with information about the firm and its offerings. Web sites also allow new product offerings to be publicized, employment opportunities to be listed, and the web site provides viewers with an initial, and lasting, image of the firm.

Customers today order both consumer products and standard business-to-business (B2B) goods over the web. This type of economic transaction is faster, less costly, and impacts the roles played by the sales manager and the sales force. For example, when customers order goods electronically, what is the role of the salesperson? In the new e-commerce marketplace, customers expect the salesperson to act as a consultant and to provide exper-tise that solves problems and creates value. This means that the sales manager transitions from being the manager of sales to the manager of the sales force – the latter being a true managerial position. Then, given the importance of this new sales environment, the sales force must be properly selected, trained, led, and compensated to become expert at solving customer problems. Sales managers must also receive pertinent and timely information about customer purchases, needs, and satisfaction levels in order to manage customer reten-tion. Technology is moving the sales function to higher levels of thought and action, which directly influences how the sales force perform their job. When these changes occur, the sales manager's role also evolves.[4]

The Internet permits customers to instantly communicate their satisfaction or lack of satisfaction about company offerings to firms in the global market. Today's customers are less willing to accept flawed product offerings in the global marketplace – the expectation is that purchased products will be world-class, and when a firm cannot or will not offer needed products customers transfer their patronage and loyalty to a competitor. Global customers invest their money with firms that provide high quality products at reasonable prices. Customer satisfaction, rather than product loyalty, is most important. Sales managers must insure that customer feedback is constantly monitored, analyzed, and necessary changes are made in order to maintain positive and sustained customer relationships. Successful global firms nurture customer relationships, referred to as Customer Relationship Management (CRM).

Web pages can also provide current and potential customers with a wealth of informa-tion about the firm.[5] By using secure passwords, order status can be monitored and buyer and seller partners can exchange information. Likewise, sellers are able to track visitors to their web page and use this electronic medium or distribution channel as a source of market research information. To make the process work smoothly it is necessary for the firm to adopt an internal marketing system that includes information sharing and working together to satisfy customer needs.

## Demographic changes

Growing diversity within both the marketplace and the workplace are clearly evident in many parts of the world today. If one examines the United States, it is clear that what was once primarily a country of European immigrants will by 2050 have become a much more diverse nation[6] (See Figure 1.1). This means that sellers must understand the needs of diverse groups of potential customers within a geographical area, unlike customers served previously in more homogeneous markets. Likewise, the future sales force will be comprised of more diverse groups of people. This suggests that sales managers will hire, train, and manage people who possess significantly diverse values and attitudes toward life and business. Therefore, sales managers in the global marketplace must understand different cultures and establish management parameters that are inclusive of diverse people within the emerging workplace.

Similar demographic changes are also occurring globally. In Europe, immigrants from India, Africa, and the Middle East work in most member countries of the European Union. Germany is actually stepping up efforts to recruit highly skilled professionals, technicians, and scientists from emerging nations.[7] These demographic trends create unique needs for customer products and services that firms must be aware of and try to satisfy when the opportunity is profitable.

Global salespersons are selected from three different categories of workers. These groups include: *local nationals* from the business location country; *expatriates*, or foreign workers who are from the same country as the headquarters or ownership country of the global firm; and *third-country nationals* who are not from either the home or the local country. Global firms employ a mixture of different categories of salespersons, but for a variety of reasons the trend is away from expatriates and toward local and third-country nationals. Such policies increase the diversity of the sales force.

## Relationship marketing

Firms in the global marketplace are modifying their approach toward their best customers or clients from that of a one-time transaction that maximizes profits to a longer-term view called "relationship marketing." While relationship marketing means many things to

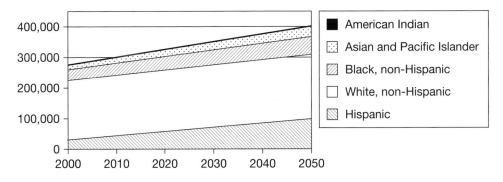

**Figure 1.1** *Projection of the US population by race*
*Source: US Bureau of the Census, release date January 13, 2000*

different parties in the exchange process, it is basically a desire to establish a long-term relationship between the customer and the supplier. A variety of motivations explain the adoption of a new customer approach by global companies. A major reason is the cost of conducting personal visits or customer sales call continues to increase. For example, in the United States, the cost of an industrial sales call is approximately $200.[8] For this reason companies cannot afford to allow their sales force to make unproductive sales calls. Firms have come to believe that a more efficient method of marketing is to establish and maintain long-term relationships with their customers. When a long-term relationship is established and nurtured, it is less necessary to spend significant amounts of money advertising to make customers aware of the product offering and then employing a sales force to stimulate demand for unwanted products/services to potential customers.

Relationship marketing also necessitates the sharing of confidential information between partners that attempt to make every encounter a "win–win" situation. Relationship partners are also expected to communicate openly and work together to further both partner's goals. These are difficult and often conflicting goals for organizations, so relationship marketing may not be ideal for all situations.[9] However, relationship marketing changes the perspective and the role of the sales force. By adopting a relationship approach to the market, the global sales force becomes concerned with making sales and maintaining satisfied customers.

Information technology improvements allow the firm to calculate the net gain/loss of conducting business with partners. That is, a supplier can calculate the profit earned, and then set appropriate service levels for all customers. In effect current or potentially profitable customers are provided higher levels of service than are one-shot customers who call and attempt to negotiate low prices and short delivery terms. In this way, firms are able to identify and nurture their most profitable accounts. Companies understand, however, that it takes time to form a relationship. This is especially true in certain cultures, like those found in Asia, where forming a close relationship can take years. It is just not possible to form a quick relationship in certain cultures. For example, Americans have been criticized for scheduling a one-week visit to Japan to conduct business with new or potential clients. At best, the Japanese will spend this time assessing the character and dependability of the American visitor, but there is little likelihood that any substantive business activity will occur.[10] In a cross-cultural business situation, decades may pass before a seller is granted proprietary information.

## Economic changes

Numerous economic changes are in progress around the globe. As these changes occur, markets become more or less attractive generators of profits. For example, in the first half of the1990s, many global firms viewed Asia as being a high growth area with significant future potential. However, with the economic crisis of 1997, global firms either scaled back or ceased their operations in most Asian countries. Asia has rebounded from the 1997 crisis, but certain Asian nations still face slow growth and other economic problems – currency devaluation, real estate overvaluation, or a lack of transferable currency. A number of global firms have responded to the latest economic changes by reentering the more promising Asian countries. However, across the Pacific Ocean, the US economy remained strong for nearly a decade.[11] Economic conditions influence the ability of the global sales force to serve their customers. Sales managers with a global perspective understand that Asian accounts might be stagnant, while at the same time US and European sales are higher than normal. In such a situation, sales managers would adjust strategies and assignments to profit from current opportunities.

## Legal challenges

Global sales managers incur different types of legal environments on a daily basis. That is, how does one conduct business when different legal systems are in place in the countries of the buyer and the seller? For example, global business operations are complicated in Russia by a legal system that is "in flux" and where uneven implementation of existing laws is a daily occurrence.[12] Disparate legal systems complicate and delay the global business process. For example, BP Amoco paid $485 million for 10 percent of Sidanko, a Russian oil company, which later went bankrupt. The firm's assets were then sold to another Russian firm for approximately $175 million, despite the fact the company reported estimated revenue of $1.1 billion per year. Only after BP Amoco sought support from the US Congress, which was appropriating money for modernizing the Russian oil industry, was the sale of Sidanko examined by the Russian legal system.[13]

Likewise, in certain Asian countries copyright and trademark protection laws are selectively enforced. When global firms begin manufacturing or distributing their goods in certain countries, competitors or even partners may simply begin producing duplicate products that utilize the existing brand name! Sales managers must work with a knowledgeable international attorney to insure that legal situations are considered and, whenever possible, the likelihood of legal problems is minimized. One way to reduce legal ambiguities is to maintain control of key product technologies. However, this approach can cause problems because when a global firm withholds information from a global partner, it is difficult to form or maintain a long-term relationship.

Also, different political environments complicate the standardization of fringe benefits offered to workers by global companies. For example, in comparison with US standards, European countries guarantee generous employee benefits. These benefits can include profit sharing, bonuses, medical and dental expenses, severance pay, and maternity and vacation allowances. While US firms devote 35 percent of wages to benefits, in Europe the figure can vary from 45 percent in Germany to 92 percent in Italy! Many European pay plans are driven by a tax system that exceeds 50 percent in the countries.[14]

## Ethical challenges

An important area for global sales managers and their organizations is defining and practicing ethical behavior. Traditionally, the sales area generates a large proportion of unethical behavior complaints. The sales area is criticized for selling products not needed, being less than truthful with buyers, and not adhering to agreed-upon sales terms. As might be expected, these sales actions erode trust between the buyer and seller and make follow-up purchases highly unlikely. Research has also shown that dissatisfied customers inform a significant number of friends and coworkers about unsatisfactory service received from salespersons.[15]

A major dilemma faced by sales managers is the ability to define what is ethical and what is not for the global sales force. Ethical standards vary by situation and certainly by culture. For example, US firms are restricted by the Foreign Corrupt Practices Act (FCPA) from making payments to foreign government officials or political parties for the purpose of making a sale or increasing profits.[16] Conversely, in Germany and Italy, bribes paid abroad can be legally claimed as a business expense.[17]

When a salesperson conducts business in diverse cultures, he or she must understand the expectations of that culture (see Exhibit 1.3). For example, in Japan gifts are normally exchanged as a means of forming and maintaining a relationship. In other countries, like Germany and Switzerland, executives prefer not to receive gifts because they feel obligated.[18] One must also be cautious of the type of gift that is extended to a potential or current customer. Cultural norms also dictate what is acceptable in regard to the recipient (employee or family member), the type of gift (trip, tangible item, or cash), and when the gift is extended (before or after the purchase).

The global sales manager must insure that the sales force understands the firm's policy regarding acceptable ethical behavior. This means there will be written codes of ethics and training sessions to educate the sales force about what the company considers to be acceptable salesperson behavior. A few firms publish expected ethical guidelines and instruct the salesperson to communicate with management when the ethical situation deviates from established rules. Global sales managers must control their sales force in order not to find themselves in an embarrassing ethical situation that will result in negative consequences to the profitability and/or reputation of the global firm. Sales managers in the global marketplace understand that unethical behavior will eventually be discovered and this publicity will find its way into a global communications network. When this happens, significant time and resources will have to be invested to correct this breach of customer and societal trust.

## CHAPTER SUMMARY

Global trade has increased significantly over the past three decades and is predicted to surpass $8 trillion by 2002.[19] Decades ago economists advised nations to specialize in what they do best, produce goods at reasonable cost, and then trade their surplus goods to other nations for the goods and services produced efficiently elsewhere. It appears as we enter the new millennium, that the nations of the world are increasingly doing just that!

However, business practices in the global marketplace have changed the roles of the sales force and the sales manager. Firms may not perceive themselves as being global competitors, but few firms compete in purely domestic markets. Therefore, even when a company supplies goods or services only to local consumers, the probability is that global firms will enter the local market with world class goods that cost the same or even less than domestically produced offerings. This suggests that nearly everyone is competing in a global marketplace whether they choose to or not!

## EXHIBIT 1.3 UNDERSTANDING DIFFERENT CULTURES

Global salespersons encounter resistance from customers in different cultures. Often this is due to global salespersons not understanding the "do's" and "don'ts" of interacting with different cultures. Understanding how to act in most cultures may be the difference between closing a sale and losing a customer. For example, simply calling someone with your palm up and raising a finger may alienate the potential customer. Listed below are specific *faux pas* one should avoid in certain cultures.

- *Arab countries*. Greet people and use your right hand when eating and drinking. Do not use your left hand to hold, offer, or receive materials, because in Arab countries the left hand is used to touch toilet paper. If you must use your left hand to write, apologize for doing so.
- *China*. Always accept and drink tea during business meetings, even if you are offered dozens of cups each day. Present materials in black and white because colors may have special meanings. Never eat or drink before your host does so.
- *France*. The French normally do not meet until after 10:00 a.m. Do not offer to meet for a business breakfast.
- *Germany*. Do not address a business associate by their first name unless you are invited to do so. Never schedule a breakfast meeting.
- *Latin America*. The clock is not taken seriously, so do not schedule more than two meetings during the day.
- *Japan*. Do not raise business issues on the golf course unless your host initiates the conversation. Do not cross your legs and show the bottom of the foot. This is insulting to the Japanese.
- *Mexico*. Do not send red or yellow flowers as a gift; these colors are associated with evil spirits and death. A better gift is a box of premium chocolates.
- *Philippines*. Rather than disagree with someone, "Yes" can have many meanings from "I do not know" to "I want to end the conversation." Criticism should never be direct, but should be offered as softly as possible.
- *Other countries*. It is offensive to use the "thumbs up" sign in the Middle East, and rude in Australia. Likewise, it is offensive in France to make the "OK" sign by forming a circle with the thumb and index finger. It is considered too personal to ask someone in the Middle East, "How is your family?"

*Source*. Andy Cohen, "Small World, Big Challenge," *Sales and Marketing Management*, June 1996, 69–73.

Therefore, sales supervisors must manage a global sales force differently than they would a domestic sales force. The major difference in this shift is that global sales managers must contend with diverse cultures and languages, unfamiliar territories, different legal systems and ethical standards, while achieving goals through a sales force that may be based half-way around the globe. As discussed in this chapter, a number of forces are expediting the globalization process. These include faster and ubiquitous communications, larger airplanes and more frequent direct flights, an increase in global trade, and populous nations like China joining the World Trade Organization (WTO). Also, *BusinessWeek* has reported that a nation's ability to absorb workers from other cultures may determine whether that nation grows or stagnates.[20]

This book examines the major areas of personal selling and sales management in a global marketplace, but first the extremely important topic of culture is presented in Chapter 2. Culture lies at the very heart of every aspect of global sales management. Culture influences who is hired, how they are trained, how they work, and how they expect to be rewarded for their contributions to the firm. Likewise, culture impacts customer expectations, ethical behavior, relationship marketing, and the partners we select around the globe. Successful global sales managers must begin by understanding and appreciating the diverse cultural influences found on our planet. So sit back, relax, and begin your journey through *Sales Management: A Global Perspective*.

## TOPICAL APPROACH OF THE BOOK

This text explores sales management in the global marketplace by presenting four distinct areas: (I) Introduction and culture; (II) Global personal selling; (III) Global human resources; and (IV) Global strategic management Issues.

Part I, "Introduction and culture," examines the emerging market economy that pervades most nations of the world and the importance of possessing a global view. Even if firms do not see the relevance of selling their products globally, competitors from other nations may invade their markets. This means that everyone is essentially competing in a global market-place. Also culture significantly impacts how business is conducted in a global marketplace and influences how businesses are administratively organized and managed and how firms interact with their salespersons. Culture also impacts all human resource areas, personal selling practices, and global management issues. The influence of diverse cultures is a complicating factor in global business interactions.

Part II, "Global personal selling," provides guidance for meeting, interacting, communicating, negotiating, and persuading the customer to partner with the global supplier. A global salesperson must be introduced, become acquainted, learn about the potential client, gain trust, and finally agree to partner in a personal setting. This sales process differs significantly around the globe. Chapter 3 examines historical, organizational, and cultural influences on the sales process. Chapters 4 and 5 introduce a sales process for the global marketplace, beginning with cross-cultural negotiating skills, and discusses the importance of ethics in all sales activities.

Part III, "Global human resources," covers the managerial responsibilities of selection, training, territory design and management, motivation, compensation, and evaluation. Each of these areas is important, because sales managers in the global marketplace must be able to select and hire highly competent salespersons. If the sales manager makes an incorrect selection decision, then the remaining stages of human resource development are less effective. Likewise, culture impacts each of these stages. What is acceptable in one culture for selecting, training, or motivating sales force members may be unacceptable elsewhere. For example, laws in most European nations set generous policies regarding vacation, termination, and unemployment benefits. In other countries, like the United States, European social policies are considered "extravagant."

Part IV, "Global strategic management issues," covers the areas of forecasting, segmenting, firm sales strategies, and customer relationship management strategies. This section provides guidance for sales managers who must understand and implement company strategies. It is imperative for sales managers in the global marketplace to understand firm strategies in order to devise successful sales strategies. This final section of the text provides managers with a comprehensive understanding of how the sales force fits into the overall firm structure.

## DISCUSSION QUESTIONS

1 How will globalization change the operation of many firms? What role will the sales manager play in this new marketplace?

2 Discuss and relate how each force within the global marketplace is increasing global business activities.

3 How are the Internet, communications, and customer relationship management affecting the role of the salesperson and sales manager?

4 If demographic trends seen in Europe and the United States continue, how will this modify the role of the sales manager and salesperson?

5 What changes must occur for a firm to form relationships with their best customers? Should a firm have close relationships with all their customers?

6 Global markets offer increased economic opportunities and threats. Explain as many of these as you can. Does this mean firms must be more agile in the future?

7 Ethical and legal considerations are important in home markets. Why do these two forces increase in importance as firms enter the global arena?

## REFERENCES

1 Anonymous (1998), "By the Numbers," *Sales and Marketing Management*, June, 14.

2 Lancaster, Hal (1998), "Learning to Manage in a Global Workplace (You're on Your Own)," *Wall Street Journal*, 231:106, B1.

3 Ohmae, Kenichi (1999), *The Borderless World*, New York: Harper Business.

**15**

4   Avlonitis, George J., and Despina A. Karayanni (2000), "The Impact of Internet Use on Business-to-Business Marketing: Examples from American and European Companies," *Industrial Marketing Management*, 29:5 (September), 441–60.

5   Honeycutt, Earl D. Jr., Theresa B. Flaherty, and Ken Benassi (1998), "Marketing Industrial Products on the Internet," *Industrial Marketing Management*, 27, 63–72.

6   US Census Bureau (2000), "Projections of the Resident Population by Race," www.pop@census.gov, January 13.

7   Zachary, G. Pascal, and Cecile Rohwedder (2001), "Germany Widens Door for Immigrants," *Wall Street Journal*, July 2, A8, A10.

8   "Sales Call Costs" (1998), *Sales and Marketing Management*, December, 31.

9   Fournier, Susan, Susan Dobscha, and David Glen Mick (1998), "Preventing the Premature Death of Relationship Marketing," *Harvard Business Review*, January–February, 42–51.

10  Ford, John B. and Earl D. Honeycutt, Jr. (1993), "Japanese National Culture as a Basis for Understanding Japanese Business Practices," *Business Horizons*, November–December, 27–34.

11  Bureau of Economic Analysis (2000), "Gross Domestic Product," July 28.

12  *1997 Russian Country Commercial Guide*, Moscow: US Embassy.

13  www.RussiaToday.com (1999), *Reuter's News Service*, October 14, 22, November 26.

14  Samli, A. Coskun, and John S. Hill (1998), *Marketing Globally*, Chicago: NTC.

15  Carr, Clay (1990), *Front Line Customer Service*, New York: John Wiley & Sons.

16  Arunthanes, Wiboon, Patriya Tansuhaj, and David J. Lemak (1994), "Cross-cultural Business Gift Giving," *International Marketing Review*, 11:4 (January), 44–55.

17  Cateora, Philip (1993), *International Marketing*, eighth edition, Homewood IL: Irwin.

18  Fadiman, A.J. (1986), "A Traveler's Guide to Gifts and Bribes," *Harvard Business Review*, July–August, 122–4, 126, 130, 132, 134, 136.

19  Berkowitz, Eric, Roger A. Kerin, Steven W. Hartley, and William Rudelius (2000), *Marketing*, sixth edition, Boston MA: Irwin McGraw-Hill.

20  Baker, Stephen (2002), "Twenty-five Ideas for a Changing World – Workplace," *BusinessWeek Online*, August 26.

## Chapter 2

# Culture and sales

This chapter presents a discussion of the makeup and impact of culture on the sales force operating in a global setting. The sales manager is provided with suggestions for making the optimal choice of salesperson for the particular cultural setting along with ways to help the salesperson to deal with customers from different cultures.

**LEARNING OBJECTIVES**

*After reading this chapter, you will be able to:*

- Understand the nature of culture and how it affects human behavior.
- Appreciate the importance of national culture as a defining set of acceptable beliefs and behaviors.
- Understand the various ways in which national culture is manifested.
- Improve relationships with foreign-born salespeople.
- Understand the cultural forces affecting the performance of salespeople.
- Select the best candidates for international sales positions based upon the various cultures in which they will be operating.

## KEY TERMS

- Culture.
- Acculturation and Assimilation.
- Power distance, Uncertainty avoidance, Masculinity/Femininity, Individualism/Collectivism, and Confucian dynamism.
- Components of culture.
- Idioms, Dialects and Vernacular.
- High context and Low context cultures.
- Nonverbal communication.

Culture affects everything that we as human beings do. It permeates our thoughts as well as our actions. The nature of culture can be thought of as: (1) communicable knowledge, (2) all that which separates humans from nonhumans, or (3) all of the historical accomplishments produced by man's social life.[1] What seems obvious is that learning is a key ingredient, and society is the primary provider of that learning. We define *culture* as: *all of the behavioral traits that we acquire from and share with the members of our society*. The point is that cultural traits are learned from the environment that surrounds us. They are not inherited. Our cultural makeup affects how we feel about and react to various societal stimuli. One problem that we constantly face is our tendency to view the actions of others from our own perspective. We basically project our culture and our cultural expectations on others. While this appears to be appropriate if we are dealing with others from the same culture, it is increasingly more likely that we will be dealing with individuals from other cultural backgrounds. It is therefore better to be sensitive and able to adapt to a variety of different cultural backgrounds.

Sales management is heavily influenced by culture, and in this globally focused business environment it is important to understand the cultural forces which shape and affect the interactions between salespeople and customers as well as the interactions between salespeople and sales managers. Sensitivity to cultural differences can enhance the chances of success in any interpersonal interactions, and it is our purpose in this book to provide the framework for understanding cultural differences as they potentially affect salespeople in a variety of business settings. If a salesperson approaches a meeting with a customer armed with knowledge of the customer's cultural background, then their words, actions, and body language can all be strategically shaped to enhance the potential for not only a positive interaction, but also the development of a long-term profitable relationship with that customer. An understanding of culture can also help the sales manager to build a personal relationship with salespeople from a variety of different cultures, thereby ensuring their success. Knowledge of cultural differences allows the sales manager to structure the global sales force to minimize the potential for cultural conflicts and thereby maximize the potential effectiveness of customer relationship building.

CASE VIGNETTE **CULTURE CLASH**

Hiroshi Hamada has a problem that he must deal with. Hiroshi is the newly appointed Sales Manager for the fledgling European Division of Tanaka Chemicals. His existing sales force is primarily made up of Japanese nationals, and they are concerned about how to deal with European customers. None of his salespeople has any experience with or understanding of European culture. He recently visited Rome, and he found himself in a difficult situation when several Italians tried to be friendly and hug him. His shock caused hurt feelings. This experience has contributed to his anxiety.

## ACCULTURATION AND ASSIMILATION

Whenever individuals gather together in communities, a cultural bond is created. Since culture deals with learned knowledge, the cultural backgrounds and understandings of each member of the group have the potential to affect or be affected by the group as a whole. An outsider who comes into contact with a new group will learn some of the values and ideas held by the group, but the self-perceived importance of their own cultural heritage will affect how much the cultural immigrant accepts of the new culture's values and teachings. The amount that is learned and accepted by the outsider is *acculturation*. When the individual is completely absorbed into the new culture, this extreme is known as *assimilation*. This rarely happens, since the individual normally retains certain tenets of their own cultural heritage. The greater the degree of discord between the new group culture and the immigrant's home culture, the greater the potential for discord, conflict, and misunderstanding. Sales managers who expect someone from a different culture to completely accept the teachings and ways of a new culture will surely be disappointed. Intuitively, it is reasonable to expect that the more similar the new person's home culture is to the new group's culture, the easier the transition and the greater the acceptance of the group's cultural beliefs and standards. If culture is created and impacted whenever individuals congregate, then an understanding of the various important communities and culture is helpful.

## THE LEVELS OF CULTURAL AGGREGATION

Individuals group together on a variety of levels. These levels are in order from highest to lowest levels of aggregation: (1) global, (2) regional, (3) national, and (4) local. Each is discussed in relation to the concerns of the sales manager dealing with a global sales force.

### Global culture

The highest level of cultural grouping occurs on a *global* level. While there is some evidence of homogenization forces at work globally that are unifying wants and needs across certain demographic segments (e.g., youth in many countries affected by what they see in movies, hear in music, see on television, and eat at global fast food outlets), it is strategically risky to approach sales management from a global cultural perspective. To assume that sales-people have the same values from different countries is problematic. Sales managers cannot expect to deal with salespeople from all different countries the same way. The cultural makeup of the sales force and the cultural makeup of the customer base must be carefully considered by the sales manager to ensure the best fit possible.

## Regional culture

The next step down in scope would be to examine large geographic regions of the world and the potential for *regional* cultural similarities and cohesiveness. But is there enough simi-larity across all countries included in Asia, Southeast Asia, or Europe? While there might be certain similarities across the countries of a particular region, it is more likely that indi-vidual country differences far outweigh any similarities. The sales manager who thinks that all Asian customers can be lumped together and chooses a Japanese salesperson to call on all Asian customers will likely have difficulties. While there are cultural similarities (e.g., religion), the historical relations between Japan and certain Asian neighbors have been strained. There is little love between Japan and Korea or between Japan and China, and although this is slowly diminishing over time, there are still problems. One sees this as well in Europe, with strained relations among a number of the countries involved. Regional simi-larities, when they can effectively be built upon, offer opportunities for sales managers interested in using third-country nationals to make calls on customers across a particular region. With the use of a salesperson from a nation perceived to be more neutral in nature with sufficient cultural similarity, this type of individual could be effectively used across a variety of countries. Examples include Swiss nationals calling on a variety of West European nations or a Singaporean calling on a range of countries in Southeast Asia. The ability of a person to handle the travel and stress of a multicountry territory would of course require careful assessment.

## National culture

The most important level of cultural aggregation exists at the *national* level. Time and again, national differences have the single greatest impact upon cultural orientation. National cultural traits are the most deep-seated and defining characteristics that are imprinted on the individual. It is important to address those national cultural traits because they are effec-tive differentiators of individual nations. The most famous mechanism for differentiation has been the four dimensions identified by Geert Hofstede:[2] Power distance, Uncertainty avoidance, Individualism/collectivism, and Masculinity/femininity. Michael Bond added a fifth dimension to the group in later work:[3] Confucian dynamism. *Power distance* deals with the perceived hierarchical structuring of the society. The more clearly articulated and rigid the power structure, the more that placement in the hierarchy will be clearly understood and significantly affect the dealings between and among individuals. India, Mexico, and the Philippines are countries where power distance is wide and there is a rigid, hierarchical

power-structured society. Everyone knows his or her status within the hierarchy and understands whether to treat the person they are dealing with as a superior, as an equal, or as
an inferior. This would have a major bearing on the structuring of a sales force, since the
hierarchical level of the salesperson affects their ability to interact on a meaningful level
with a potential customer. If someone perceived to be lower in the power structure calls
upon a superior, the potential for cultural conflict is heightened. In more egalitarian societies like Australia, Israel or Ireland, power structuring is far more loose, and the potential
for conflict is minimal.

Another dimension is *uncertainty avoidance*, which focuses on the way the society deals
with risk. The higher the level of perceived risk, the greater the need to prepare for uncer-
tainties. In risk-averse countries like Japan, Greece or Portugal, everything has to be clearly
laid out and prepared before proceeding. This can be seen in the inability of the individual
to act on his or her own initiative for fear of making a mistake. In a country like Singapore
or Denmark or Sweden, there is little concern over taking an action and then worrying
about the consequences of that action. The global sales manager can see the potential for
conflict if a Danish salesperson is calling on a Greek customer with the goal of quickly
closing the sale.

One of the most important dimensions of national cultural difference is *individualism/
collectivism*. This dimension centers on the importance of the group as opposed to the individual. In societies where the group is more important, like Japan, Thailand, Pakistan, or
Venezuela, whatever is done by the individual must be done with the health and well-being
of the group in mind. The group or community must be protected at all costs, and the individual should not make decisions that might reflect badly on the group. A salesperson from
a collectivist nation would need permission from the group before taking actions, which
could be frustrating for a customer who is from an individualistic nation and wants to take
actions in their own best interest and wants to reach an agreement quickly. People from
collectivist societies are more likely to want to discuss the situation with their superiors and
reach group consensus before proceeding. This type of contrast can clearly be seen when
considering the nature of CEOs in Japan and the United States. In Japan, the CEO should
be the embodiment of all the beliefs and values of the company, but the American CEO is
often seen as the entrepreneurial spirit who goes in their own direction. While this is an
overgeneralization, the sales manager who does not pick salespeople carefully given the
nature of the customer base, particularly with regard to this dimension, risks alienation
from the beginning. Not a wise strategy in this day and age of relationship marketing and
customer relationship management (CRM).

The last of Hofstede's original national characteristics is *masculinity/femininity*, which
deals with the types of traits that are most valued by the society: those associated with
masculinity or femininity. Masculine traits involve the importance of strength, success,
confidence, and the importance of competitiveness, while feminine traits include nurturing,
building personal relationships, compassion, and concern for improving quality of life. In
feminine nations, wealth is not as important as quality of life, and large and ostentatious is
not as valued as small and quiet. Examples of feminine countries include Sweden, Denmark,
Norway, Chile, and Thailand. Masculine countries include Japan, Austria, Venezuela, and
Mexico. The sales manager who hopes that the Chilean salesperson can cover all South

American countries may experience trouble when it comes to sending him or her into Venezuela.

The final dimension is *Confucian dynamism* that focuses on time differences. Countries that rate high on this dimension are more long-term-focused and value commitment and persistence. Countries high on this dimension are primarily Asian nations influenced by the teachings of Confucius. One sees a good comparison in the United States with its short-term, profit-driven financial perspective as opposed to Japan with its longer-term perspective when establishing a presence in a new foreign market. The US firms will be focused heavily on immediate profitability rather than committing for the long run and being willing to wait until operations become profitable.

## Local culture

Finally, culture can be found at the *local* level as well. Here the local community can have an impact on the views and actions of the individual. This local community may be comprised of the district, city, or even neighborhood areas in which the individual lives. While these communities have their own cultural orientations, they do not appear to define the individual's outlook as significantly as the national culture.

## Managerial considerations

Since national culture is the most influential in shaping an individual's behaviors and attitudes, a series of managerial suggestions are provided for the sales manager dealing with a global sales force. Even the use of expatriate salespeople requires an understanding of national cultural dimensions since they will interact with people from other nations. It is important to note that it is not automatically problematic to send someone who represents a culture that is on one extreme of these traits to call on someone from a country on the other end of the spectrum. What is important is that the *chances* of cultural conflict should be minimized to enhance the probability of successful relationship building between salesperson and customer. One way to minimize conflict is by making the salesperson sensitive to the cultural differences that might exist and to avoid behaviors and language that might be misconstrued and create animosity. For the sales manager, the understanding of and sensitivity to these defining cultural characteristics are imperative for the most effective strategic structuring of the sales force. Strategically, periodic cultural training sessions for salespeople make a great deal of sense, especially when the sales manager is dealing with salespeople who travel outside their home countries. It should also be stressed that cultural training is just as important for the sales manager, since they will potentially be interacting with salespeople from different cultures, and their expectations of those individuals will be affected by the cultural orientation. The culturally sensitive sales manager is better prepared to not only place salespeople effectively in the field but also to manage people from different cultures. The biggest problem is encountered culturally when untrained individuals expect everyone to act and see things from the same perspective.

## THE COMPONENTS OF CULTURE

If culture is so important in our thoughts and actions, it is important to examine the various components of culture. Understanding the five national cultural dimensions presented above is a good starting point; however, to ensure the best possible results for the sales force, a deeper understanding of national culture's impact on the individual is important. Cultural components are an excellent mechanism for gaining this understanding. They can be defined as: *the various ways in which culture is manifested in the thoughts, words and actions of a society.* Each cultural manifestation will now be discussed (see Figure 2.1), examples of differences found in potential sales settings will be provided, and suggestions for handling these potentially problematic situations will be presented.

### Communication

*Verbal*

A major area for cultural conflict revolves around the use of language. For communication to effectively take place, the meaning of various words and phrases must be clear. It is helpful at this point to review the interpersonal communication process. The person initiating the communication begins with an idea in mind that they want to convey to the receiver. This idea is then translated into a series of signs and symbols for the purposes of communication. This is the function of language. It serves as the mechanism for allowing ideas to be transmitted. The translation of ideas to language is known as encoding, and the process by which the receiver translates those signs and symbols back into ideas is called

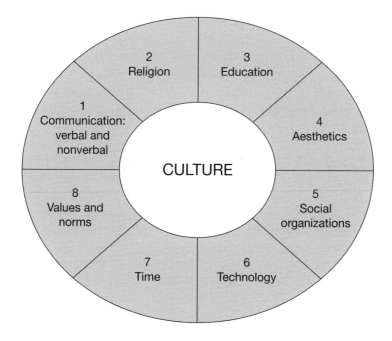

**Figure 2.1** *The components of culture*

decoding. What both parties hope in this process is that the original ideas that were in the head of the sender are the same ideas which are understood by the receiver. If the words and phrases are not clear to both parties, the potential for miscommunication is increased. This miscommunication is possible between the sales manager and salesperson and the salesperson and the customer. The key is to be sensitive to the language differences that might exist between the two parties and to seek clarifications wherever possible so that the chances of mutual understanding are increased. When dealing with other than one's native language, there are three problem areas often encountered in communications:[4] (1) simple carelessness, (2) the use of multiple-meaning words and, (3) the use of idioms.

*Simple carelessness* refers to the problem inherent in not doing the proper homework ahead of time. It involves the inappropriate or accidental use of a word. Obviously this could be grounds for major offense, but luckily this can easily be avoided by using a dictionary for that language. In some instances, when the language barrier is too high between the sales manager and salesperson or between the salesperson and the customer, it would be better to make use of a qualified bilingual interpreter. Strategically, it would not make sense to continually make use of an interpreter to help the salesperson communicate with the customers. It would be beneficial in that situation to hire a salesperson who is bilingual or at least near-fluent in the language of the customers. This is especially important when building meaningful long-term relationships with customers.

A more difficult problem is the use of *multiple-meaning words*. In this situation a word might be used that has a primary meaning that is very different from a secondary meaning, and may be the grounds for conflict. Languages like Japanese are problematic in this regard because the meaning of some words is derived from the context in which the word appears. This requires the individual to be careful in their word selection to avoid problems. This is more likely to arise when the salesperson using the foreign language can speak the language but might not be aware of local or regional uses of the word. This might arise when using a third-country national to call on customers in several countries within the same region (e.g., a Venezuelan calling on customers in Colombia, Peru and Chile). Probably the most effective way to deal with this problem is for the salesperson to be as deferential to the customer as possible and make it clear that they would not mean to offend in any way and be able to ask questions if necessary about the right words to be used.

The use of *idioms* is the most troublesome issue in the use of a particular language. The reason for this is that an idiom is a grouping of words that have no literal translation. In English a typical example is the phrase "raining cats and dogs." By itself this word grouping is nonsensical. Trying to translate an idiomatic expression literally will often get the individual into trouble. At the least it will cause confusion, but more seriously it could be seen as offensive. This potential problem is easily eliminated by avoiding the use of idiomatic expressions altogether. The sales manager is always well advised, either when dealing with foreign salespersons or when selecting salespeople to call on foreign customers, to counsel against the use of any kind of idiomatic expression. When in doubt, simply find other ways to convey the message.

A few additional language considerations. A few other aspects of language can also be troublesome. The strategy is to be sensitive ahead of time so that you have the best chance to avoid conflict before it ever begins. First of all, remember that in some societies, there are actually different forms of language that are appropriate when addressing a superior as opposed to an equal or inferior. The sales manager should ensure that the salesperson always begins deferentially with formal language (as though addressing someone who is a superior) when speaking to a potential customer. It is always best to play it safe and err on the side of deference. It will usually put the customer in a position of magnanimity. They can always say that there is no need to speak so formally, but it is best for them to take the lead.

Another language concern involves countries where a variety of *dialects* are spoken. Dialects refer to different languages that may be spoken within a particular country. This may be more evident in less developed countries where there are groups or communities that live relatively isolated from one another and where there is no standard language. In such an environment there is little choice but to find a bilingual expert to serve as translator. Knowing that the salesperson will be responsible for covering an area in which potential customers speak a particular dialect will certainly enhance chances of success. Forewarned is forearmed!

Another issue is the use of *vernacular*, which is language that is being created over time. New words and phrases are always being added to languages as advancements are made. One can easily see this in the array of words added to many languages connected with technological advances (e.g., the development and growth in the use of the Internet as a communication medium). In many countries there are a variety of new words and phrases resulting from computer advancements like e-business, electronic commerce, web pages, servers, and firewalls. Staying current in the language patterns is important, especially for the salesperson being asked to call on customers in different countries. It is always helpful to see if there are important words or phrases associated with business operations and society that might come up in conversation. A good way to prepare for this is through the inclusion of new words and phrases in language training seminars for company salespeople.

A final note on language: Hall's "high context versus low context cultures." Edward Hall[5] suggested that an important distinction between cultures (often in terms of nations) involves the distinction between high context and low context cultures. In a *high context* culture communication can take place without any words being spoken. The meaning is dependent upon the context. This is the kind of situation where people are so similar in nature that what is not said is just as important as what is said. This situation will occur when you have nations that are homogeneous. Japan, Saudi Arabia and a number of European countries fit into this category. In a sales situation, the sales manager has to make sure that the salesperson understands that in these types of cultures, contract negotiations are subject to change as new individuals enter the negotiation process. In the *low context* culture subtleties are lost. Here the words are the key to successful negotiations. Everything must be clearly spelled out, and the actual contract becomes the important focal point. A low context country is one in which there is heterogeneity within the population. In nations where there are sizable immigrant populations, like the United States, Australia, and India, everything must be clearly spelled out for the parties involved during a sales negotiation.

## Nonverbal

The issue of context points up the importance of nonverbal communications. This is critical to any sales negotiation setting, and as a result, the sales manager must include nonverbal communication training for the global sales force. Research has shown that much of what is important in a sales negotiation process is the nonverbal communications that take place. As a result, it is important for salespersons to understand the various types of nonverbal communications as found in Table 2.1. Each is briefly described below, with sales examples presented for illustration purposes.

*Appearance/grooming* focuses on how an individual dresses and keeps their head and facial hair. Different cultures look differently at dress and grooming. Formality often is manifested in clothing and appearance, and a country like Japan with its hierarchical society is less tolerant of an informal appearance and grooming than is a country like Australia. *Tone of voice/speech patterns* focuses on loudness and softness of response, clarity of response, and shrillness of response. Anger is easily manifested in loudness, while timidity is found in quiet and hesitant speech. Much can be conveyed from speech patterns. *Timing of responses* deals with how long it takes to respond when a question is asked. Responding too quickly may indicate a lack of proper consideration of what was asked, while too slow a response might be viewed as avoidance. *Posture* involves sitting or standing. In some countries sitting and not offering someone else a seat (forcing them to stand) can be seen as offensive and stand-offish behavior. *Use of space* refers to how much distance is left between the salesperson and the customer. In countries like Italy, closeness is expected, while it would be seen as highly offensive in Asian countries like Korea, Japan, or China. In these countries personal space is highly prized, and invasion of the space is inappropriate. *Sense of smell* deals with how the individuals smell to each other. In some countries daily bathing is not as important as it is in other countries. Even the use of perfume, cologne, or deodorant may be thought of very differently in more relaxed cultures. Some countries in the Middle East and northern Africa do not bathe daily, owing to limitations on access to bathtubs and showers. *Hand gestures* can be inappropriate or offensive because they convey something other than what was intended. The use of the thumb and forefinger touching while the other fingers are held up is a sign of "OK" in the United States, but this gesture is seen as obscene in some European nations. Knowing what is meant by that culture with different hand signals/gestures is extremely important. *Physical contact* focuses on the use of touch when communicating. Some cultures accept a pat on the back or a touch on

**Table 2.1** *Types of nonverbal communication*

Appearance/Grooming

Tone of voice/Speech patterns

Timing of responses

Posture

Use of space

Sense of smell

Hand gestures

Physical contact

Eye contact

Body angles

the arm, while other cultures find it incredibly offensive. Again, Italians like to be close in terms of space and give hugs and pats on the back. Conversely, these gestures could be quite offensive to Japanese, Koreans, or Chinese. *Eye contact* deals with looking straight into someone's eyes or not. In countries like the United States, avoidance of eye contact can be seen as evasive and grounds for distrust, yet in other countries direct eye contact is seen as peering too far into an individual's hidden self (obviously more apt to be found in less developed countries). Finally, *body angles* refer to how one positions oneself to the other person. Face-to-face can be seen as confrontational, while looking slightly up at the individual is seen as less offensive. This would involve the concept of bowing in Japan, where it is always a good idea for the salesperson to show deference by bowing a little lower than the Japanese customer.

Communication considerations. Obviously, the better prepared the salesperson is to understand verbal and nonverbal communication issues, the greater the chances of relationship building with potential customers. In order to effectively pave the way, it is imperative for the sales manager to know who the customers are that the salespeople will be calling on and to prepare them for what to expect. Cultural training/sensitizing will greatly enhance the chances of success. How can this information be gathered? By asking former salespeople who have called on these types of customers. If former salespeople are not available, then ask someone from the target culture. The key is to avoid actions and words that could be considered offensive. The salesperson does not want to set off mental "alarm bells" in the mind of their customer from the beginning because they didn't dress appropriately or offended the person by being too pushy.

## Religion

Religious beliefs have an important bearing on interpersonal dealings. The sales manager dealing with a salesperson as an employee needs to understand how religion can affect that person's actions and behaviors. Religious holidays/celebrations/obligations can affect the hours that are imposed on the salesperson. Times may need to be kept open for the salesperson to pray, and followers may not work during high religious seasons. Certainly the thirty days of Ramadan offer challenges for the sales manager. But religious insensitivity can create an intolerable work environment or conflict. Religious beliefs may also dictate what an individual can consume. Alcoholic beverages may be forbidden (as for Muslims), and certain foods may also be seen as religiously inappropriate (beef for Hindus). Simply attending a luncheon or dinner could be seen as an intolerable experience for an individual feeling social or corporate pressure to consume something viewed as inappropriate by religious standards. Religion can also shape an individual's feelings about dealing with males and females in a business setting. If women are seen as lesser than men in religious teachings, then imagine the difficulty for a female sales manager having to deal regularly with male salespeople, or a female salesperson calling on male customers. In some Middle Eastern countries, women are expected to be subservient in all ways to men, even to walk behind them. How can a potential male customer in this type of environment develop a long-term relationship with a female salesperson? These types of situations set up conflicts that can be extremely stressful for the individuals involved. The sales manager must be aware of religious teachings and beliefs and deal with them accordingly.

## Education

The level of education will also have an effect upon the success of the salesperson operating in a foreign culture. Certainly the number of years of education of the individual will have a bearing on their success when dealing with others. It is difficult for a prospective customer to be called on by a salesperson who does not at least have the same educational learning and background. The lack of knowledge could be the basis for a conflict that would be insurmountable. Obviously there would need to be as much similarity as possible in the educational experience of the salesperson and that of the customer, but more education would be better than less for the salesperson because they would be better able to adapt to perceived differences. Having the equivalent of a university/college education allows salespeople to be better prepared to deal with a variety of educational backgrounds. The hard part is to find university graduates in a variety of countries who desire sales as a career path. As business schools in different countries add courses to their curricula which focus on professional selling and sales management, the increased exposure should raise awareness about the attractiveness of sales careers and the pool of interested candidates will grow. The sales manager who is willing to visit business schools and make guest lectures may be able to build important bridges for future employment purposes. It is clear that what will make college students interested in sales careers is greater knowledge of the benefits associated with sales careers. Lack of knowledge is a hindrance that can be eliminated.

A critical issue for overseas placement of a salesperson, if they bring their family with them, could depend upon the nature of the educational system in their home country. This issue becomes particularly problematic when competitiveness and high test scores determine success in professional careers. This is the situation faced in Japan, for example. The problem is that if a Japanese national is chosen for an overseas sales job, they would potentially put their children in peril of losing competitiveness. If a child scores poorly on the various levels of exams, they will not be able to enter the "proper" schools, with the end goal being to get accepted into the highest ranked universities (e.g., Tokyo University or Waseda). The child being separated from the home educational system loses valuable in-school instruction. As a result, fear of losing competitiveness may put heavy stress upon the family. The salesperson would not be able to afford to keep their home back in Japan, and moving the family overseas puts them in jeopardy educationally. This type of stress can negatively impact that person's performance. What often occurs is that some families in this position are not able to return home until after the children finish their university education in their adopted countries. Understanding the nature of the educational system in the home country of a potential salesperson can help in identifying the best candidate for the position.

## Aesthetics

Aesthetics deals with what a society finds beautiful and visually appealing. This can apply to dress and apparel or to artwork or to such things as the presentation of food or musical tastes. This could certainly affect the potential salesperson from a dress and appearance standpoint. Such things as length of hair, smell, facial hair, decoration with jewelry or other types of facial adornment are all influenced by the home culture. Usually what is seen as visually appropriate by the individual is based upon their cultural makeup. The dress and appearance of the individual are directly linked with nonverbal communications, and the suggestions presented earlier should be considered here as well. Also, if an individual is expected to make sales presentations or to develop sales promotional literature, the appearance of these materials would be affected by their personal aesthetic orientation. It would therefore be wise for the sales manager to look for similar aesthetic expectations whenever possible between salespeople and their intended customers.

## Social organizations

Social organizations deal with the kinds of groups the individual belongs to in the culture. This includes the family, community groups, special interest groups, and work groups. The sales manager must assess how well the individual works in group settings, particularly when the company uses sales teams. It is important to consider that relationships can be significantly affected by the variables of age, income, ethnic heritage, social status, or gender. Sales managers may find themselves having difficulties dealing with their various sales force members because of perceived disparities in any or all of these variables, and this may also be true for salespeople dealing with customers. Problems may arise when males in patriarchal societies are asked to work for females (in a superior position). Imagine a work force of Japanese males answering to a female sales manager. This would create enormous personal conflict. Imagine older individuals in hierarchical societies answering to younger supervisors. This may also be seen when someone from a more affluent background is asked to deal with someone from a poorer background. This might be found when using someone from a more blue-collar area of a country to call on customers who are primarily white-collar. The words used, the social graces, and a variety of what might be seen as "inappropriate" traits might put a severe strain on any potential working relationship.

## Technology

This focuses on the tools and material aspects of culture. Knowing how advanced the potential salesperson's society is helps to match them up with the technological sophistication of potential customers. It is important that the salesperson understands the technological limitations of the potential customer. This might also affect the performance of the salesperson in a multicountry setting if they are given a laptop computer to record their sales calls or market potential projection figures. It would therefore be helpful to check the individual's technological literacy when assessing the proper fit of salesperson to global sales territory. It is also important to consider that the products being sold may have a technological sophistication that is either more advanced or less advanced than what is readily available and expected in a foreign country. Being ahead of the technological curve can result in salespeople trying to sell products in a market that is not ready for those products, which could be just as problematic as asking salespeople to sell products in a market where the products are seen as already obsolete. This technological gap can also occur because of the technological sophistication difference that might exist between sales manager and salesperson and/or between salesperson and foreign customer. Taking the time to ensure similarities among the players can improve the chances for long-term profitable relationships.

**29**

## Time

The concept of time is quite important for the sales manager to understand as a component of national culture. How the salesperson handles scheduled meetings with potential customers will influence initial impressions and relationship-building potential. The issue is the role of the clock in business as well as social settings. Some countries, like Germany and Japan, are focused on meeting at precisely scheduled times. Being late is a cultural affront that could make it very difficult to build goodwill again with that individual. You have potentially wasted their valuable time and have treated them as though they are not important. The opposite approach to time can be seen in such countries as Mexico, where delays are always involved. Time can also cause friction between the sales manager and the salesperson when they come from different time orientations. If the salesperson is from a relaxed time culture, it is helpful if the sales manager is sensitive about time and helps the salesperson adjust to the new situation gradually. Old habits, as we are all aware, are slow to change. If the sales manager is more relaxed about time than the salesperson, then it may be necessary to be more attentive to time schedules at least for a while until the individual has adjusted to the new schedule. These same suggestions are appropriate for the salesperson dealing with customers from different time orientations.

## Values and norms

The final component of culture deals with values and norms that are culturally ingrained. What countries expect, in terms of group and individual behavior, will in many cases be different. The value system that exists in the country sets the standards of acceptable behavior for the population. Some of the major value orientations are seen in the following list:

- Hard work as opposed to relaxation/leisure.
- Egalitarian as opposed to patriarchal decision making.
- Conservativism as opposed to liberalism.
- Female submissiveness as opposed to female liberation.
- Ethnocentrism as opposed to polycentrism.

The point is to be sensitive to the disparate values held important in different countries and see that the placement of salespeople into these work environments is done with the expectation that similarity enhances success, while major differences can be difficult to overcome in relationship building. Imagine the difficulty encountered in Western Germany when the Berlin Wall fell and West German companies were expected to hire former East German workers who had very different values regarding the work ethic. Owing to regular shortages of materials, East German workers often took breaks or ended their work days early. This was not the case for West Germany, where hard work was highly valued.

Besides work orientation, the nature of decision making can be an area for cultural conflict. Egalitarian societies, where decisions are made jointly between husbands and wives, can be stressful for individuals from patriarchal societies where the male has always been the important decision maker. Cultural conflict could also arise from the level of conservativism/traditionality versus liberalism/modernity. Individuals from conservative societies may feel that we should continue to do things the way we always have while those from liberal societies may feel that change (even change for the sake of change) is highly valued. An issue that can be particularly traumatic for female salespeople or sales managers involves dealing in a professional capacity with individuals from societies where women are expected to be submissive/subservient to men. It is very difficult for female sales representatives to call on older Japanese customers, since they do not give credibility to women in professional roles. Imagine sending female employees into countries where women walk behind men, completely cover their faces and the rest of their bodies, and remain silent.

Finally, one of the most difficult cultural concerns in a global context involves the difference in perspective of those from ethnocentric countries as opposed to those from polycentric countries. *Ethnocentrism* involves the view that the way things are conducted in the individual's country is the way that things should be done around the rest of the world. This attitude has gotten many American firms into trouble as other countries do not have to accept the American corporate way of doing things. *Polycentrism* involves thinking of the world as made up of many different ways of doing things. It assumes that each country has its own effective mechanisms, and when entering each country, the outsider should adapt to the ways that things are done in the newly entered country. *Taking an adaptive posture will always be reacted to more favorably than an ethnocentric posture.* Attempting to adjust to the culture of a foreign country and its people will usually be seen as positive by individuals from that culture. Rigidity does not engender warm feelings.

## BUILDING BETTER RELATIONSHIPS AS A MANAGER WITH SALESPEOPLE

Given all of the cultural concerns raised, what can the global sales manager do to develop better working relationships with the multicultural salespeople that they will be managing? A number of practical suggestions are worth considering. First, the best basis for a successful relationship is through cultural sensitivity and awareness. We all as humans have the tendency to "project" our cultural values and perspectives on to others with whom we interact. Since these foreign individuals do *not* come from the same culture, little should be taken for granted. The following skills and abilities are essential for multicultural managers:[6]

- Respect for others.
- Tolerance of ambiguity.
- Ability to relate to people.
- Being nonjudgmental.
- Ability to personalize one's observations.
- Empathy.
- Persistence/patience.

The most important point is that it does not take significant time or effort for the sales manager to read up on culture and become more sensitive to the cultural backgrounds of their salespeople. This sensitivity helps to build warmer and better working relationships.

The second issue involves unclear instructions that might be given to a salesperson by the sales manager that lead to poor or even unacceptable results. Obviously, the job of the sales manager is to communicate clear instructions to the salesperson and not to take anything for granted. Do not assume that you are automatically "in tune" with the foreign salesperson. There is every opportunity in two-way interpersonal communication to clarify whether the ideas have been effectively communicated. The point is that the manager can obtain immediate feedback to questions to see if the individual truly understood what was being said. Avoiding this clarification step is potentially worse than the alternative. The following suggestions will help the global sales manager to enhance their chances of clear and meaningful communications with foreign salespeople:

- Speak slowly and clearly.
- Avoid the use of idiomatic expressions.
- Try not to appear impatient or irritated.
- Periodically stop and ask what the salesperson understood or whether clarification is needed.

Lastly, it is important to know where to turn for additional cultural information when, and if, it is needed. The following is a helpful list of readily available books that focus on different cultures, cultural expectations, and mannerisms:

- *Do's and Taboo's around the World* by Roger E. Axtell, third edition, New York: John Wiley & Sons, 1993.
- *Do's and Taboos around the World for Women in Business* by Roger E. Axtell, Tami Briggs and Margaret Corcoran, New York: John Wiley & Sons, 1997.
- *Do's and Taboos of Hosting International Visitors* by Roger E. Axtell, New York: John Wiley & Sons, 1990.
- *Do's and Taboos of Humor around the World: Stories and Tips from Business and Life* by Roger E. Axtell, New York: John Wiley & Sons, 1999.
- *Do's and Taboos of International Trade* by Roger E. Axtell, New York: John Wiley & Sons, 1991.
- *Dun and Bradstreet's Guide to doing Business around the World* by Terri Morrison, Wayne A. Conaway and Joseph J. Douress, Englewood Cliffs NJ: Prentice Hall, 2000.
- *Gestures: The Do's and Taboos of Body Language around the World* by Roger E. Axtell, rev. edn, New York: John Wiley & Sons, 1998.
- *Kiss, Bow, or Shake Hands: How to do Business in Sixty Countries* by Terri Morrison, Wayne A. Conaway, and George A. Borden, Avon MA: Adams Media Corporation, 1995.
- *Managing Cultural Differences* by Philip R. Harris and Robert T. Moran, Houston TX: Gulf, 2000.

## CHAPTER SUMMARY

Culture shapes the behaviors and expectations of human beings. If the sales manager understands the nature of culture and how it is manifested, he or she can enhance the chances of success for the sales force in a variety of ways. First, they can choose the appropriate individuals given the nature of their potential foreign sales territories based upon cultural fit. Second, they can arm the salesperson with a cultural sensitivity that will enhance the chances of building a meaningful long-term relationship with potential customers. Finally, culturally aware sales managers can be better prepared to develop their own relationships with the various members of their sales force.

## DISCUSSION QUESTIONS

1   What is national culture, and why is it so important for the global sales manager?
2   What are the dimensions of national culture that were identified by Geert Hofstede, and how might they affect a salesperson in a variety of country settings?
3   Identify the various types of nonverbal communications and provide examples of cultural problems for each.
4   What are high context and low context cultures, and how would they potentially affect a global sales force?
5   What are idioms, and why are they so troublesome for sales encounters?
6   How might time be a cultural problem for an international sales encounter?
7   What are the seven skills and abilities that are important for multicultural managers?
8   How can global sales managers enhance their chances of clear and meaningful communication with foreign salespeople?

## REFERENCES

1   Kroeber, Alfred L., and Clyde Kluckhohn (1963), *Culture: A Critical Review of Concepts and Definitions*, New York: Vintage Books.

2   Hofstede, Geert (1980), *Cultures Consequences*, Newbury Park CA: Sage Publications.

3   Bond, Michael H. (1988), "Finding Universal Dimensions of Individual Variation in Multicultural Studies of Values: The Rokeach and Chinese Value Surveys," *Journal of Personality and Social Psychology*, 55, 1009–15.

4   Ricks, David A. (1993), *Blunders in International Business*, Cambridge MA: Blackwell Business Books.

5   Hall, Edward T. (1976), *Beyond, Culture*, Garden City NY: Anchor Books.

6   Axtell, Roger E. (1990), *The Do's and Taboos of Hosting International Visitors*, New York: John Wiley & Sons.

# Part II

# Global personal selling

## Chapter 3

# Personal sales in a global context

This chapter covers four basic topic areas: a short history of the sales profession, sales force orientations, different sales force jobs, and ethics.

### LEARNING OBJECTIVES

*After reading this chapter, you will be able to:*

- Discuss the evolution of the sales profession from early trader to that of a professional.
- Compare and contrast the six firm orientations on the operation of the sales force.
- Explain how sales force objectives can vary, based upon industry, location, and culture.
- Compare and contrast the five distinct sales careers discussed in this chapter and understand that there are variations of each career listed.
- Understand the importance of ethical behavior and social responsibility for professional salespersons.
- Compare and contrast the utilitarian and deontological approaches to resolving an ethical dilemma for each of the five potential areas discussed in this chapter.

**KEY TERMS**

- Industrial revolution.
- Production, Product, Sales, Marketing, Relationship marketing, and Global firm philosophies.
- Selling support, Account maintenance, Account winners, Inside sales, and Direct sales positions.
- Teleological and Deontological ethics.

## INTRODUCTION

It is important to understand the myriad forces that affect personal selling in the global marketplace. The previous chapter explained the impact culture has upon the global sales force. In the global marketplace, culture is the paramount force that influences all sales actions. For example, culture dictates the approach taken by the global salesperson when interacting with a current or potential customer. This chapter builds upon culture by introducing additional areas that significantly impact both sales management strategies and salesperson behavior. These topics include a background of personal selling and sales management, firm philosophies that drive the sales force, activities engaged in by the sales force, different sales force jobs, and concludes with a discussion of ethics and five ethical dilemma categories faced by salespeople in the global marketplace. The purpose of this chapter is to provide an explanation of forces that influence the global sales force.

## SALES PROFESSION EVOLUTION

The salesperson of the twenty-first century is quite different from his or her predecessors. Armed with higher-quality information made possible through information technology, today's salesperson possesses greater levels of formal education, is better trained, and is more astute than earlier generations of salespersons. Readers may note that earlier and less professional sales representatives made "pitches" that had little to do with the needs of their prospective clients. This behavior may be attributable to sales management practices that encouraged and rewarded aggressive market behavior. Today's sales professionals understand cross-cultural interactions and the need to form long-term relationships with their partners. In contemporary business the salesperson must know how to listen, to speak only when appropriate, and to be technically competent in order to solve problems for the client. In other words, today's sales professionals operate in a complex environment that surpasses previous sales force practices.

Selling, in some form, has existed since man began living in settlements. History records Marco Polo and the silk trade operating between Europe and China, Phoenician merchants trading in the Middle East, and Chinese merchants and traders plying the Pacific Rim in search of wealth. Early merchants traveled through frontier regions bartering and purchasing goods that were sold in the city and, in return, selling manufactured goods that originated in the cities. For a variety of reasons, a number of cultures viewed the sales profession unfavorably. In early China, for example, national prosperity was based upon agriculture rather than commerce. This resulted in merchants being assigned a status below those of peasant farmers, artisans, and soldiers.[1] However, the role of the sales force in conducting commerce became more specialized and well defined in Western cultures during the industrial revolution.

The *industrial revolution*, which began in the mid-1700s, resulted in the construction of large manufacturing facilities that were operated for maximum efficiency at locations distant from consumers. With this arrangement, it was economically prudent to hire representatives to operate as "middlemen" between the production facilities and merchants and final consumers. Industrial firms dispatched salespersons, armed with samples of finished goods, to visit distant markets to attract and meet with potential buyers. In effect, professional salespersons became the eyes and ears of large firms and the communication path with the marketplace.

Beginning in the twentieth century, the world was introduced to the telephone, air travel, and other technological advances that greatly influenced sales management practices. Salespersons began receiving formal sales training, were assigned exclusive sales territories, and learned canned sales presentations. Canned sales presentations attempt to standardize the interaction between the buyer and the seller, by insuring that the salesperson covered selected topics in the sales presentation.

Between 1914 and 1945, the countries of the world experienced World Wars I and II and the Great Depression. During the economic downturn of the 1930s, many firms expected their sales force to move items in a stagnant marketplace. The Great Depression was followed by World War II, which resulted in product rationing and pent-up consumer demand. Beginning in 1945, with the signing of peace treaties in Europe and the Pacific, nations shifted their attention to commercial pursuits. Also during this period, more firms came to acknowledge the importance of understanding their customers and behaving ethically and professionally. In many Western societies, the salesperson gained status for the significant contribution they make to the success of the firm. However, in the former Soviet and Chinese planned economies, sales and marketing functions were not always valued.[2] Today, Chinese citizens are modifying their attitudes toward business and are beginning to understand that gentlemen can seek profits and still be righteous. This value shift will profoundly change the status of business in the most populous country in the world.[3]

At the dawn of the twenty-first century, firms expect salespersons to be professionals. This means the salesperson is well trained, dependable, helpful, and professional in their daily behavior. Attempts to manipulate the customer during sales presentations are not considered or practiced. Sales professionals work diligently each day solving problems for their customers – in business-to-business markets – and the average citizen is unaware that this activity takes place! Suffice it to say that the salesperson plays an extremely important role in the global economy of the twenty-first century.

## FIRM PHILOSOPHIES

Firms in the global marketplace tend to practice one or more basic business philosophies or orientations. Therefore, it is important for sales managers and salespersons to understand how each philosophy results in a different emphasis being placed upon the roles and duties of the sales force. Orientations also dictate different levels of power, influence, and prestige within the firm for the sales, engineering, and manufacturing functional areas.

### Production philosophy

Companies that adhere to a production philosophy focus on economies of scale derived from efficient and increasing production quantities. This approach may be appropriate, especially when market demand exceeds supply. If the firm can accomplish production efficiencies, then the goods produced can be marketed at lower costs, which should result in higher sales levels. Most experts agree that efficient production is necessary for supplying standardized goods to a "mass" or global market.

When firms follow a production philosophy, sales force activities are often viewed as an afterthought. One role of the sales function is to allocate scarce goods to customers. Or sales personnel are expected to travel and communicate the availability and price of goods to distant customers. Likewise the sales force or sales department is rarely, if ever, consulted before changes are made to products and pricing is controlled outside of sales and marketing. The role of the sales force is to help the firm find buyers for the goods once they are manufactured.

### Product philosophy

Other firms believe that designing a "better mousetrap" will result in customers beating a path to their door. These firms may be approaching or have surpassed a point of economic equilibrium – supply meeting demand – which necessitates organizations to differentiate themselves from competitors. This means that engineering and design aspects of the business – like quality, durability, and functionality – are viewed as being the most important functions. This is because managers assume that customers purchase goods primarily because of these qualities.

In this circumstance, the sales force takes orders and delivers goods. However, the firm's primary focus is on the product, rather than the customer. The sales force plays a less significant role in providing needs satisfying goods to the marketplace. As an engineer informed one of the authors: "The important job is design and manufacture; anyone can sell the product."

## Sales philosophy

When markets become saturated with goods, firms may come to believe that customers will purchase only when they are stimulated. This may occur when it is difficult to differentiate based upon product features or capabilities. When this situation arises, firms may assume the best option is to hire sales personnel whose job it is to persuade customers to purchase the firm's product(s). The goal is to make the sale, and often any method that results in success is tolerated. Sales-oriented firms believe that success is guaranteed by sales revenue increases in each business period.

For firms that follow a sales orientation, the sales force is viewed as a necessary evil that is tolerated as long as forecasts are met. When sales goals are not met, then the sales force may receive threats of dismissal or offers of rewards if they work harder and accomplish more. Firms that ascribe to this philosophy fail to understand that it is difficult for the sales force to be successful when there is no differential advantage. In other words, the sales force is supposed to use its ability to persuade and convince customers to buy a product that may not satisfy customer needs. These firms attempt to sell what they can make, rather than what is needed or wanted by the marketplace.

## Marketing philosophy

A firm that pursues a marketing philosophy wants to produce goods that satisfy customer needs; believes that market research will uncover customer needs; that only customer-desired goods should be produced; and that profitability instead of sales revenue defines success. Firms believe that both buyers and sellers will benefit from such an orientation. In other words, customer needs are measured through market research and goods are manufactured to address these needs. The role of the sales force, like that of all members of the market-oriented firm, is to produce satisfied customers.[4]

The marketing philosophy has been criticized for a number of reasons. First, when asked, customers may not always know what they want or need. Second, respondents may not know their long-term needs nor understand emerging technologies that can be incorporated into current products. Finally, following a marketing philosophy does not guarantee firm success.[5]

## Relationship marketing

In the 1990s, more firms began implementing a marketing philosophy that resulted in an extended period of buyer–seller interaction. From a financial perspective, the customer becomes a stream of income. Rather than spending large sums of money advertising and using the sales force to pursue potential customers, firms believe it is more efficient to build relationships that result in long-term business built around "win–win" encounters. A number of business-to-business firms have practiced a form of relationship marketing with their best customers, but they may not have always pursued an established relationship marketing orientation. The sales force works to solve problems that result in more efficient business for their customers and does not attempt to sell unneeded or unwanted products. Similarly, customers do not pursue strategies aimed at reducing the selling price by pitting suppliers against one another.

However, not all customers may want a relationship with their suppliers and firms should not attempt to form extensive relationships except with their best customers.[6] What many firms are able to do today, because of advances in information technology, is to gauge the degree of profitability generated by each customer. This results in firms providing varying levels of service to different customers.

## Global philosophy

World-class firms practice a global orientation. This means that global firms understand there are segments of customers in most countries that desire world-class products. The firm views the world as one market and approaches it with a unified strategy that allows lessons learned to be applied globally, while saving money in the process.[7] Global firms seek to create greater value for their customers by standardizing to gain economies of scale, but localize or customize the product whenever necessary to satisfy customers.

Workers, including sales personnel, are recruited worldwide. The global or transnational firm seeks to produce the highest quality products/services, at the lowest possible prices, while "delighting" their customers. The role of the global salesperson is to be culturally and linguistically competent, to interact with global customers to establish long-term relationships, and to serve as the global firm's representative to customers. This means the global salesperson must be highly educated, experienced, competent, and an equal member of the corporation's business team.[8]

## Importance of firm orientations

When presented with a discussion of the different firm philosophies or orientations, the reader may assume that firms evolve through each philosophy. While this evolution may appear to be intuitive, it seldom happens. Based upon the firm's world-view, a single orientation may be adopted and followed until forced to change by declining sales and customer losses. Generally firm orientations, and the underlying organizational culture, do not change easily or frequently.

Firms can adopt and follow one or more of these philosophies and be successful. Each philosophy has its place depending upon the marketplace. It can also be argued that certain aspects of each orientation are important for the success of the firm. Global customers expect low manufacturing costs, excellent design, and having their needs met. The firm wants to form a relationship with its best customers because this orientation appears to generate lower-cost customers. Likewise, the firm expects the sales force to work the marketplace to reach new customers or to find outlets for products that have been overproduced or under-engineered. However, while a firm's orientation may change slightly, depending upon the market situation, the firm normally adheres to a single orientation more than the rest.

An important reason for potential sales managers and salespersons to understand firm approaches to the marketplace is that the firm's philosophy will impact their own role in the organization. It is imperative, for this reason, that all salespersons understand the market orientation practiced by their firm. By being aware of the firm's general orientation, salespersons and sales managers can ascertain the expected role they will play, as well as their ability to succeed in the organization. In effect, by understanding the orientation practiced by the firm, the salesperson can better understand the likelihood that they can be satisfied in the workplace.

## SALES FORCE ACTIVITIES

The functions performed on the job by the salesperson to accomplish tasks vary by job type, industry and country. While the uninitiated may believe that all sales jobs are the same, this is not true. Selling jobs differ considerably. These differences include both the types of activities the salesperson engages in and the frequency of performing the activity. This implies that sales success is dependent upon understanding which activities are important and being able to effectively perform these tasks. In turn, sales force activities directly influence sales force management and sales training issues.

Several studies conducted in the United States found that salespersons perform a number of similar job-related activities: direct selling, customer service, working with managers, managing information, working with others, training/recruiting, entertaining, and out-of-town travel. There is little doubt that all salespersons perform many of these activities in their day-to-day job. However, the degree of intensity found in working with managers and others, entertaining, and traveling can vary considerably. Such forces as the stage of product life cycle, competitive situation, budget, and salesperson experience directly impact the salesperson's ability to perform these sales activities.

Since sales activities vary by industry and location, then it appears certain that the sales job also differs by culture. In a study of industrial salespersons in Germany, Denmark, and the United States, this is precisely what was found.[9] The study reported that salespersons from all three countries engaged in such common activities as closing a sale, monitoring competition, overcoming objections, studying market trends, and providing/receiving feedback. Conversely, few salespersons provided maintenance, delivered products, created advertising, stocked products, or installed equipment. Interestingly, the activities reported by German and US salespersons were more similar than those performed in Denmark. German firms engage in training customers and setting up displays more often than their US counterparts. American salespersons, on the other hand, report a greater focus on prospecting (94 percent US versus 41 percent for German and 38 percent for Danish firms). US salespersons also expedited customer orders at higher levels than German and Danish salespersons. Danish salespersons reported higher levels of helping customers with inventory, making demonstrations, and engaging in significantly less activity with regards to entertaining clients and traveling overnight. Some variations are attributable to respondent

**43**

differences and the fact that Denmark is a smaller country that may not require overnight travel. What is obvious is there are clear differences in the type and frequency of sales force activities. This is extremely important for salespersons and sales managers to understand and to use to their advantage in the global marketplace.

## PERSONAL SELLING JOBS

A wide variety of personal selling jobs exist around the world. These include everything from retail salespersons that stand behind a counter until approached by customers to telephone salespersons that call unknown customers trying to sell unneeded or unwanted goods/services. However, there are a number of general job classifications that assist in the understanding of the sales profession. In this section, we discuss selling support, account maintenance, account winners, inside salespersons, and direct sales positions.

### Selling support

Selling support refers to individuals who utilize their expertise to advise customers about the firm's products/services through the dissemination of information, samples, and personal visits. Examples of selling support jobs include pharmaceutical and technical salespersons. Pharmaceutical salespersons are also called *missionary salespersons* because they meet with physicians and hospital pharmacists to convert the buyer to a believer in the medicine. The *technical salesperson* serves a similar function by meeting with engineers, manufacturing managers, and quality control managers and providing technical information and product samples that convince the buyer organization that the seller's products are of high quality. In most cases, neither the pharmaceutical nor the technical representative makes a direct sale. That is, physicians prescribe medications for their patients and hospitals order direct from the manufacturer. In technical sales, an account representative presents a written proposal to the buyer to finalize the purchase. Selling support personnel must possess high levels of expertise, have solid interpersonal skills, and be excellent problem solvers.

### Account maintenance

In a number of industries the salesperson's goal is to maintain an ongoing relationship with current customers. This means the salesperson regularly calls upon their accounts, takes orders for products, resolves problems, and maintains positive relationships. Account maintenance salespersons provide outstanding service and work to make the customer dependent upon these services. In the grocery business, manufacturers' representatives interact with the store manager, assist with merchandise stocking, pricing, and returns, and gain the best possible shelf space for their product line.

Account maintenance salespersons are also called *order takers*. This name derives from route salespersons that are employed by wholesalers, who regularly call upon an established customer base, taking orders and replenishing standard product items. In most cases, order takers do not create new business. Account maintenance salespersons may assume responsibility for the account after the customer begins buying from a salesperson responsible for opening new accounts.

## Account winners

Salespersons who are categorized as account winners open new accounts and introduce new products to potential or established accounts. Firms making a push to expand their market share or increase the number of customer accounts rely upon account winner salespersons. An account winner's role may be to visit accounts with the goal of opening the account and then turning the account over to an account maintenance colleague. Also, a salesperson who "grows" the number and size of current customer accounts falls into this category. "Growing" an account means that the initial purchase levels are small but the salesperson works with the buyer to increase the dollar amount and number of products/services purchased from the supplier.

## Inside sales

Inside salespersons occupy a wide array of job descriptions. These individuals do not physically travel to customer locations, but handle phone, fax, or computer inquiries and orders placed by established and new customers. Telemarketing salespersons can also operate actively by calling customers and selling products/services. Conversely, an inside salesperson can assume a more passive role by answering phone calls generated by customer need or by advertisements that direct them to toll-free numbers. When customers call to place orders, it is customary for the inside salesperson to cross-sell by asking about related items that might also be needed by the customer. For example, if a firm calls a supplier and orders copier paper, the salesperson would ask if the caller also needed toner and/or print cartridges.

## Direct sales

Direct sales positions exist in a number of industries and include retail, life insurance, real estate, and investment sales. This category includes direct sales firms like Amway, Tupperware, and Mary Kay that have spread from the United States to many Asian and European locations. The qualifications for a direct salesperson varies widely, based upon the need for licensing – insurance, real estate, and investments – and the intangibility of the product. For example, higher education and specialized skills are needed to sell stock portfolios to wealthy investors, but these same qualifications are not necessary to sell consumer items to friends and acquaintances. Direct sales occur more frequently today in the global marketplace. Many of the firms listed above have expanded their business in emerging markets where aspiring entrepreneurs or housewives can work hard, serve their client base, and turn a profit.

## ETHICAL FORCES

Ethics and ethical behavior have many meanings. In the global marketplace ethical behavior suggests that the salesperson, and the firm they represent, make decisions based upon sound moral principles. In business, however, a firm must make a long-run profit in order to remain solvent, so we can already see a dilemma. Businesses must balance the need for

**45**

profitability with the needs of society. This means the firm and the salesperson must at times make compromises. As a result, society has developed rules to guide firms in their search for profitability that do not implicitly harm society. For our purposes, business ethics is defined as "moral principles and standards that guide behavior in the world of business."[10] Society ultimately determines if a firm's actions are ethical and the response that occurs when actions are viewed as being unethical.

Being an ethical firm also means that the company is socially responsible. This infers that the firm will maximize its benefit while minimizing any negative impact upon society. However, it is not always simple or easy to identify when a firm or salesperson behaves ethically. We now explore a number of moral philosophies that provide differing views of ethical behavior.

## Teleological philosophy

A teleological moral philosophy focuses on the outcome or consequence of an action. An example of this might be pleasure, knowledge, success, or career growth. Moral philosophers refer to teleological ethics as *consequentialism*. Two important teleological philosophies influence business decisions – egoism and utilitariansim.

*Egoism* refers to acceptable behavior in regard to individual consequences. In effect, egoists believe ethical decisions should maximize the benefits of the individual. These benefits may take the form of success, wealth, fame, or power. When making an ethical decision, the individual makes choices based upon his or her personal self-interest. An example of egoism is when a salesperson for Westinghouse Philippines knows that the medical scanning machine he sells routinely fails to operate and requires weekly maintenance. But the salesperson does not inform the prospective customer about this potential problem because it might affect the current purchase decision. Completing the sale would result in success, wealth (a sales commission), and possible fame (from managers and colleagues) for the salesperson.

*Utilitarianism* is similar to egoism, but the utilitarian seeks the greatest good for the greatest number of people. The ultimate goal is to make decisions that result in the greatest total utility for everyone affected by the decision. A cost–benefit comparison is conducted by a decision maker that calculates the utility of the consequences and then selects the course of action that results in the greatest utility for all parties. For example, when the same Westinghouse Philippines salesman determines through a cost–benefit analysis that a large number of patients will receive superior medical treatment based upon information derived from the equipment, that physicians, nurses, and hospital workers will benefit both professionally and financially, and the hospital will gain prestige and funding from this state-of-the-art equipment. Therefore, the salesperson decides that the total utility for all parties greatly exceeds the negative aspects of divulging the potential maintenance defect.

A concern when cost–benefit comparisons are made is that a manager can influence the decision by how he or she defines and weights the consequences to both beneficiaries and non-beneficiaries. In other words, it is possible for a decision maker to exaggerate the benefits and downplay the negative impact of the action on affected parties. In effect, two managers might conduct independent cost–benefit analyses of the same ethical dilemma and reach very different conclusions.

## Deontological philosophy

This moral school believes that ethical decisions should be made based upon the rights of individuals and their intentions. Unlike utilitarians, deontologists believe that some actions are never justified, regardless of the consequences. For example, in deontological philosophy, it is never acceptable to harm an individual because such action infringes the rights of the individual as a person. In utilitarian theory, one might be able to justify the death of an individual if it leads to greater utility for others. Deontological believers are influenced by the German philosopher Kant and state that there are moral absolutes against killing, stealing, lying, etc., and under no circumstance can these actions be justified. One way to determine whether an action is ethical is to ask a person, "If your behavior was viewed by everyone, would you still do this?"

Deontologists can also be grouped into those who adhere to certain rules and those who focus on the nature of the acts. Deontologists who adhere to rules believe that reason and logic can be used to formulate moral principles. An example is the Christian "Golden Rule," which advocates that all people be treated as we would like to be treated. Some deontologists examine the "act" to determine ethicality, and employ the principles of equity, fairness, and impartiality to make and enforce decisions. This ethical school believes that people know that certain acts are right or wrong, no matter the consequences or rules. Deontologists might say, in regard to the previous example of the Westinghouse Philippines salesperson, that he should not fail to disclose the maintenance problem with the scanning machine, since he wants the buyer to be open in her discussion with him.

It should be clear that there are numerous ways to assess the ethical correctness of an action. Each school of philosophy has clear guidelines for determining ethical behavior. However, it is possible for each of these ethical schools of thought to believe that their course of action is ethical and yet disagree with one another!

## Ethics in the global marketplace

Potential ethical dilemmas abound in the global sales marketplace. In this section discrimination, the use of bribery, product issues, pricing issues, and behavior/compliance issues are discussed.

### Discrimination

US laws prohibit discrimination of persons based upon race, color, sex, religion, or disabilities in hiring, termination, and promotion decisions. According to one author, it is common practice to ask job applicants to provide information about their marital status, birth date, age, citizenship, and language competences in cultures that are "being oriented" instead of "doing oriented" found in the United States.[11] However, discrimination in some form appears to exist in nearly all nations of the world. One has only to look at the treatment of immigrants in certain areas of Europe, the aborigines in Australia, and women in Japan to view discrimination in real terms. Discrimination is often justified because of cultural norms, but these norms come into conflict when two or more cultures interact to conduct business.

One example of discrimination in sales relates to firms not being able to utilize women as sales representatives in Middle Eastern countries and Japan. Managers from more egalitarian countries face the dilemma of assigning men to service accounts in cultures that discriminate at the expense of not allowing women to advance in their careers. A contrasting alternative is to impose practices from outside the customer's culture – by trying to force cultures to deal with women. However, this action will almost certainly lead to business failure.[12]

## Bribery

In many cultures the payment of bribes to facilitate business is an accepted practice and goes by many names (see Table 3.1). Bribery seems to be endemic in certain parts of the world (see Exhibit 3.1) and is an accepted tradition in areas of Africa, the Middle East and Asia.[13] Bribes tend to be more common when firms are involved in large construction projects, military hardware, turnkey efforts, and large equipment contracts. Likewise, when economies are not transparent, like those found in many emerging nations, it is necessary to spread a lot of "grease" or bribes to initiate business.[14] In the United States, the Foreign Corruption Practices Act (FCPA) prohibits US firms from engaging in bribery. This means that US firms must operate under different rules than companies with headquarters located in other countries. However, to complicate matters, when global sales representatives fail to offer "gifts" at appropriate times, the potential client can become offended by this "*faux pas*" and break off negotiations.[15]

## Product issues

This ethical dilemma occurs when products that are banned in one country are shipped and sold in another, usually less developed, nation. Often these products have been identified as being dangerous or defective in the home country. Rather than destroying the product, the manufacturer ships the good to a less developed nation where it is sold to local consumers without fanfare.

**Table 3.1** Local terminology for bribery

| Country | Term | Local meaning |
|---|---|---|
| Brazil | *jeito* | influence or reciprocity |
| Ethiopia | *gubo* | bribe |
| Egypt | | |
| Greece | *ladoma* | bribe |
| India | *baksheesh* | gratuity or gift or alms |
| Turkey | | |
| Mexico | *mordida* | a little bite |
| Philippines | *lagay* | bribe |
| Southeast Asia | *kumshaw* | bribe |
| Zaire | *matabiche* | bribe |

Source: Roger E. Axtell (ed.) *Do's and Taboos around the World*, New York: John Wiley & Sons, 1990

## EXHIBIT 3.1 BRIBERY RAMPANT IN EASTERN EUROPE

More than 3,000 firms that operate in Eastern Europe report that bribery and corruption are "endemic" in Eastern Europe and the former Soviet Union. Even after a decade of rule since the collapse of the former Soviet Union, companies report that "bribe taxes" range from 2.1 percent of annual revenues in Croatia to 8.1 percent in Georgia. They claim that when this "bribe tax" is added to official taxes levied by the countries, the burden is excessive and impacts economic enterprise. What is surprising is that Eastern European countries that are often categorized as having transitioned to free markets, like Hungary and Poland, are reported to require bribes from firms at higher percentages than in Russia.

The study, which was conducted by the World Bank and the European Bank for Reconstruction and Redevelopment, reported that direct government intervention in the area economy had been reduced since the fall of the centrally planned governments. However, the study noted that some governments continue to favor certain firms with subsidies and loan forgiveness. Also, a small number of indigenous firms exert tremendous influence over decisions made by central governments. The study concluded that, even though bribery and corruption remain a problem in Eastern Europe, freedom and economic choice in the marketplace expanded over the 1990s.

*Source.* John Reed and Erik Portanger, "Bribery, Corruption are rampant in Eastern Europe, Survey finds," *Wall Street Journal*, November 9, 1999, A21.

Most people are aware of the controversy over Nestlé selling infant formula to poor African consumers through sales representatives dressed in nurses' uniforms. The mothers then diluted the baby formula with polluted water to save money and a number of infants died from this practice. As a result, an international boycott was initiated and, subsequently, Nestlé agreed to stop promoting infant formula in Africa and to label the product with disclaimers. In this case, there was nothing wrong with the product. A second example is US tobacco manufacturers who are under pressure to reduce advertising and promotional efforts for their product in the United States. One alternative strategy has been to move to other markets – in this case the global marketplace. Activist groups have criticized US tobacco companies for selling a product in emerging markets that clearly harms consumers. In response, the governments of emerging nations have responded that increased tobacco sales result in higher tax revenues and additional jobs for their citizens. Also, these government officials state that local consumers do not have high life expectancies and they enjoy consuming tobacco.

### Pricing issues

Global firms adopt different pricing schemes around the world and this results in some practices being viewed as "discriminatory." This means that consumers are charged different prices for an identical product without a logical reason for doing so. Price discrimination is legal in the United States as long as price differences can be justified based upon costs.

**49**

When consumers from two nations are charged different prices, it is discriminatory unless valid reasons can be justified for these practices. Valid reasons include tax, tariffs, transport, or higher manufacturing expenses. In the United States, firms must adhere to the Robinson–Patman Act, which states that a seller must charge any industrial buyer the same price for goods as long as the conditions of purchase are identical. But price discrimination is routinely practiced in many nations.

Japan and other countries have been criticized for "dumping" or selling products outside the home country at lower prices than charged in the home marketplace. Pharmaceutical firms have also been criticized for charging citizens of developed nations higher prices for drugs than in less developed countries. Critics call this "gouging." There is little doubt that pricing is a complicated issue in global sales transactions. However, charging different prices to consumer segments, gouging, and dumping all result in some consumers having to pay more than a fair price for their products. The dilemma comes with defining the word "fair." Fair for whom?

### Behavior/compliance issues

In addition to ethical dilemmas encountered in the marketplace, salespersons are expected to adhere to or comply with internal rules and ethical expectations. These include honest dealing with management and colleagues, prudent management of resources, and complying with company policies and regulations. To operate successfully, persons within an organization must be able to depend upon the promises of their managers and colleagues. Promises must be kept or affected persons need to be notified. Managers must not make promises to salespersons that are presented to customers that cannot or will not be honored. In Western societies this is known as firm or individual integrity.

As a representative of the firm, the salesperson must responsibly manage company resources while they are in the office or traveling. This can range from wasting time in the office making unofficial long distance phone calls or playing computer games on a personal computer to staying in more expensive hotels than necessary when visiting customers, and rationalizing the action by stating that sales expenses are covered by the firm. Salespersons must always be mindful that it is unethical to expend their firm's money on unnecessary activities, even though they are personally pleasurable.

Also, the salesperson must behave ethically when filing expense vouchers at the conclusion of a company business trip. This means that the salesperson should file a claim for reimbursement for the exact amount expended during the trip to conduct company business. Travel expenses are not an alternative form of sales force compensation. Likewise, it is important for the firm to clearly state what are and what are not acceptable travel expenses and to reimburse fairly and promptly when a business trip is completed. In this area, both the salesperson and the firm must be fair and honest with one another. It should be evident that ethical behavior is a two-way street.

## Ethical codes of conduct

In response to ethical dilemmas, and to provide employees with ethical guidelines, firms adopt and distribute ethical codes of conduct. Without an ethical code of conduct, the individual salesperson is left to interpret acceptable behavior based upon the practices and expectations of colleagues and managers. A code of conduct is a policy statement that lists specific acceptable behaviors.[16] These behaviors, which are organized into five areas, can be either internal or within the organization and external or between the salesperson and customers, suppliers, and partners. Sales managers must consistently demand high levels of ethical behavior and utilize rewards and punishments to motivate sales personnel to adhere to ethical codes of conduct.[17]

Even when firms adopt and publish a code of ethics, not all ethical dilemmas can be resolved. This is because ethical dilemmas occur in gray areas that present sales personnel and sales managers with situations not previously experienced. However, without a code of ethics, the sales force has little guidance upon which to base decisions in the office and field. For a code of ethics to be successful, it must be specific, the sales force and other employees must be trained, and a neutral office must audit compliance.[18]

In business – whether domestic or global – the sales force should attempt to behave ethically and be socially responsible in all business dealings. The problem is that determining what is ethical depends upon the individual's perspective or situation. Most salespersons in the global marketplace would not knowingly break a law, harm the environment, or discriminate against others. When discussed in an abstract manner, moral dilemmas are straightforward and easy to understand. The problem occurs when a salesperson finds him or herself in a situation where the laws are nonexistent or ambiguous, where local customs include ethically questionable practices, and when a firm will do anything to win the contract.[19]

Global firms often rely upon local laws to guide their ethical dealings. However, established law can only establish a "floor" of acceptable dealings above which ethical behavior should be practiced. That is, ethical behavior requires the salesperson operating in the global marketplace to behave at a higher standard than simply following legal precedence. In effect, current laws are responses to former breaches of ethical behavior.[20]

There are three ethical principles global sales managers can employ to help distinguish between correct and incorrect behavior.[21] These principles include:

| Ethical principle | Question |
|---|---|
| ■ Utilitarian ethics | Does the action maximize the benefits of all parties? |
| ■ Rights of the parties | Are individual rights respected? |
| ■ Justice of fairness | Are the actions just and fair for all parties? |

Answers to these questions should assist global salespersons and sales managers in determining whether their actions are ethically correct. One final question individuals might ask themselves, when confronted with a vexing ethical dilemma, is: "How would I feel if my parents (or children) were to learn about my action?"

## CHAPTER SUMMARY

This chapter presented forces that impact personal selling in the global marketplace. These include a brief history of the sales profession, firm orientation, ethical dilemmas faced by the sales force, and specific sales jobs. It is important to understand where the sales profession originated in order to understand current firm practices and perceptions. The firm's orientation toward the marketplace directly affects the role played by salespersons, the expectations of sales personnel by the firm's management, and policies established for current and potential customers. Nearly all salespersons encounter ethical conflicts as they engage in business activities. These may be internal or external ethical dilemmas. Finally, the type of sales position significantly influences the role, skills, and expectations of the sales force. By understanding these forces, the salesperson can play a more informed role in the organization. This greater awareness of market-related forces also aids the salesperson to understand the "what, why, and when" aspects of their job.

## DISCUSSION QUESTIONS

1   What role has technology played in the evolution of the salesperson?

2   Compare and contrast the focus of the firm orientation on the sales force.

3   How do the situational variables of industry, location, and culture influence sales force activities?

4   Discuss the distinct job categories presented and how necessary skills and resultant activities can vary between sales jobs.

5   What are some outcomes of unethical sales force behavior? How might questionable behavior affect buyer and seller relationships?

6   Why is it so difficult to define ethical sales force behavior?

## REFERENCES

1   Seagrave, Sterling (1995), *Lords of the Rim*, New York: Putnam.

2   Lupton, Robert A., Earl D. Honeycutt, Jr., David P. Paul, and John B. Ford (1997), "The Appeal of a Personal Selling Career in Slovakia: Implications for Global Marketers," *AMA Educators' Proceedings*, Chicago: American Marketing Association, 259–65.

3   Quanyu, Huang, Richard S. Andrulis, and Chen Tong (1994), *A Guide to Successful Business Relations with the Chinese*, New York: International Business Press.

4   Drucker, Peter (1973), *Management: Tasks, Responsibilities, Practices and Plans*, New York: Harper & Row.

5   Houston, Franklin S. (1986), "The Marketing Concept: What it is and What it is Not," *Journal of Marketing*, 50:2 (April), 81–7.

6   Fournier, Susan, Susan Dobscha, and David Glen Mick (1998), "Preventing the Premature Death of Relationship Marketing," *Harvard Business Review*, January–February, 42–4, 46, 48–51.

7   Derryberry, Jennifer (1999), "What it Really Means to go Global," *Sales and Marketing Management*, 151:12 (December), 93–4.

8   Ohmae, Kenichi (1999), *The Borderless World*, New York: Harper Business.

9   Moncrief, William C. (1988), "A Comparison of Sales Activities in an International Setting," *Journal of International Consumer Marketing*, 1:1, 45–61.

10  Ferrell, O.C., and John Fraedrich (1991), *Business Ethics*, Boston MA: Houghton Mifflin.

11  Usunier, Jean-Claude (1996), *Marketing across Cultures*, London: Prentice Hall.

12  Ferrell and Fraedrich (1991).

13  Fadiman, A.J. (1986), "A Traveler's Guide to the Gifts and Bribes," *Harvard Business Review*, July–August, 122–4, 126, 130, 132, 134, 136.

14  Xu, Gang "Jerry" (2001), E-mail correspondence, July 12.

15  Arunthanes, Wiboon, Patriya Tansuhaj, and David J. Lemak (1994), "Cross-cultural Business Gift Giving," *International Marketing Review*, 11:4, 44–55.

16  Ferrell and Fraedrich (1991).

17  Honeycutt, Earl D., Jr., and John B. Ford (1993), "Ethical Dilemmas in the Automotive Industry," *AMA Educators' Proceedings*, August, Chicago: American Marketing Association, 352–8.

18  Smith, N. Craig, and John A. Quelch (1993), *Ethics in Marketing*, Homewood IL: Irwin.

19  Anonymous (1997), "Corruption: Stop the Rot," *Business Asia*, January 13, 2.

20  Honeycutt, Earl D., Jr., Myron Glassman, Michael Zugelder, and Kiran Karande (2001), "Determinants of Ethical Behavior: A Study of Auto Salespeople," *Journal of Business Ethics*, 32:1 (July), 69–79.

21  Cateora, Philip R., and John L. Graham (1999), *International Marketing*, Boston MA: Irwin McGraw-Hill.

# Chapter 4

# Cross-cultural communication, negotiation and the global selling process, I

This chapter covers cross-cultural communication, negotiation, and the initial steps of the selling process.

## LEARNING OBJECTIVES

*After reading this chapter, you will be able to:*

- Understand the interpersonal communication process and how the salesperson can ensure that there is a true understanding with potential customers.
- Discuss the negotiations process and how the salesperson can use it to enhance their chances of successfully making points in negotiations with potential customers.
- Explain the preliminary steps in the global selling process used to strategically prepare the salesperson for face-to-face meetings with prospective customers.

## KEY TERMS

- Encoding, Decoding, and Noise.
- Shadowing and Role-playing.
- Sense making and Sense giving.

## INTRODUCTION

This book is written for the sales manager who will lead a global sales force. Much of the material presented in Chapter 2 details cultural sensitivity and training activities to enhance the sales force's chances of success in the field. This chapter, and the next, build upon this cultural background by explaining three processes that significantly affect cross-cultural selling. In order for a salesperson to achieve success in sales, it is imperative that he or she understands: (1) how interpersonal communication occurs, (2) the nature of the negotiations process, and (3) the steps involved in the selling process. The smooth functioning of these three processes is complicated by differing cultural backgrounds of the two main players – the prospective buyer and seller. Armed with the cultural knowledge that serves as a fundamental component of this book, proper strategic preparations can be undertaken by the sales manager to ensure their sales force has the necessary knowledge to close the sale. This chapter presents the first two processes and the initial steps of the selling process. The remainder of the selling process is discussed in Chapter 5.

## THE INTERPERSONAL COMMUNICATION PROCESS

The first requirement for success in sales is to insure that the salesperson can effectively communicate with current and potential customers. Of course, the communication of ideas from the sales manager to the salesperson is just as important as communication between the salesperson and potential buyer. The interpersonal communication process, shown in Figure 4.1, begins with an idea in the mind of the person who wants to communicate that idea to another person. That idea must be translated into a form that enables it to be communicated. This requires the translation of the idea into a series of signs and symbols (language), known as *encoding*, which is used for communication.

These signs and symbols are then transmitted by means of a communication medium (e.g., spoken words, written words). The receiver next attempts to translate the received signs and symbols into an idea, which is called *decoding*. Of course, it is important that the idea received by the potential customer match as closely as possible with the original thought in the salesperson's mind. What makes this a challenge is that during the communication process, *noise* or distortion can significantly affect what is heard and understood by the receiver. Imagine the noise potential when a UK salesperson initially meets with an impor-

CASE VIGNETTE **PREPARING FOR MIDDLE EAST NEGOTIATIONS**

Robert Fraser, a sales manager for a large defense contractor in California, is scheduled to travel to the Middle East next month to discuss sales of aircraft and tanks to the governments of that region. This will be Fraser's first trip to this area of the world and he wants to make a favorable impression. He wonders what type of preparation he should undergo to insure he can successfully interact without offending his hosts.

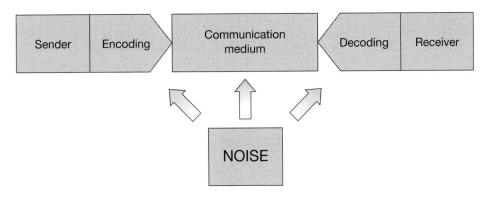

**Figure 4.1** *The interpersonal communication process*

tant Korean customer who has only a limited understanding of the English language. Given this disparity, then add to the communication challenges the distractions that exist in a normal business workplace environment (e.g., manufacturing processes, other conversations, outside noises), and it becomes clear how noise can seriously affect what is actually heard and understood by each party. Now, think about how cultural awkwardness between the buyer and seller can exacerbate the situation.

Fortunately, in an interpersonal context, immediate feedback can be used to clarify the ideas involved in the communication effort. The sender can ask the receiver what they understood was communicated, which permits further explanation or clarification, when necessary. The important role of the salesperson is to insure that he or she understands the language of the potential customer as well as possible so that an accurate meeting of minds occurs.

Often, in cross-cultural settings, inability to understand contextual nuances of the language leads to misunderstandings. When the salesperson calling upon the potential customer is unsure of the language involved, then it is imperative that he or she employs a bilingual interpreter who can assist the two parties in reaching a meaningful agreement. In the event that the salesperson does not know the buyer's language, then just having sales materials written in that language by experts does not ensure that a meeting of the minds will occur, since there is no way for the two parties to effectively seek clarification. Clarification in communication is the key to success, and the interpreter brings a necessary component to the first meetings between buyer and seller. It may be possible, with language training, that later meetings will not require an interpreter, but this may only be viable once a solid relationship been built between the salesperson and the cross-cultural customer. It is important to remember that cultural awareness, covered in Chapter 2, provides the salesperson with tools to minimize the impact of noise and distortion during the communication process.

## THE NEGOTIATION PROCESS

In addition to clarity of communication between the parties, a clear understanding of the negotiation process is integrally important to sales success. When the sales manager understands what is involved in this important process, then he or she can provide helpful training for the salesperson to understand how to arrive at the best position in any negotiation. The negotiation process is shown in Figure 4.2 and each component of the process is discussed

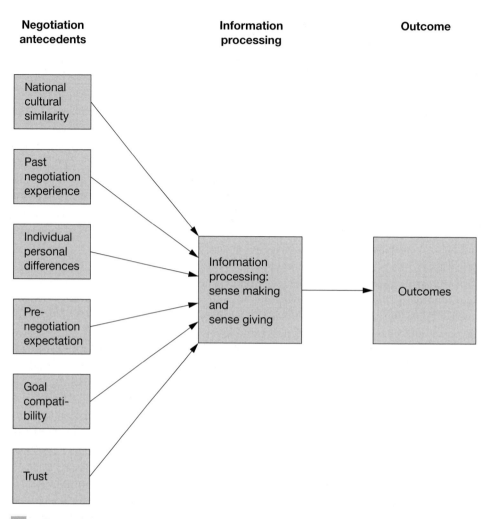

**Figure 4.2** *The cross-cultural negotiation process*

below. The first section focuses on the antecedents to negotiation, which include the perspectives the salesperson and prospective buyer bring to the sales negotiation process. The second section involves the negotiation process components, sense making and sense giving, where the parties attempt to process the relevant information. The final section covers the outcomes of the negotiation process.

## Antecedents to negotiation

### National cultural similarity

One of the most important things the salesperson and prospective cross-cultural customer bring to the negotiation process is their basic national cultural makeup. Chapter 2 discusses national cultural characteristics, and what becomes clear by understanding culture is that the more similar the cultural backgrounds of the parties involved, the greater the chance for understanding and agreement between the parties. Of course, this is made more diffi-cult in the business-to-business sales process; however, if sales teams are utilized, then the more similar the members of the sales team are to those of the prospective buying group, the greater the chance of clear understanding among all parties involved. Intuitively, cultural differences create a potential for misunderstandings and perceived behavioral discrepancies; however, it is the purpose of this book to sensitize the sales manager to culture and its impact and, as a result, minimize the potential for conflict in interactions. This certainly includes the negotiation process. One cautionary note is that the salesperson should not make assumptions about what the cross-cultural customer is thinking or feeling unless both parties are from the same or a similar culture. It is easy to become overconfident and assume that there is complete agreement when in fact there is not. With proper knowledge and preparation, even negotiating parties from widely disparate cultures can reach lasting and beneficial agreements. In such situations preparation and sensitivity are the keys to guiding the other party to a successful outcome.

## Past negotiation experience

Research shows that the more experience the salesperson brings to cross-cultural negotia-tions, the greater their flexibility in dealing with and guiding cross-cultural customers to successful negotiation outcomes. The global sales manager can provide training to compen-sate for lack of negotiation experience. One training method is to have their most successful and seasoned veterans teach new salespeople what to expect and how to handle themselves during negotiations. This training should be conducted on a periodic basis, by a variety of veteran salespeople that offer suggestions and give help to less experienced salespeople. Other helpful techniques involve: (1) allowing inexperienced salespeople to *shadow* or accompany seasoned veterans to observe how they conduct themselves in different cross-cultural negotiations settings with opportunity for debriefing afterwards or (2) *role playing*, where veterans put trainees through mock negotiations in either or both roles as buyer and seller and subsequently critique them on their handling of different situations. It is partic-ularly helpful to videotape role-play exercises and show the trainees how they did. Trainees also learn a great deal when they watch themselves and hear helpful suggestions from more experienced colleagues or supervisors. Significant improvement is often seen when trainees take part in follow-up role-playing exercises.

## Individual personal differences

While national cultural characteristics and past experience are both important influencers in the negotiation process, other individual personal characteristics are also important. Personal characteristics contribute to each person's individuality and include enduring characteristics like personality, intelligence, and creativity along with such transient char-acteristics as mood or emotion. The important issue is the ability of the individual to recognize inherent differences and to be sensitive about how they can affect the negotiation process. Even in collectivist cultures, like Japan, where individuality is often suppressed for the betterment of the organization, there are personal traits that can emerge in negotiations and which need to be considered. For example, imagine how traveling for thirty hours or

**59**

more could affect the negotiating abilities of a Japanese buyer who has come to negotiate a long-term supply contract with your company. The buyer would be tired and potentially in a poor mental state to reach agreement during the sales meeting. It would be best to offer that person the opportunity to sleep and be refreshed before beginning sales negotiation meetings. It is equally important to recognize that in these types of collectivist cultures, individual powers are often minimized for the protection of the group as a whole, which potentially impact the negotiation process in profound ways. A Japanese corporate customer may not have the authority to make the important decisions involved and a series of negotiations may be required before the sales agreement can be successfully reached. One way to effectively deal with personal individual differences is to learn as much as possible about the particular individual before any face-to-face meeting so that their personal actions or mannerisms can be put into the proper context. The more the salesperson knows about the potential customer, the better prepared they will be to recognize differences and avoid situations where these differences could negatively affect personal negotiations. It is also important for the salesperson to be trained to recognize how their own moods or emotions could negatively affect their dealings with others and to avoid conflict before it happens.

## Pre-negotiation expectations

The expectations the parties bring with them also have a significant bearing on the success of the sales negotiation process. Some sizing up of the expectations of each of the parties is necessary so that potential conflict can be minimized. It is important to remember that compromise is a necessity in most negotiation processes (especially in cultures where negotiations are an important part of daily life). Take for example countries like Italy where the enjoyment of the negotiation process can affect people in their daily lives as when buyers go to street vendors to buy goods. The thrill of the negotiation process in that situation drives the dealings. This suggests that the potential seller needs to plan for compromise so that an initial offer is set artificially high to allow negotiations to proceed and the buyer is given the satisfaction of making personal gains by paying a lower price than was originally proffered. Suppose that the salesperson came to the table with a price that was the lowest that they could offer. Where would the buyer have room to gain any personal satisfaction? Obviously, when the salesperson possesses knowledge about the negotiations expectations of the cross-cultural buyer, the better position they will be in to succeed in negotiations. This requires the salesperson to spend time listening to and possibly acting as a problem solver for the buyer.

## Goal compatibility

Another factor that affects the success of the sales negotiation process is the compatibility of the parties' goals. The closer that these goals are in sync with one another, the greater the possibility of reaching a successful agreement. As a result, it becomes imperative for the salesperson to determine the buyer's goals. Careful listening may be the best way to ascertain the nature of not only the buyer's personal goals, but also the goals of their organization. If the negotiations are in a business-to-business context, the goals of the organization normally take precedence over the personal goals of the buyer. Another important point to make is that national culture may have a significant effect on goal compatibility, since buy-

 **60**

ers from collectivist countries are more focused on the goals of the organization that they represent than their own personal goals.

## Trust

The final antecedent to negotiation is trust. In this case, this means the trust the individual has for the other person or persons involved in the negotiation process. The greater the amount of mutual trust that exists among the negotiating parties, the greater the chance for a successful agreement. Trust focuses on the issue of the integrity among the individuals involved and their perceived benevolence. If integrity is clearly established, and it is believed that the other parties are concerned about the well-being of all involved, then the information that is shared will be relatively free and open, and the negotiation process will work smoothly. Obviously, if the salesperson has had prior dealings with the potential cross-cultural buyer, trust may be easier to establish. However, if there have been no prior dealings, then there will probably be reluctance to openly share relevant information. In this situation, it becomes extremely important for the salesperson to act to build trust as quickly as possible. This can be accomplished through openness, honesty, and a sharing of important information. Providing important information is a sign of trust, and the show of trust on the part of one participant can break down the walls of distrust. If the salesperson has never dealt with the potential buyer, it may be possible to determine trustworthiness by seeking references from others who have had dealings with that individual or group of individuals. The key is to conduct homework ahead of time to find out whatever you can about the other parties involved in the sales negotiation process.

## Information variables

The important information-related variables that interplay with each other during the negotiation process are *sense making* and *sense giving*. They capture the actual information conveyance and processing the parties participate in during negotiations. Each is described in detail below.

## Sense making

Sense making involves the way in which an individual assigns meaning to the information presented by one or more parties involved in the sales negotiation process. It is concerned with the attempt to understand the offer being presented or the stand being taken by the other party or parties. The communication process discussed earlier plays an important role, since the effective use of feedback is integral to sense making. When the salesperson has trouble understanding the logic of the buyer's stance, clarity of logic can be established through further discussion. Sense making is enhanced by clear communication.

## Sense giving

Sense giving involves how effectively the individual attempts to communicate the necessary information that allows the other party or parties to make sense of his or her position in

**61**

the sales negotiation. When any of the negotiating parties withhold information, then it becomes more difficult to assign appropriate meaning to the extended offer. Again, clear cross-cultural communication must occur to effectively give meaning to the recipient of the conveyed information. Chapter 2 provides suggestions on how to clearly and meaningfully communicate with those from other cultures.

## Outcomes

Intuitively, an appropriate outcome for the sales negotiation process is a successful agreement. As a result, inability to reach a meeting of minds is an unsuccessful outcome. There, of course, may be a need for further meetings, especially when the individuals negotiating must seek permission from those higher in the organization before finalizing the agreement. The minimum goal of the salesperson for any negotiation should be complete agreement with those involved on exactly where they stand and what needs to be done at that point to successfully complete the process. Leaving things unstated or "up in the air" enhances the chances that there will be no successful outcome to the process. At a minimum, the salesperson should always summarize the stances of the parties and clarify the next steps that will be involved before buyer or buying group members leave the negotiation.

Practical suggestions for improving the sales negotiation process. Given the nature of the sales negotiation process, some practical suggestions will help the sales manager to understand what information must be given to their salespeople to enhance their chances of success in cross-cultural negotiations. First James Sebenius, at Harvard Business School, suggests that it is important for the party entering the negotiation to ascertain: (1) who the real players are in the negotiation and (2) who has the authority to make the necessary decisions.[1] Once such matters are clearly understood, effective strategies for handling negotiations can then be mapped out.

One of the most effective lists of suggestions for what to do and what not to do in cross-cultural negotiations is the following list of "dos" and "don'ts":[2]

Do:

- Know your subject and be well prepared.
- Specify clear objectives and know your bottom line.
- Develop personal relationships but be careful not to be manipulated.
- Seek opportunities for informal get-togethers, since that is where most initial contacts will be made.
- Meticulously follow protocol: cross-cultural parties are often more conscious of status than Americans.
- Understand national sensitivities and do not violate them.
- Assess the flexibility of your opponent and the obstacles he or she faces.
- Understand the decision-making process and build upon your position by taking advantage of each step.
- Pin down details.

Don't:

- Look at everything from your own definition of what determines a rational and scientific viewpoint.

- Press a point when others are not prepared to accept it.
- Look at things from your own narrow self-interest.
- Ask for concessions or compromises that are politically or culturally sensitive.
- Stick to your agenda if the other party has a different set of priorities.
- Use jargon that will confuse the other side.
- Skip authority levels, since you will need middle management to implement the agreement.
- Ask for a decision that you know the other side can't or isn't ready to make.
- Differ with members of your own team in public.
- Stake out extreme positions; be consistent in your approach.

Finally, understanding the communication process, clarity, cultural sensitivity and awareness of how mood and emotion can affect the process increase the chances that meaningful communications will occur, and this enhances the chances for success in reaching a successful sales agreement.

## THE GLOBAL SELLING PROCESS

The third important process for success in global sales is the selling process. Clear communications and effective negotiations are necessary once there is a face-to-face meeting between buyer and seller, but the seven steps of the global selling process have been proven in corporate use for generations, and when performed correctly, help the salesperson conclude the sale. The seven steps are: (1) finding customers, (2) preparing, (3) relationship building, (4) product offering, (5) offer clarification, (6) securing the purchase, and (7) maintaining the relationship.

Salespersons follow specific steps that, when successfully implemented, result in prospective or existing customers making a purchase. In the global marketplace, it is necessary for salespersons to follow a more diverse sales process than they might in domestic markets. That is, in a homogeneous domestic market, the salesperson can follow a similar sales process for many of their customers. However, in a multicultural or global market, salespersons must alter the sales process to account for cultural variations. Depending upon the salesperson–customer relationship, which is formed by cumulative interactions, different amounts of time and effort must be devoted to each process step.

Personal selling is "the" principal promotional tool utilized by the sales firm in the global marketplace. In some cultures, personal selling receives even greater emphasis when local laws restrict advertising and salespersons are inexpensive to employ. For example, in China, a US medical equipment firm hires physicians and nurses to sell to other health care providers.[3] In many developing nations low wages permit the firm to hire and deploy a larger sales force.[4] The first two of the seven steps of the selling process are presented below, with the remainder coming in Chapter 5.

### Finding customers

The first step in the sales process, finding customers, consists of two actions: (1) identifying sales prospects and (2) insuring that these potential clients are worthy of additional effort being invested in converting them from prospect to customer. For example, the French firm Cerestar compiled a list of thousands of possible corn starch users in China. Company sales representatives then began to cold call to assess actual customer needs from trading firms, distributors, and representative offices. The sales force found this process to be frustrating because many potential customers were reluctant to talk to strangers and others were bankrupt. In the end, less than 10 percent of the firms on the original list were qualified as potential customers.[5]

### Identifying sales prospects

Depending upon the industry and local custom, global salespersons may devote a portion of their work day searching for and contacting new customers. A multitude of reasons explain why a salesperson must find new customers. These include current customers going out of business, relocating, switching to competitors, and even dying! This is why, in certain industries, a salesperson must allocate a significant portion of time to generating new customers. In industrial or business-to-business (B2B) sales, less emphasis is placed upon finding new customers. This is because there are fewer B2B customers, and these accounts have been initially qualified – perhaps by analyzing their SIC code and making a personal visit – and it is rare for new manufacturers to enter the market after the product reaches the maturity stage. However, one global sales manager reports that his job is to enlarge the upper part of the funnel by finding more customers for his sales force to call upon.[6]

In certain sales positions, like insurance, auto sales, and copiers, the customer's needs are temporarily satisfied once the product or service is delivered. It is then possible for the salesperson to "grow" these accounts by having the customer trade up to higher priced or higher quality products/services. In the interim, the salesperson must identify new customers while waiting for existing clients to repurchase. Although there are a large number of sources for finding potential customers, this discussion is meant to be less than complete. Suffice it to say that salespersons have a significant number of methods for finding new customers (see Exhibit 4.1). A few methods employed to locate potential customers are presented in detail below.

*Customer recommendations.* Satisfied customers can provide the salesperson with a list of his/her friends and colleagues who have a need for the product. In fact, in certain industries it is standard practice for salespersons to ask the customer to provide two or three potential "leads" that might also benefit from purchasing the product represented by the salesperson. The salesperson should not pressure the customer for these names if they are reluctant to offer them and should realize that in certain cultures it is not appropriate behavior to share information about friends or business associates. Most salespersons believe there is no better recommendation than that of a satisfied customer.

*Centers of influence.* There are influential persons in every community who can recommend potential customers to the salesperson. These leaders – be they civic, religious, or business – should be cultivated for sales leads over breakfast or lunch once or twice a year. The salesperson must be careful not to use the leader's name with the customer unless agreed to by the center of influence. Likewise, the salesperson must be subtle in these meetings and must share information of value in a "*quid pro quo*" relationship with the leader.

# EXHIBIT 4.1 METHODS OF FINDING CUSTOMERS

Over the years, creative sales personnel and managers have established a large number of methods for identifying potential customers. Methods of locating new customers can be organized into four categories – internal to the firm, external to the firm, promotional sources, and personal sources/actions. Multiple examples of each source are explained briefly below.

*Internal sources*

- Company records – examine existing records for previous customers or contacts.
- Inactive accounts – former customers who stopped purchasing.
- Junior sales personnel/sales associates – use less costly or new personnel to call or contact potential customers through cold calls or identify through research.
- Telemarketing:
    - Inbound – calls to toll-free numbers requesting information about products.
    - Outbound – calls by sales associates to qualify and establish sales meetings.
- Phone/mail inquiries – inquiries to the firm about products or special offers.
- Caller identification – phone numbers of people who have dialed the firm.
- Other company salespersons – firm salespersons that work in other territories/ products.
- Service department – notification by service manager that product cannot be repaired.
- Credit department – notification that customer is seeking credit approval.
- Surveys – market research information that customer completes
- Current large accounts – potential needs among other departments or divisions.

*External sources*

- Satisfied customers – ask customer for name of potential customers.
- Endless chain – ask each customer for three to five names; always more than closing ratio.
- Center of influence/community contact – individual in community who can provide information about new firms, managers, or company plans.
- Networking – social relationships that provide business-related information.
- Professional society/civic meetings/social events – opportunities to network and seek information about potential customers.
- Contact agent – external firms that are paid to identify/qualify potential customers.
- Friends and acquaintances – family and friends can suggest potential customers.
- Non-competing salespeople – information shared between salespersonnel from different industries about potential customers that need products from both.
- Salesperson swap meet – special meeting to exchange names between noncompeting salespersons.
- Cultivate visible accounts – make cold calls to visible accounts in territory.
- Chamber of commerce – business organization has membership list of existing and new members.

- Engineering departments of potential customers – technical information about future customer needs.
- Lists:
    - Broker lists – lists of potential customers purchased from list broker.
    - Clubs, universities, companies – membership lists of these groups
    - Computerized databases – databases available from state or credit sources.
- Directories:
    - Industrial directory – directories published by specific industries.
    - Business directory – directories published for specific locations.
    - Local, state, national directories – government-sponsored directories.

*Promotional sources*
- Broadcast media – radio/television commercials with phone number.
- Contests – register to win a free product; nonwinners are potential purchasers.
- Group parties/meetings – meetings of neighbors, church groups, or friends.
- Internet – responses to web site or e-mail messages.
- Media advertising – print advertisements with phone number of mail-in postcard.
- Direct Mail – outgoing mail that informs potential customer and provides phone number or contact information for salesperson.
- Trade publication ads – ads in magazine or journal that focuses on industry.
- Shows – shows that exhibit product or introduce new model(s) for one or more companies.
- Trade shows – large shows where all competitors for industry are present.
- Educational seminars – meetings where new laws or technologies are explained to potential customers. Interested attendees can be identified.
- Sales letters – direct mail signed and sent by salesperson.
- Business-related articles in publications – similar to public relations; a technical article about a new product or an article about a personality that requests individuals wanting to learn more about the product or engineering knowledge to contact the company.

*Personal actions*
- Observation – maintaining a watchful eye on new businesses.
- Cold calling – stopping by unannounced and talking to manager/purchaser.
- Spotters/bird dog – agent who sends potential customers to salesperson and, when successful, is paid a commission.
- Business card referral system – similar to spotters; business card given to potential customer, who returns to salesperson for a discount, free gift, etc.
- The itch cycle – contacting former customer just before normal repurchase cycle.
- Orphan adoption – taking over accounts when salesperson leaves firm.
- Technical advancement – contacting customers who have earlier model.
- Claim staking – claiming customers not being serviced by other salespersons.

*Lists.* Numerous lists are available for identifying prospective clients. These lists may be as basic as a summary of members of a church, synagogue, or mosque, country club, sports club, property owners' association, or university alumni association. A salesperson must be cautious when utilizing organizational lists so that it is not transparent to the prospects that a salesperson is calling upon group members.

Firms or salespersons can also purchase prospective customer lists from professional agents or firms that derive their data from new product registrations or, in countries where permissible, government databases such as drivers' licenses or voters' lists. These databases may not be current, since in today's highly mobile society people regularly relocate because of business transfers or personal choice. In many cultures, citizens are reluctant to provide personal information to market researchers or government agents, so there will not be lists available in these cultures.

*Publications.* It is possible for the salesperson to learn about new business openings by gathering information from the business section of the newspaper or local business period-icals. In some B2B industries there is a trade journal that publicizes new product introductions, plant openings, and acquisitions/mergers.

*Referrals.* Potential customers can be referred by company maintenance personnel and sales colleagues. For example, a salesperson from another territory may learn of a need that exists at an office or manufacturing plant located in your territory from his customer. In certain industries, the maintenance manager will notify the salesperson when a customer has requested maintenance on a product that needs to be replaced. In most cases, these sources pass the salesperson's name or business card to potential customers that make contact with the salesperson.

*Advertising-generated.* Many industrial firms advertise their products/services and provide either a postcard the reader can use to request additional information or samples. These advertisements also provide avenues for contacting the company in the form of a toll-free phone number, web site, or e-mail address.

## Qualifying

Once a sufficient number of potential customers is generated, they must be evaluated and prioritized based upon relevant criteria. This step is equally important because not all poten-tial customers qualify for additional sales emphasis, based upon one or more of the following reasons:

- *Money* Can the customer afford to buy the product? Do they have cash, credit, an open account, or an item to trade that results in both the buyer and the seller being better off? In Asia, salespersons monitor the funding status of their customers to insure time is not wasted on customers who do not have the money to purchase.[7]
- *Authority* Does the individual or location the salesperson works at have the authority to purchase? Can they commit or obligate the firm or themselves by signing a purchase order or contract?
- *Need* Does the buyer need the good? In other words, will the buyer or the organization gain utility from purchasing the product/service?

**67**

- *Fit* Does the potential buyer's organizational culture fit the culture of the seller? If the buyer's culture is totally divergent from that of the seller, then the ensuing exchange will likely be frustrating and not worth the required effort. One example of a poor fit is when the potential buyer requests that the seller offer a reduced unit price by lowering production standards. Depending upon the importance of the buyer, a decision to conduct business based upon fit will be made by upper management (see Exhibit 4.2).

One expert claims that Chinese salespersons often fail to qualify their customers, because business is still practiced based upon personal relationships or "guan-xi" rather than business potential. This suggests that in certain cultures, the salesperson must be more closely supervised and directed. When customers are to be "qualified," the manager must set clear

## EXHIBIT 4.2 ARE ALL CUSTOMERS A GOOD FIT?

When global firms initiate business contacts with new customers, the cultural and economic fit between the two firms should be investigated. Situations encountered in China by global firms aptly illustrate this point. Even with membership in the World Trade Organization (WTO), global firms know that making a sale in China does not mean you will get paid for the goods. As a result, high levels of credit or "accounts receivable," caused by a lack of working capital, are constraining growth in the Chinese marketplace. Global firms now add "receivables" to a long list of difficulties that include fake products, incompetent joint venture partners, protectionism, and government regulations. These problems impact global and domestic firms that conduct business with government-owned enterprises in China. When government-sponsored firms fail, a chain reaction of events is created: the bankrupt firm cannot pay distributors and distributors are unable to pay their suppliers.

In response, Nike and other global firms restrict or deny credit to problem accounts. While this approach retards growth, Nike believes the economic health of the brand and business are maintained. Asimco, an automotive parts supplier, took a different approach and pays managers a bonus based upon the joint venture's earnings, which are affected negatively by accounts receivable. Some government-run companies pay Asimco through barter, like receiving trucks as payment for parts. This requires Asimco to use the trucks in its business or sell them on the open market. As a result, Asimco sells fewer products in China and more to other Asian countries. Procter & Gamble and Gillette adopted different approaches to deal with errant payers. Both global firms demand mortgage guarantees, which means that if a debtor fails to pay, their property must be forfeited. Gillette also requires third-party guarantees. Gillette believes the third-party guarantee system is very effective for securing payment. Gillette is also paying closer attention to financial statements, assets, and distribution systems to assess the financial viability of potential customers. Therefore, a global firm would be wise to not conduct business with a firm unless an acceptable fit exists between the buyer and seller.

*Source.* Trisha Saywell, "Accounts Unreceivable," *Far Eastern Economic Report,* July 6, 2000, 66–8.

goals along with a path to achieve those goals.[8] In response, one Chinese manager states that business in China is "still largely unstructured and irrational." A customer that is disqualified today may become a qualified customer tomorrow and then it will be too late to develop a relationship.[9]

If the answer to any one of these four qualification questions – money, authority, need, and fit – cannot be "yes," the salesperson is wasting time by calling upon the prospective buyer. Because an industrial sales call is expensive, firms can ill afford to have their professional sales force calling upon customers who cannot or will not purchase a product. Such behavior misdirects both the time and talent of the sales force. An old American sales proverb is that "a good salesperson can sell ice to an eskimo." However, in today's global market the correct attitude is that a good salesperson has no desire to sell a product to anyone who has no need for the item.

## Preparing

Successful salespersons spend significant time preparing for meetings with potential customers. In fact, a professional salesperson devotes time to learn about the qualified prospect, their culture, their organization, product line(s), competitors, and past relationship history between the buyer/seller firms. Today's salesperson must average four or five sales calls before making a sale.[10] In culturally diverse global markets, where it is necessary to get to know the partner well and form long-term relationships, the requisite number of sales calls will be even higher. For example, before major decisions are made in Japan, preliminary meetings are held to discuss what will happen during the decision meeting. In this way both parties know beforehand any controversial issues that may arise, as well as the outcome of the meeting.[11]

During the preparation stage, the salesperson can gain information from existing company files, customer relationship management (CRM) software, the potential customer's web site, and commercial sources such as magazines, newspapers, and commercial sources. Also, when interacting with different cultures it is essential to seek information about the cultural norms and expectations from salespersons and managers who have worked successfully in the culture, from resource books and, as appropriate, from consultants. In most situations, the more that is known about the prospective customer, the greater the probability of identifying and satisfying existing needs and forming a long-term relationship. It should be obvious, based upon the time that must be devoted to this effort, that the salesperson can make this type of commitment only for potentially profitable customers.

Before meeting with the prospect, the salesperson should insure that he or she can correctly pronounce the prospect's name. One technique for gaining this knowledge is to call the prospective customer's assistant or company receptionist to confirm the appointment, which insures the salesperson hears and correctly pronounces the prospect's name. One of the authors telephoned a Philippine office to confirm an appointment and pronounced the manager's name in Tagalog, the national language. It was quite a surprise to learn the manager was an American with a Spanish-appearing family name that was pronounced quite differently. Other information about the prospect, such as hobbies, interests, and likes/dislikes, also makes getting acquainted easier and may shed light upon the type of gift the prospect would value.

The salesperson should also anticipate the types of products the prospect will need and how these products will satisfy those needs. The salesperson should possess an accurate understanding of how their products compare with competitors' and why the prospect is purchasing or might prefer a competitive product instead of the one being offered. In other words, the salesperson should have a plan for approaching the prospect that anticipates questions and concerns that may be raised during the initial meeting(s). Such planning should be repeated for future meetings as well.

Formal presentations should be compiled, using professional software or transparencies as dictated by technology and culture. In developing countries like India, it may be risky to use high-technology equipment for sales presentations.[12] Therefore, global salespersons should prepare transparencies or flip charts as a backup for computer-generated presentations. It is also prudent for the salesperson to practice the formal presentation for important customers in the presence of technical and managerial staff. In so doing, the sales presentation can be reviewed for clarity and technical competence. This process also insures the salesperson's presentation accurately portrays management's point of view.

## CHAPTER SUMMARY

Global sales managers must be prepared to provide their global sales force with the necessary tools to ensure sales success. The interpersonal communication process affects the success of communications between the salesperson and their prospective customer. The sales negotiation process is also important, since it affects the ability of the salesperson and the prospective customer to reach an acceptable agreement. Finally, the seven steps of the personal selling process are important, as they help the salesperson to organize their efforts toward building a meaningful relationship with the prospective customer and produce sales in both the present and the future. This chapter presented the first two of these processes and the steps of the selling process leading up to the initial meeting with the prospective customer.

## DISCUSSION QUESTIONS

1   What is the interpersonal communication process, and why is it so important for the global salesperson?

2   What are the different antecedents to negotiation, and how can the global salesperson deal effectively with each?

3   What is the difference between sense making and sense giving, and why are they important in the sales negotiation process?

4   What are some suggestions for things to do and things not to do during the sales negotiation process?

5   What are the seven different steps of the global selling process?

6   What are six different mechanisms for identifying potential customers that could be used by the global salesperson?

7   Why is preparation so important for the global salesperson?

8   How would customer relationship management software be used during the preparation stage by the global salesperson?

## REFERENCES

1   Sebenius, James K. (2002), "The Hidden Challenge of Cross-border Negotiations," *Harvard Business Review*, March, 76–85.

2   Herbig, Paul, and Hugh Kramer (1992), "Dos and Don'ts of Cross-cultural Negotiations," *Industrial Marketing Management*, 21, 287–98.

3   Xu, Gang "Jerry" (2001), E-mail communication in response to questions, July 12.

4   Terpstra, Vern, and Ravi Sarathy (2000), *International Marketing*, eighth edition, Fort Worth TX: Dryden Press.

5   Lawrence, Susan V. (2000), "Formula for Disaster," *Far Eastern Economic Review*, October 5, 52–4.

6   Xu, Gang "Jerry" (2001), E-mail communication in response to questions, July 12.

7   Xu, Gang "Jerry" (2001), E-mail communication in response to questions, July 12.

8   Miller, Chip E. (1996), "US Techniques not Best for Chinese Sales Reps," *Marketing News*, November 4, 5.

9   Xu, Gang "Jerry" (2001), E-mail communication in response to questions, July 12.

10  Morris, Michael, Leyland Pitt, and Earl Honeycutt (2001), *Business-to-Business Marketing*, Fair Oaks CA: Sage Publications.

11  Daft, Doug (2000), "Coke's New Formula," *Far Eastern Economic Review*, April 20, 64–5.

12  Honeycutt, Earl D., Jr., John B. Ford, and Lew Kurtzman (1996), "Potential Problems and Solutions when Hiring a Worldwide Sales Team," *Industrial Marketing Management*, 11:1, 42–54.

# Chapter 5

# The global selling process, II

This chapter concludes the global selling process begun in Chapter 4.

## LEARNING OBJECTIVES

*After considering this chapter, you will be able to*:

- Understand the relationship-building step of the global selling process and how the salesperson can make the best impression when meeting the prospective buyer and ultimately gain their trust and cooperation.
- Discuss the product offering step of the global selling process and how the salesperson can best prepare for and make the most effective sales presentation to the prospective buyer.
- Explain the offer clarification step of the global selling process and how the salesperson can anticipate possible questions asked by the prospective buyer.
- Describe the importance of the relationship step of the global selling process and how the salesperson can effectively build a long-term relationship with the prospective buyer.
- Recognize and minimize the potential for unethical practices in the global selling process.

## KEY TERMS

- Guaranteed, Referral, Personal, and Benefit Introductions.
- Buying center.
- Stimulus response, Mental states, Need satisfaction, Problem solving, and Consultative selling presentations.
- Role conflict.

## INTRODUCTION

This chapter builds upon basic knowledge in Chapter 4 that discussed the: (1) interpersonal communication process, (2) sales negotiation process, and (3) initial steps of the global selling process. Chapter 5 completes the remaining five steps of the global selling process, beginning with the first face-to-face meeting between the global salesperson and the prospective cross-cultural customer. It is important to remember how the interpersonal communications and the sales negotiation processes are interwoven into the five personal selling steps. That is, within each of these five steps there are opportunities to both communicate with and influence the customer toward a mutually beneficial agreement. Now the remaining steps of the global selling process, that include a number of illustrative cross-cultural examples, are discussed.

> CASE VIGNETTE **FORMING A RELATIONSHIP**
>
> Whenever Jennifer Smythe travels to Asia for her American company, she is often uncomfortable about trying to form relationships with her current and potential hosts. She knows that men managers accompany clients to *karaoke* bars and that they keep late hours whenever they are in-country. Since this seldom happens to Jennifer, she feels that she is being discriminated against, but does not know how to change the situation.

## RELATIONSHIP BUILDING

This third step of the global sales process includes meeting, making a favorable impression, and gaining the trust and cooperation of the potential customer. In some cultures relationship building happens quickly, while in other cultures it takes longer to form a relationship. There are a number of ways to meet the prospect, that include:

- *Guaranteed introduction*, when the salesperson meets the prospect in the presence of a mutual friend or business acquaintance that speaks positively of each person and serves as a reference or guarantor for each party.
- *Referral introduction*. In some cultures it is acceptable to inform the potential customer upon meeting for the first time that a mutual friend has referred the customer to them.
- *Personal introduction*. In some cultures, salespersons introduce themselves personally or, as in Japan, through a ritual exchanging of business cards.
- *Benefit introduction*. The salesperson introduces him/herself by asking if the buyer would like to save money, time, or gain some type of benefit.

In addition to greeting the prospect, it is important to know appropriate greetings and phrases in the prospective buyer's language (see Table 5.1). In most Asian cultures professional business cards, printed on one side in the local language, are essential. For example, in Japan, the formal exchanging of business cards has taken the place of personal introduc-

**Table 5.1** *Greetings and toasts*

| Country | Thank you | Toasts |
| --- | --- | --- |
| Arabic | Shu-kran | No alcohol, none |
| China | | |
|    Mandarin | Shay-shay | Kam-pay |
|    Cantonese | Doe-jay | Yum-sing |
| France | Mare-see | Ah-votre-sahn-tay |
| Germany | Dahnk-ah | Pro-zit |
| Greece | Ef-ha-ri-sto | Stin-igia.sas |
| Italy | Grahtz-ee | Sah-loo-tay |
| Japan | Arr-I-gah-toe | Kam-pai |
| Philippines | Sa-la-mat | Mag-ta-gay ta-yo |
| Portugual | Ohb-ri-gah-toe | Sah-ude |
| Russia | Spa-see-bow | Nah-zda-roe-vee-ah |
| Scandinavia | Tak | Skoal |
| Spain | Grah-see-as | Sah-lood |

tions. At a minimum, the salesperson must understand how and when to bow or shake hands, rudimentary phrases in the national language, and local etiquette for eating and drinking. Such cultural expertise can be acquired through cross-cultural training prior to undertaking international travel.

Cultures differ slightly in how relationships are formed, but trust is an essential relationship component, regardless of the culture. That is, the buyer and seller must trust one another to do what is promised and they must be able to depend upon one another.[1] Getting to know a Japanese buyer means formal business meetings during the day and forays to karaoke bars at night, where singing and drinking extend until the early morning hours. At karaoke bars, both the buyer and the seller can observe one another's actions in a social situation where prescribed roles are played.[2] A buyer and seller in Japan may also visit a *riokan* or hot spring resort to relax and become better acquainted. The *riokan* provides an opportunity to relax in a hot mineral spring, receive massages, consume sake, smoke, and talk. In effect the buyer and seller are establishing rapport.[3] Only after long periods of establishing rapport and trust do discussions move to important business issues. In cultures like Japan, business does not occur quickly.

## PRODUCT OFFERING

Sales presentations are both formal and informal in nature. That is, the salesperson makes a formal proposal that communicates the offer to the buyer and the firm. However, the salesperson also makes informal sales presentations to members of the *buying center* from the first meeting until the actual contract is awarded (see Exhibit 5.1). In other words,

## EXHIBIT 5.1 WHAT IS A BUYING CENTER?

In business-to-business (B2B) sales encounters, the salesperson works within a buying center that is comprised of a large number of people. These individuals play different roles within the buying center that affects the salesperson's interactions. Generally, there are at least five different roles played within a buying center. It is possible, but not likely, that one person can play all roles, but generally speaking there are a large number of parties that have to be contacted and served. The buying center parties include:

- *Initiator* – the person who initiates a request for a product. This could be a supervisor that reports a defective computer monitor to the purchasing department.
- *User* – the individual who will use the computer monitor.
- *Influencer* – any individual or department that has influence over the standards or brands that will be considered by the firm. This can be engineering, quality control, or upper management.
- *Buyer* – a person or team that makes the purchase decision. In this scenario it could be the purchasing agent that is responsible for computer hardware or a team that is comprised of representatives from different firm departments.
- *Gatekeeper* – any person(s) that restrict(s) the salesperson from information or entry to buying center parties. Often this is a secretary, receptionist, or purchasing agent.

The job of the B2B salesperson is to first identify who plays what role in the buying center. While this may appear intuitive, buying center parties have been known to exaggerate their importance in the purchase decision. Then, once the parties have been identified, the salesperson's role is to provide each individual or team with the correct amount and type of information they will need to make a favorable purchase decision. The more time the salesperson can spend with influencers and deciders will increase the salesperson's ability to gain a favorable purchase response. Conversely, misidentifying the roles played within the buying center and not providing pertinent information to buying center parties will result in a reduced probability of making the B2B sale!

every meeting with buying center members result in the salesperson "selling" the benefits of their product(s), listening to buyer concerns, and allaying concerns by adjusting the offer or providing additional information.

Most salespersons utilize one or more personal selling approaches that include stimulus response, mental states, need satisfaction, and problem-solving methods. The first two approaches – stimulus response and mental states – can be traced to the early days of sales. The next two approaches, need satisfaction and problem solving, have been discussed for several decades. A fifth approach, consultative selling, is also practiced. All five approaches are discussed in this section. It is important for global salespersons to understand each approach and to utilize the appropriate one for the selling situation. That is, what works in

Paris may not be effective in Peoria. Most firms find that one or a combination of these sales approaches results in higher salesperson success. Global salespersons also understand that an effective sales presentation and interaction with the customers may require a mixture of approaches. That is, successful salespersons must adapt their sales approaches to customers.[4] This discussion begins with the least and moves to the most complex customer approaches.

## Stimulus–response

Stimulus–response theory originated in early animal behavior experiments. In personal selling, the salesperson tries to supply appropriate stimuli through words and actions. An automobile sales manager once explained that his goal during a sales presentation was to stimulate ten "yes" answers from prospective customers prior to asking for a final agreement on purchasing the automobile. That is, the sales manager would ask: Do you like the style of the automobile? Is the ride comfortable? Does the stereo sound luxurious? The goal of each question was to elicit a "yes" response. Once a predetermined number of "yes" answers was reached – for this sales manager it was ten – he would then ask for the major decision to purchase the automobile.

Many firms that employ stimulus–response presentations do so in conjunction with canned sales presentations. In this way less experienced salespersons can follow a script or make a logical presentation from memory that incorporates stimuli for the potential purchaser. However, in significant or "high involvement" purchases, the customer plays an important role in the buying process. Sales experts define the sales situation as a "dyad" of two individuals – the buyer and the seller. The stimulus response–approach requires that the salesperson dominate the sales call, which is unlikely when dealing with a professional purchaser. A second concern is that stimulus–response approaches are normally not flexible enough to allow the buyer to interrupt or digress to other subjects. When diversions occur, the presentation can lose its focus.

The stimulus–response approach is often employed by sales personnel that sell lower priced goods, under time constraints, to consumers. An example is telemarketers who sell replacement windows, credit cards, or seek donations for charities. Telemarketing sales managers know the salesperson has one chance to communicate with potential customers about the product and the goal is to present the offering as quickly and efficiently as possible.

## Mental states selling

In reaching a purchase decision customers are believed to pass through the four stages of attention, interest, desire, and action (AIDA). The salesperson's goal is to follow a prepared sales presentation that begins by gaining the prospective buyer's attention and then logically moves through the three remaining stages. Like stimulus–response, the salesperson dominates this sales approach. Interruptions and questions during the mental state approach can impede the process and make it difficult for the salesperson to discern the buyer's stage.

When salespersons use the mental states approach, prior planning is essential before initiating the sales call to insure a logical and well organized presentation. The salesperson must also listen carefully to the buyer and read their body language to understand their purchase inclination. However, it may be difficult to gauge the customer's actual purchase stage. When this happens, the salesperson spends too little or too much time trying to move the customer into the next purchase stage.

Like stimulus response, the mental state approach is not customer-oriented. That is, the needs of the customer are of less interest to the salesperson than making the sale. This approach is also questionable in most, if not all, business-to-business situations. Employing this sales approach on potential customers from a different culture is also problematic because of diverse thought processes and cultural expectations. However, canned portions of sales presentations appear to have benefits (see Exhibit 5.2).

## EXHIBIT 5.2 ARE THERE BENEFITS FROM CANNED SALES PRESENTATIONS?

Many sales managers and salespersons believe that canned sales presentations are rigid and unwieldy monologues. And, based upon some telemarketing presentations, it is easy to understand how this generalization can be made. However, canned sales presentations may be appropriate for newly hired sales personnel and they are helpful when preparing for sales calls where routine questions may be asked.

When firms hire new sales representatives, especially those with little sales experience, the firm can provide a scripted sales presentation the salesperson can employ during initial sales calls. This does not mean the salesperson meets the buyer and immediately goes into a scripted presentation. What happens is that the salesperson gains confidence by having a logical presentation committed to memory. This presentation insures that all pertinent information is shared with the buyer and that most buyer concerns are addressed by the "neophyte" salesperson. The more times the salesperson makes the presentation, the easier it will be for them to feel natural and spontaneous.

Likewise, when a salesperson makes a sales call, the buyer may ask redundant or similar questions. For example, a question constantly asked one of the authors was "What does the name TRW mean?" In response, the salesperson could have committed to memory a history of their company. Similar caches of information can be stored in memory about products, delivery options, and product comparisons against competitors. The use of canned portions of a sales presentation does not mean the salesperson responds to a question from the buyer in a monotone voice. Like any educated professional, there is some aspect of memorization required to be competent. When used correctly, canned or prepared presentations can be helpful and will increase the presentation skill levels of the global salesperson.

*Source.* Marvin A. Jolson, "Canned Adaptiveness: A New Direction for Modern Salesmanship," *Business Horizons*, 32 (January–February 1989), 7–12.

## Need satisfaction

In this approach, the salesperson meets and dialogues with the customer with the goal of identifying and satisfying a need. The salesperson meets with the customer, asks general questions that are narrowed when potential needs are identified, and proposes a solution that generally relates to the purchase of the seller's product or service.

The need satisfaction approach is better received, because the focus is on satisfying customer needs. This is especially true of preliminary meetings that are held for fact finding prior to making formal presentations or submitting written proposals. However, customers become suspicious when a salesperson continues to probe for nonexistent problems or recommends products/services that are not in the best interests of the firm.

## Problem solving

Problem solving is an extension of the needs satisfaction approach. However, more time is devoted to examining problem or situation alternatives. For example, if a customer reports that shipping costs are increasing significantly, the salesperson would conduct an audit of the firm's entire shipping system. This action might require a team of experts to analyze this problem area or companies have developed standard laptop computer programs that perform an audit based upon customer-provided information.

Once the audit or analysis is completed, the salesperson submits a report or makes a formal presentation detailing a solution for the area of concern. Perhaps the recommendation is that the customer should contact a competitor that can best satisfy their needs. Problem solving works best for industrial accounts that rely upon logic and analysis to make purchase decisions.

## Consultative selling

Consultative selling requires the salesperson to assist the buyer, by employing the expertise of the selling firm, in reaching their strategic goals. In effect the sales organization enters a partnership where they are entrusted with the buyer's strategic goals and works to help the buyer reach their objectives. Consultative salespersons must be highly qualified, in order to become an expert on the buyer's products, industry, and competitors, and to assist the buyer even when an immediate sale is not imminent. In effect, consultative selling requires the salesperson to possess specific skills (see Exhibit 5.3). This partnership must be reciprocal, in that the buyer understands that the selling firm has to be profitable and information must be shared with the salesperson. It is important for the sales firm to establish a "value-added approach" and to realize that the salesperson will not recommend a product/service unless it advances the customer toward their strategic goals.

## Buyer–seller meeting

In professional sales situations, the salesperson meets the buyer at an appointed time. In some cultures it is acceptable to be late, while in other countries arriving late is viewed

## EXHIBIT 5.3 CONSULTATIVE SELLING SKILL SET

Sales practitioners state that a salesperson must demonstrate how their product or service will result in higher customer profits. This ability permits the firm to charge higher prices and maintain solid margins. However, consultative selling requires the salesperson to possess and have the ability to employ certain skills:

- *Add value* – the salesperson must communicate how profits will increase based upon the adoption of the product recommended.
- *Follow up* – once the product or service is purchased, the salesperson must track the results and quantify the value of the purchase.
- *Be a marketing consultant* – the salesperson must learn from the customer what they need and then construct a program that will accomplish the customer's goals without lowering price and profits.
- *Be a problem solver* – work with the customer to manage the program and solve problems as they arise.
- *Think long-term* – provide top quality customer support that reinforces the purchase decision.

*Source.* William F. Kendy, "Consultative Selling," *Selling Power*, September 2000, 53–5.

negatively. In emerging nations like the Philippines, where it is difficult to arrange reliable transport and Manila traffic is often at a standstill, arriving late is more acceptable than in developed nations like the United States, Great Britain, and Germany. When meeting potential customers in the Middle East, a sales rep may ask for an appointment and be told: "Let us meet at ten in the morning, *ansh Allah*." The customer means that the meeting will occur at 10.00 a.m., "Allah willing." Should the customer be detained from the meeting for any reason, there is a logical reason for the absence.[5]

Once the meeting begins, the salesperson's goal is to make a favorable first impression. In most cultures this means being appropriately dressed, smiling, and making positive comments about the buyer and their firm. Once initial pleasantries are completed, there may be a discussion of sports, hobbies, or families; then, the buyer and seller move to discussing mutual business interests. However, Japanese sales meetings are formal and initiated by the exchanging of business cards, bowing or shaking hands, and discussing matters unrelated to business. These preliminary discussions provide each side with an opportunity for "sense making" about the prospective partner's attitudes, ability to communicate, and willingness to listen. Depending upon the situation and number of visits made by the seller, it may be appropriate to present an appropriate gift to the buyer. Finally, in Japan, the buyer and seller do not call one another by first names – this would infer that proper respect is not being shown.[6]

Global sales calls are lengthy, less structured, and involve give and take buyer–seller exchanges. Most of the time it is necessary for the salesperson to discuss in depth the buyer's business situation and needs. To assume that the salesperson can be taught a "slick" or canned sales presentation they can employ against the buyer is unrealistic. In B2B sales situations, sellers who fail to focus upon the needs of the buyer will seldom be allowed to return for a follow-up visit. To shut the selling firm out of future business the buyer only has to "be unavailable," or be "too busy," when the seller requests an appointment.

Once the buyer and seller discuss and identify a problem or need that can be satisfied, it is time for the seller to communicate "how" their product/service can be of value. At this time the salesperson responds with proposed solutions to the buyer's need(s). This is why it is important for firms to hire highly competent salespersons who can create value for the customer. Most buyers today are not satisfied when a salesperson responds with "Let me talk this over with my experts and get back to you." Buyers wonder why an "expert" is not sitting in front of them!

Professional salespersons often begin their sales presentation by identifying and restating customer needs as understood from earlier meetings. The salesperson should also confirm buying the firm's goals regarding price, quality, delivery, and reliability. Once the buyer and seller are certain they are beginning at the same point, the salesperson explains how their product/service satisfies the buyer's needs, along with a discussion of how this offer will further the buyer's goals.

## OFFER CLARIFICATION

Once the presentation is completed, the salesperson should expect questions. Buyer questions, concerns, or requests are normal in any sales situation. In most cases, the buyer asks questions to clarify the seller's offer or asks for concessions. It is important, during this phase of the sales process, that the seller utilizes their finely honed abilities of listening, reading body language, and listening for subtle comments to identify buyer concerns.

The buyer may respond to the sales presentation by asking for test results or samples that can be evaluated for suitability and/or reliability. Or the buyer may ask for additional written data about the recommended product/service. Whatever the request, it is important that the salesperson respond positively, promptly, and professionally. In many cultures salespersons must be prepared to negotiate during this phase of the sales process. For example, if the buyer asks whether a shorter delivery schedule is possible, the seller can respond that it may be possible if the buyer shares inventory levels and expected purchase information in advance with the seller. Buyers will probably request price concessions, but marketing theory tells us that it is difficult to sell on price alone. That is, the seller should not attempt to base their offer solely on price, unless this is the strategy adopted by upper management. A wiser approach is to discuss the total value provided by the product offering. Total value includes such attributes as the product, service, training, maintenance, warranty, and trade-in options.

While negotiations may take place during all meetings, this tends to be the step where most of the serious negotiating and concession making occurs. Therefore, it is important to review the basics of negotiations presented in Chapter 4, which guides the global salesperson toward reaching mutually beneficial agreements.

## SECURING THE PURCHASE

Many personal selling books illustrate "closing" techniques that force the buyer to agree to the purchase of the product/service. Again, in professional sales situations, these closing techniques are inappropriate and seldom work. For example, one consumer sales technique is "closing on a decision" where the seller asks the buyer if they want a product in red or blue? Once the answer is proffered, then the buyer has committed. However, in B2B meetings buyers provide this information to all prospective vendors. That is, product type, color, and expected purchase quantities are known in advance by the B2B buyer and all sellers. When it is time for a purchase decision to be made, most professional sellers communicate directly with the buyer and ask: "Since my offer meets your needs, should we do business?"

However, national culture influences different decision-making styles. In Asia, firms follow several different avenues before reaching a purchase decision. In Thailand decisions tend to be made from the top down, while Japan operates upward from lower levels to the CEO.[7] In other cultures, the salesperson waits for the seller to raise the issue of purchase. For example, after decades of being deluged by government propaganda, Chinese consumers are skeptical of a salesperson who "bellows his wares."[8] This suggests that a slow approach to securing a sale is a more effective one in China.

## MAINTAINING THE RELATIONSHIP

The final stage in the sales process, maintaining the relationship, is extremely important. Once the sale has been made it is time to implement the agreement. This means that once the customer has agreed to purchase the product, the salesperson should work closely with the buyer. The buyer should have a single point of contact that can answer questions, resolve problems, and represent the needs of the buyer to the seller. By maintaining this relationship, the salesperson will retain an excellent position for making additional sales and remaining at the top of the "choice ladder" when the buyer again needs a product/service available from the selling firm.

As discussed in Chapter 3, firms are adopting a "relationship" approach with their best customers. However, global firms know that forging a relationship has potential pitfalls and there are recommended rules to follow in global markets (see Exhibit 5.4). When European customers form relationships with their suppliers, they place great importance on salesperson integrity. This means the global firm must develop a corporate structure that allows the salesperson to deliver on promises. One way to insure the salesperson makes and keeps their word is to include sales personnel in pricing, delivery, and manufacturing decisions, and insure that global salespersons regularly visit the factory to remain current about new manufacturing techniques and processes. In Europe suppliers build and maintain customer loyalty by not promising more than they can deliver. Fast talking, hard selling salespersons will not survive for long in Europe.[9] Similarly in Japan, suppliers must conform to exacting local product standards if they are to succeed.[10]

Global firms take customer satisfaction very seriously. For example, Japanese firms expect their suppliers to provide free after-sale service.[11] A number of global firms track customer satisfaction levels, which impact raise and promotion decisions and are a part of the salesperson's annual performance review.

## EXHIBIT 5.4 FORGING GLOBAL RELATIONSHIPS: LESSONS LEARNED

Global firms have learned, through trial and error, a number of lessons that reduce the likelihood of failure when forming relationships. Each of the lessons is discussed below.

- *Take as few partners as legally allowable*. This is because each additional partner increases the complexity of doing business. Avoid a fifty–fifty ownership arrangement, that will result in neither partner being able to make quick decisions.
- *Adopt and follow international management practices*. This means that internationally accepted accounting, customer service, marketing, and ethical practices must be adopted and practiced. While this rigid approach may result in lost market share in the short run, this step will minimize illegal activities.
- *Begin small*. It is more pragmatic to enter a market in a small way. This reduces the probability of disaster and allows the global firm to change directions or leave the market quickly, when necessary.
- *Listen carefully to partners*. It is essential for global managers to listen to their partners, but to not follow them blindly. Do not stake your business on what your partners tell you.
- *Do not view the country as a single market*. Most countries have different regional needs, wants, customs, business practices, and income. Think and act locally.
- *Be wary of government policies*. Government policies and regulations are important for global competitors, but can change rapidly. Be cautious when basing entry strategies upon existing policies.
- *Keep your ear to the ground*. Global sales firms must watch the local business climate. A successful business model in one market does not insure success in another marketplace. This is because business climates change independently of one another.

*Source*. Fons Tuinstra, "Shampoo Wars," *Asiaweek*, January 21, 2000, 48–9.

## ETHICAL CONSIDERATIONS

Personal selling is an area fraught with opportunities for ethical abuse, and as a profession, salespersons are thought to possess low ethical standards. However, there are logical explanations for this situation. First, some firms operate under a sales orientation that dictates that high levels of sales activity or pressure are necessary to succeed. This is why many of the sales "tricks of the trade" were developed to maneuver the buyer into a position where they were forced to say, "Yes." At other times, the salesperson may simply not tell the truth to make the sale. This is where the term *caveat emptor*, or "buyer beware," originated in US legal parlance, because the judiciary system declared that consumers must be suspicious of items offered for sale and that the customer had a responsibility to understand purchase conditions. While a number of firms still practice a sales orientation, this is not advocated or practiced by firms that believe business success occurs when the buyer and seller mutually benefit from a relationship.

Salespersons are criticized for unethical behavior and for being untruthful, but much of this behavior can be traced to management. That is, sales managers set unrealistic goals and demand that the sales force achieve those goals regardless of the actions needed to do so. Managers must set realistic goals and hold salespersons accountable for violating ethical behavior guidelines. If a sales manager advocates ethical behavior and then rewards a salesperson who acts unethically to make a large sale, it will be difficult to enforce ethical behavior in future sales actions.

One explanation for why a salesperson is perceived to act unethically during the sales process is that the salesperson is a boundary spanner that attempts to bring the buyer and seller firms together. This means that the salesperson must get the two parties to agree to terms and conditions, which is no easy task. As seen in Table 5.2, the salesperson occupies a difficult position when initial positions are staked out by the buyer and seller. At the greatest distance, the sales organization informs the salesperson that the buyer is to be sold the standard product, at the highest possible price, with minimal service obligation, and the longest delivery time. The buyer, on the other hand, wants to buy a modified product, at an economical price, with high service levels, and short delivery time. In effect the buyer and the seller begin their discussions at opposite ends of a continuum. How then, is the salesperson to resolve this dilemma?

The salesperson generally has little power over either the sales organization or the buyer. Therefore, the salesperson must accomplish their job through negotiation and compromise – the salesperson must convince the seller to lower the price and negotiate with the buyer to pay a higher price. The same is true for modifying the product, delivery time, and service commitment.

*Role conflict* occurs when a salesperson is constantly placed in a position where he or she tries to meet the disparate expectations of numerous parties. For example, the sales organization believes the salesperson is a tool of the company that will go into the field and sell the product at the highest possible price that results in the greatest amount of profitability. The buyer, on the other hand, believes the salesperson will meet their needs. The salesperson's family also expects time and attention will be devoted to them.

**Table 5.2** The salesperson and role conflict

| Seller position | Salesperson | Buyer position |
| --- | --- | --- |
| Highest possible price | Price | Lowest possible price |
| Standard product | Product | Modified product |
| Long delivery time | Delivery | Short delivery time |
| Low service commitment | Service | High service commitment |

What is problematic for the salesperson is that all parties setting expectations have an ability to reward and punish the salesperson. The sales manager can reward the salesperson for correct behavior by giving a pay increase, a new company car, a new cellular phone, a bonus or a better territory. If the salesperson does not behave the way the manager expects, the sales manager may punish the salesperson by taking away perquisites, raises, or territories. The sales manager can even punish the salesperson by assigning a less convenient territory that will result in a lower salary. Similarly, the buyer can reward the salesperson with larger and additional orders and can punish the salesperson by withholding an order. The salesperson's family can reward him with emotional support and love when his behavior meets their expectations and withhold this support when actions fails to meet their expectations. What should be obvious is that the salesperson cannot possibly meet the expectations of all these different parties.

Therefore, the salesperson must attempt to satisfy the demands of all parties, which is no small task. The salesperson can act in one of several ways. First, the salesperson can meet with the buyer, lay out the seller's position and then say "take it or leave it." However, the likely outcome is that few buyers would continue the sales process. Secondly, the seller can totally withdraw from the situation since there appears to be little likelihood that the parties can be satisfied. This behavior would not work since the salesperson must interact with the customer to be successful. Third, the salesperson can work with both parties to reach a compromise. This is what most salespersons do, work with the buyer and seller and bring them together through compromise. To reach a compromise the salesperson has to utilize diplomatic skills to resolve different positions. This necessitates that the salesperson not be totally blunt with either of the parties, because the goal is to work with each party to understand the position of the other and then to compromise to reach an acceptable final agreement. If the salesperson were completely inflexible with either party, the negotiation process would break down and the agreement would be in jeopardy. The way the sales process works may explain why salespersons are sometimes characterized as being dishonest during the sales process.

However, it is important to reiterate that ethical dealings with the customer are essential for establishing an atmosphere of trust, cooperation, and maintaining a business relationship. Unethical behavior may help the salesperson and sales firm reach short-term sales goals, but this behavior will not maintain long-run customers. As soon as a customer learns of unethical salesperson behavior, they will seek a more reliable and trustworthy business partner.

## CHAPTER SUMMARY

This chapter completes the global sales process that consists of seven steps: (1) finding customers, (2) preparing, (3) relationship building, (4) product offering, (5) offer clarification, (6) securing the purchase, and (7) maintaining the relationship. Each of these steps is interdependent and early steps must be successfully practiced for later steps to work correctly. Cultural forces impact all stages of the global sales process. This means that salespersons who call upon customers from diverse cultures and backgrounds must understand how the sales process needs to be modified to accommodate customers' distinctive needs. Finally, an explanation of why the salesperson is viewed to be unethical during the sales process and why it is essential to behave ethically was presented. A final point to remember is that no "for profit" firm can remain in business unless sales are made. Hence the sales process – in one variation or another – is practiced by every for-profit business and many not-for-profit organizations.

## DISCUSSION QUESTIONS

1   What are four different mechanisms that can be used by a global salesperson to meet a prospective buyer?
2   What is the benefit of the global salesperson making informal sales presentations?
3   What are the five different approaches that the global salesperson can use in making a sales presentation to a prospective buyer, and under what circumstances would each be appropriate?
4   What kinds of questions might the prospective buyer have for the global salesperson after the sales presentation has been made?
5   How can the global salesperson effectively secure the sale with the prospective buyer?
6   What are important considerations for the global salesperson in maintaining long-term successful relationships with the prospective buyer?
7   What are some opportunities for ethical abuse that might emerge in the global selling process, and how can they be avoided?
8   What is role conflict, and how might it affect the global selling process?

## REFERENCES

1   Daft, Doug (2000), "Coke's New Formula," *Far Eastern Economic Review*, April 20, 64–5.

2   Ford, John B., and Earl D. Honeycutt, Jr. (1992), "Japanese National Culture as a Basis for Understanding Japanese Business Practices," *Business Horizons*, 35:6, 27–34.

3   Eppler, Dianne B., Earl D. Honeycutt, Jr., John B. Ford, and Edward Markowski (1998), "The Relationship of Self-monitoring and Adaptiveness to the Performance of Real Estate Sales Professionals," *Journal of Business and Economic Studies*, 4:2, 37–51.

4   Eppler, Honeycutt, Ford, and Markowski (1998).

5   Acuff, Frank L. (1993), *How to Negotiate Anything with Anyone Anywhere around the World*, New York: Amacom Books.

6   Axtell, Roger E., ed. (1993), *Do's and Taboos around the World*, third edition, New York: John Wiley & Sons.

7   Daft, Doug (2000), "Coke's New Formula," *Far Eastern Economic Review*, April 20, 64–5.

8   Tuinstra, Fons (2000), "Eight Things You Didn't Know about Chinese Consumers," *Asiaweek*, April 28, 42–6, 51.

9   Flynn, Brian H., and Kathleen A. Murray (1993), "Your Sales Force May be Your Weak Link," *Journal of European Business*, 5:2, 45–8.

10  Tung, Rosalie L. (1984), *Business Negotiations with the Japanese*, Lexington MA: D.C. Heath.

11  Tung (1984).

Part III

# Global human resources

## Chapter 6

# Global sales organizations

This chapter presents the steps in designing a sales organization. Additionally, concepts that influence organizations, common structures found in the global marketplace, and multiple channels are discussed.

## LEARNING OBJECTIVES

*After reading this chapter, you will be able to:*

- List and explain the steps involved in analyzing and building a sales organization.
- Discuss the relationship between company, marketing, and sales goals.
- Explain the influence of market complexity, customer location, and market variations on market effectiveness.
- Discuss the impact of generalist versus specialist, centralization, span of control, and line and staff positions on sales force structures.
- Compare the positive and negative aspects of geographical, product, market, functional, and combination sales force structures.
- List and discuss organizational structures found in the global marketplace.
- Explain the multiple sales force options available to firms.
- Understand when it is time to evaluate and modify a sales organization.

## KEY TERMS

- SWOT analysis.
- 80/20 principle.
- Global account management.
- Piggyback marketing.

## INTRODUCTION

Organizational design can be a planned process or a series of random events in managing the sales force. Some firms haphazardly enter into this process, while other companies follow an objective process for selecting a sales force organizational structure that includes extensive analyses of: current and potential customers, the market environment, competitors, company assets, and the firm's ability to serve the marketplace. Based upon this analysis, decisions are made about the number, type, and assignment of sales personnel. All sales force organizational decisions – whether planned or accidental – are directly influenced by the socio-economic, legal, and cultural variations found in the marketplace.[1] When design decisions are haphazard, these variations can push and pull a firm in different and even opposing directions. Conversely, when the decisions are part of a logical process, the design decisions are more likely to be optimal ones.

Even firms that have a large number of established customers in the global marketplace continually examine their territory design so that customers receive maximum service at minimum cost. Other firm objectives that influence sales force design include balancing the sales force work load, insuring that all accounts are assigned to a sales representative, implementing an effective two-way communication channel between the firm and the customer, and organizing the sales force structure to facilitate an objective sales force evaluation program.

This chapter outlines the steps to analyze and build a sales organizational structure, integrates organizational concepts that influence sales force organizations, describes the most frequent ways to organize the sales force, details sales structures in global markets, and examines multiple sales force options.

CASE VIGNETTE **WHICH SALES ORGANIZATION?**

Tameka Johnson can help move her sales organization into the global market – if she can just find the right way to organize it. After a decade of profitable direct exporting, the company expanded by forming partnerships in Europe and Asia. These partnerships place Tameka's company on the brink of even more profitable sales – provided the sales contacts can be made and maintained in these markets. The corporation has now decided it will be even more profitable to serve the market directly with a company sales force, rather than selling through partners. As a result of this upper management decision, Johnson must decide how to organize the firm's sales force for the marketplace. Having never organized a sales force to serve the global market, Johnson must make numerous decisions that will directly influence the ability of the sales force to simultaneously achieve firm objectives and satisfy customer needs.

## ANALYZING AND BUILDING A SALES ORGANIZATION

Sales organizations try to balance the needs of three competing forces: (1) the customer, (2) the firm, and (3) the business environment. The steps in this process include assessing and designing a sales organization that best matches the distinctive needs and operating styles of current and potential customers. To accomplish this goal, an analysis of the current sales force is performed (see Figure 6.1). First, a thorough environmental analysis is conducted, which includes Strengths, Weaknesses, Opportunities, and Threats (SWOT). This process identifies both internal and external demands and constraints on the firm. Second, based upon this analysis, essential sales force activities are determined. Third, managers select a sales force organizational structure that best matches market conditions. A subdecision within this stage is allocating the appropriate number and type of organizational positions that are necessary to conduct sales activities. The final two steps involve recruiting and selecting individuals to staff the organization and evaluating the effectiveness of the organization. Since all organizations evolve over time, the sales structure must be periodically assessed to remain effective. Now, let's take a more detailed look at each stage of the organizational building process.

### Analyzing the environment

Sales organizations are formed and develop for a variety of reasons. While sales structures are designed to accomplish activities, organizational shape is also influenced by individual strengths, geographical locations, and the need to satisfy management's personal preferences. It is also human nature for managers to build an empire to further their own desire for power and status. When this happens, sales functions and responsibilities can become

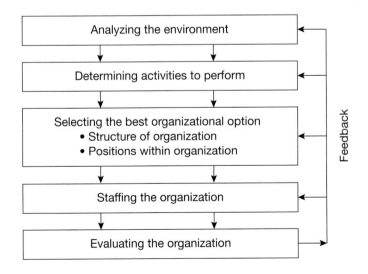

**Figure 6.1** *Analyzing or building a sales organization*

organized illogically. As a result, sales force effectiveness and company profitability may suffer.

In reality, organizations are often structured around activities and personalities. This is because managers face conflicting goals when designing organizations. On one hand, activities and responsibilities are supposed to be assigned to organizational positions without regard to the talents or preferences of current employees. However, to make the most of the talents of the sales force, and to retain good salespeople, sales managers have ample reason to organize around the talents and preferences of current employees.

When analyzing the business environment it is necessary to examine the firm's goals, market and buyer behavior, the competitive situation, and the sales force organization.

## Firm goals

Overall company goals are set at the highest levels of management through the company business plan. Top management defines the business through a mission statement, which consolidates and creates synergism among the firm's stakeholders. Most mission statements focus on markets served, rather than products manufactured, because buyer needs are more constant than the products that serve those needs. During this goal-setting stage, company executives also determine which parts of the organization receive funds for growth and which are to generate funds.

Based upon the business plan, a marketing plan is drafted to achieve the goals (see Figure 6.2). In concert with the marketing plan, the sales plan details actions or tactics necessary to meet marketing plan goals. Both the marketing and sales plans are driven by the roles assigned in the company business plan. When a firm like General Electric, that has a number

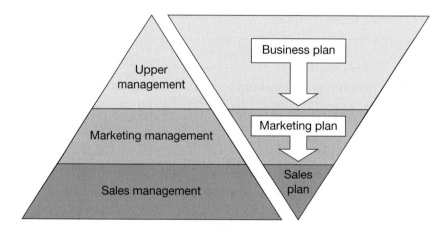

**Figure 6.2** Organizational level and planning

of business units, is structured by product, the sales force also organizes around this structure. This is because GE's product line is too broad and diverse for a single sales force to adequately represent all products in the marketplace.

## Market and buyer behavior

No matter what type of business, the sales force is a boundary spanner that links the firm to the marketplace. To insure peak effectiveness, the sales organization is structured to maximize the opportunity to satisfy customer needs and minimize obstacles that reduce high service levels. At least three characteristics influence market effectiveness.

- *Market complexity*. This characteristic depends upon the number of customer categories supplied by the selling firm. Categories include industry, language spoken, cultural variations, and legal requirements. Each additional customer category served increases the complexity of use and the need for a separate sales force.
- *Customer location*. It is common for manufacturers to have discrete site locations, each of which may purchase independently. Or customers may buy at a central location, then ship to disparate locations. When customers employ centralized purchasing with decentralized operations, salespersons seldom call upon headquarters and manufacturing sites in the field. In this situation, success will depend upon the sales force working together. The sales manager must effectively coordinate the efforts of a sales force that operates in multiple locations.
- *Market variations*. Because the marketplace is constantly in flux, few static sales organizations succeed in the long run. Firms understand that technologies change, customers enter and leave the marketplace, and product life cycles are now shorter in duration.[2] Therefore, it is important for the sales organization to be adaptable to market variations, be technically oriented, and provide superior after-sale service.[3]

## Competitors

The next component is gathering information that provides an accurate understanding of competitors and their sales organizations. A first step is identifying major competitors. To be fully cognizant of existing as well as potential competitors, it is necessary to identify both direct and indirect competitors. Once noted, the sales manager conducts a comprehensive SWOT analysis that documents how each category of the organization ranks in comparison with identified competitors. With this information, managers can identify existing competitive strengths and weaknesses in comparison with those expected from the proposed sales organization. Sales management must understand the customer buying process and insure the sales force organizational design matches the buying process. This means that sales managers must either adopt a sales force structure that delivers a level of service consistent with competitors or establish an organization that is distinctly superior. The goal should be to design a sales organization that is both efficient to operate and provides customers with superior benefit over competitors.

## Deciding upon an organization

Although extremely important, determining which organizational option to select is seldom an easy task for the sales manager, since each company faces different market and competitive factors and pursues disparate actions to succeed in the marketplace. It is necessary for the sales manager to select specific criteria for determining which sales organization best matches customer needs and organizational strengths. For global sales forces, such criteria as stage of economic development, technological sophistication of the product, and management orientation will influence the structure of the organization.

## SALES FORCE ORGANIZATIONAL CONCEPTS

A number of organizational concepts also influence sales force structures in the global marketplace. These factors include a generalist versus specialist approach, centralization of decision making, management span of control, line versus staff coordination, and the ability to coordinate and integrate the sales force.

## Generalist versus specialist

A firm that follows a generalist approach assigns the sales force to serve all customers within a specific geographical area. This means the salesperson calls upon all customers within a region, regardless of their need, and represents the firm's complete product line. The generalist approach works well when customers have similar needs and the product line is not complex. Such a focus allows the sales force to gain an understanding of the economic and competitive conditions within the territory and to minimize travel expenses.

However, when the firm's product line is broad and deep, the sales force will likely specialize by product. When individual markets have distinct needs, then the sales force may be organized around the industry or firm. The basic idea behind specialization is that an individual can master and perform a limited number of tasks at a higher level of expertise. Conversely, specialization increases the need to coordinate and communicate within the firm.

Three comparisons allow managers to arrive at the best decision about the specialization of the sales force:[4]

- Cost versus payoff of specialization.
- Client coverage versus product/application knowledge.
- Flexibility of operations.

## Centralization

Centralized firms make decisions at higher levels of the organization. When a firm allows lower level managers or workers to make decisions, then the firm is more decentralized. Although few firms are totally centralized or decentralized, most favor one of these orientations.

As companies adopt a relationship marketing approach toward the marketplace, they find it difficult to remain centralized. When firms use sales teams and leadership strategies, they must move away from centralized management. The spread of technology, which allows customers to gather information about competitors' products and pricing, requires decisions to be made more quickly than in the past. Also implied by relationship marketing is a need for highly qualified salespersons who can address customer needs on the spot rather than after lengthy consultations with headquarters. In effect, decentralization empowers the sales force to make decisions that produces satisfied customers.

## Span of control

Span of control refers to the number of persons that report to a single manager. For complex and customized product lines, the span of control is lower than for standardized products and customer needs. Also, in more centralized organizations, managers have smaller spans of control. When the organization is flatter, the manager's span of control is broader. Generally speaking, the degree to which each salesperson – and perhaps each customer served by that salesperson – represents an important or expensive resource, the more time the manager should devote to the salesperson. In effect the manager's time represents the efforts the company believes it should invest in developing, guiding, and monitoring a resource. Like many guidelines, span of control has been strongly affected by trends in the technological, economic, and sociocultural arenas. In today's world of e-mail and virtual organizations, the sales manager can closely monitor the activities of many salespeople. Industrial consolidation has created a situation in which more sophisticated and educated buyers demand ethical and professional treatment. In effect these powerful buyers aid the manager by keeping the salesperson focused on delivering a high level of quality service.

There is no rule for "ideal" span of control; however, Table 6.1 provides guidance for sales managers. Technical sales and industrial products – both of which necessitate custom solutions – result in smaller spans of control. Conversely, routine trade sales activities allow a wider span of control.

## Line versus staff positions

In a sales organization most salespersons fall within a line organization, which means that they report directly to a sales manager. Looking at Figure 6.3, one can follow the "line" upward

**Table 6.1** *Suggested span of control ratios*

| By selling task | | By product type | |
|---|---|---|---|
| Technical selling | 7:1 | Industrial products | 6:1 |
| Missionary selling | 10:1 | Consumer products | 8:1 |
| Trade selling | 12–16:1 | Services | 10:1 |

Source: James E. Bell Jr. and William O. hancock, "Optimizing Sales Organization Size," *Business Perspectives*, 8 (Winter 1972), 21

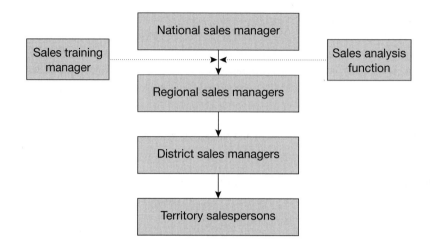

**Figure 6.3** *Line and staff organizational positions*

from territory salesperson, to district sales manager, to regional sales manager, and to national sales manager. A line position denotes that these managers retain authority for setting goals, allocating funding to achieve those goals, and evaluating the outcomes of sales force efforts.

Staff personnel are more specialized in their activities and help the salesperson generate revenue. Support functions may include sales training and sales analysis. Staff managers neither generate sales revenue or supervise line workers, but provide the sales force with specialized support to improve field sales performance.

A number of firms have outsourced staff responsibilities to outside vendors in order to provide services to the sales force at a lower cost without incurring the fixed costs generated by staff not directly engaged in sales or production activities. Outsourcing increases the need for coordination between the sales organization and the vendors contracted to provide these services.

## Selecting the best organizational option

Firms organize their company sales force around geographical, product, market/customer, function, or a combination of these factors. Each of the methods for organizing the sales force is discussed below and Table 6.2 consolidates the advantages and disadvantages of each organizational structure.

### Geographical

A firm organizes along geographical lines because it is simple, reduces duplication of effort, and insures that customers are assigned to a specific salesperson. Depending upon the number of accounts located within a geographical entity, a salesperson may be assigned a group of customers within an entire country, metropolitan area, province, city, county, or

**Table 6.2** *Positive/negative aspects of territory design*

| Structure | Positive aspects | Negative aspects |
|---|---|---|
| Geographical | Simplicity | Generalist approach |
| | Efficiency | Unequal territories |
| | No duplication | |
| Product | Product knowledge | Duplicated sales effort |
| | Applications knowledge | |
| Market | Customer knowledge | Duplicated sales effort |
| | Applications knowledge | |
| Functional | Job knowledge | Coordination efforts |
| Combination | Customer knowledge | Economies of scale issues |
| | Market knowledge | |

zip/postal code. However, a quick analysis of customer location generally confirms that geographical territories must be modified to compensate for differing sales potentials and customer needs.

Geographical sales territories have many positive aspects. First, every customer located within a territory is assigned to a single salesperson. Second, geographical groupings allow reduced travel costs and improved call efficiency. Third, geographical territories can be easier for sales managers to administer and evaluate.

However, when salespersons are assigned a geographic territory they become product generalists that may not be as familiar with all products when the firm manufactures an extensive product line. It can also be difficult to equitably organize geographic territories. Some customers are concentrated in a small area, while other territories require the salesperson to spend greater amounts of time traveling.

## Product

When firms offer complex or broad product lines, or when these products are complex in nature, the sales force is organized along product lines. The major benefit of organizing by product is that the salesperson can acquire higher levels of product knowledge that can be utilized to solve customer problems. But, when a firm has numerous product lines, such as appliances, medical, aircraft, and credit, then a separate sales force is required for each major product line.

Conversely, customers can become confused or resentful when multiple salespersons from a single firm call upon the same account. Perhaps this is because buyers perceive that it is less efficient to meet with numerous salespersons from the same firm. If a product-focused sales force does not provide satisfactory service, then this organizational structure is not the best way to serve the customer base. For example, Xerox USA was organized into three, product-related, sales force structures: computers, copiers, and office work stations. Because of customer complaints about service, the sales forces were combined into a single "Team Xerox."

## Market

Product applications vary by industry; therefore, some firms assign their sales force by market or type of organization. These assignments are necessary to maintain a close relationship with the client or closely monitor the customer's needs.[5] For example, a sales force can be organized around such industry categories as automotive, computer, consumer goods, military/government, and telecommunications. A market-organized sales force allows the salesperson to become an expert on and to follow trends within a single firm or industry. It is standard practice for a seller to exclusively assign one or more individuals, as sales advocates, to global firms like IBM, Daimler-Chrysler, Ford, Toyota, Unilever, or San Miguel to insure customer needs are met. Firms may also have a global sales manager assigned to coordinate the interactions between seller organization personnel.

A major disadvantage of organizing the sales force by market is that customers can be widely dispersed, which results in significant travel. For example, within the computer industry, Dell Computers is located in Texas, Gateway in South Dakota, Microsoft resides in Washington State, Acer in Taiwan, and Toshiba in Japan. One can easily see the vast geographical diversity and purchasing power of these large computer firms. In most cases, manufacturing vendors assign their sales forces in the computer industry by firm. This generalization about travel problems with market assignment does not always hold true, since Japanese manufacturers of automobiles and electronic goods locate in close proximity to one another and suppliers for efficiency. Finally, sales downturns in one industry or customer locale can lead to costly and possibly disruptive sales force structure realignments.

## Functional

Firms can also structure their sales force based upon functional or job activities. That is, a firm may have a salesperson that opens the account and then turns the servicing of the account over to another salesperson. Likewise food salespersons utilize sales teams that include a lead salesperson, and sales associates, that stock shelves and handle inventory and/or merchandising issues. In some emerging nations, where it is more economical to hire salespersons, global firms have added sales associates that travel the countryside promoting new products and supporting the regular company sales force.

Functional structures allow specialization. A disadvantage of functional sales organizations is that coordination needs increase and sales support personnel may not possess the depth of knowledge or service consistency offered by other specialists.

## Combination structures

When a firm is large, has multiple product lines, and operates over wide geographical areas, the sale force is organized around combinations of geography, product, market, and function. This means that a company like General Electric can organize its sales efforts along the lines of medical, consumer products, appliances, and aircraft divisions. Given this vast array of products, GE might divide the aircraft division sales force into markets – military and civilian aircraft – and geography – North America, Europe, and Asia. Therefore, a GE aircraft salesperson could be assigned military aircraft accounts in the European Union. Depending upon the size of the territory, the salesperson might call upon customers only in one or more nations – military aircraft manufacturers in France, Germany or Great Britain.

## SALES STRUCTURES IN GLOBAL MARKETS

In global markets, distribution strategies vary from country to country. An excellent example is the practice of selling automobiles at retail outlets in the United States, while using door-to-door automobile salespersons in Japan.[6] Likewise, cultural context influences sales practices. Expatriates are utilized in low context or individualistic countries like Germany, while high context or collectivist nations like Japan use local salespersons with cultural knowledge only they would possess.[7]

Global firms organize their sales forces similarly to domestic structures.[8] Even when there is a wide array of available alternatives, global firms still organize their sales force along simple geographical territories within a single country or region. Global firms that offer broad product lines, large sales volumes, or operate in large, developed markets prefer specialized organizational structures, such as product or customer assignment. In small markets, like those seen in most emerging nations, it is economically inappropriate to assign sales specialists by customer or product category.[9]

Global firms also organize the sales force based upon culture. Certainly the homogeneity or heterogeneity of languages spoken in the targeted market is an essential aspect to consider. For example, firms may divide Belgium by language – French to the south and Flemish in the north – and combine Austria and Germany because of each nation's use of the German language. Similarly, Switzerland may be organized into different regions reflecting French, Italian, and German language use. Conversely, a number of global firms combine Central America into a single sales territory.[10] Sales force managers must always be sensitive to the fact that while countries may be geographically close, each nation possesses distinct customs and values.[11]

**Table 6.3** Guidelines for organizing global sales forces

| Structure | Appropriate conditions |
|---|---|
| Geographical | Undeveloped markets |
| | Small sales volumes |
| | Similar languages/cultures |
| | Single product line |
| Product | Established market |
| Market | Broad product lines |
| Combination | Large sales volume |
| | Large/developed markets |
| | Distinct languages/cultures |

When determining the appropriate sales force structure, it is prudent to carefully assess the overseas market in terms of: (1) geographic size, (2) sales potential, (3) ease of customer access, (4) customer expectations, (5) current selling practices, and (6) language(s) spoken. A global firm that lacks sensitivity to the conditions found in local markets and copies its home market sales organization increases the likelihood of disastrous sales results.[12] To reduce the probability of this happening, Table 6.3 provides guidance for organizing global sales force territories.

## MULTIPLE SALES FORCE OPTIONS

Firms often employ multiple or parallel sales forces to serve customers. This section reviews the myriad ways firms service their customer base in the global marketplace.

### National account management

National account management refers to serving the needs of large customers that have multiple locations throughout a region or nation. Many firms service national or key accounts separately because a majority of their sales are derived from these accounts. If we look at the *80/20 principle*, we understand that approximately 80 percent of a firm's sales are generated by 20 percent of their customers. This means that, in order to form long-term relationships, firms must provide superior service to customers that generate large quantities of sales and profits. These special relationships mean that one sales executive, located at corporate level, is responsible for maintaining satisfied customers. When customer locations do not overlap, the account manager can be placed at the divisional, district, or territory level.

The sales force calls upon and services major or national accounts, with a senior salesperson serving as the manager for formulating and coordinating plans and directing sales efforts.[13] In such cases, the major account manager coordinates sales teams from different departments or specialties. In such organizations, the sales team works directly with influencers and deciders within the buying center. Firms that utilize this approach include Revlon and Anderson Windows.

### Global account management

Global account management organizes company assets to serve the needs of customers located around the world. Since a global firm may have each stage of its value chain located at different sites, it is necessary to manage the larger accounts based upon multiple global locations. For key global accounts, an account manager is assigned to customer headquarters to oversee the account team assigned to the client. This team normally consists of members that specialize in product design, applications, logistics, sales support, and marketing.[14]

Global accounts can be managed using one of three distinct approaches. First, firms have traditional sales organizations in each country, with a Global Account Manager (GAM) coordinating programs across countries. Second, is a matrix organization that shares responsibility between the Global Account Manager and National Account Manager for global accounts. The third option is to transfer key accounts from the traditional organization to the GAM, and leave program implementation to the local sales forces. Most global firms use the first two options, but the trend is toward the last alternative.[15]

## Company agents

Company sales agents represent the firm although they are independent businessmen and women. There are myriad types of agents, a number of which are discussed below. Each can be categorized and described in terms of the array of services they provide.

### Manufacturer's representative

These agents represent a number of related but non-competing product lines within a geographical area. In such relationships the manufacturer is commonly referred to as the *principal*. Manufacturers' reps do not take title to goods and have little control over pricing. Manufactures' representatives possess a number of advantages that include:

- Superior selling skills.
- Immediate coverage for new principals.
- Reduced costs and increase potential per call.
- Few fixed costs.
- Territory stability.

However, manufacturers or principals may feel the representative does not provide equal time for their products, but simply moves to another product line when an apparent buyer need is not uncovered. Also, manufacturers' reps have been criticized for paying too little attention to generating new accounts, not following up on provided leads, carrying too many product lines, and not communicating well with the manufacturer. To maintain a productive partnership, it is important for principals to understand and nurture the goals of manufacturers' representatives.

### Independent agents

There are a wide variety of independent agents. A number are discussed briefly in this section.

*Selling agents* act as the marketing department when they are responsible for the complete marketing of the product.

A *broker* represents either the buyer or the seller, with the major function being to bring the parties together and assist in negotiations. Brokers can work both as long-term continuous agents or on short-term independent transactions.

*Independent telemarketers* represent firms that may not have the personnel to perform telemarketing or as an outsource agent that performs the function at a lower cost to the manufacturer.

*Piggyback marketing* is an innovative distribution strategy that allows one manufacturer to actively distribute the products of another, thereby making fuller use of distribution channels and increasing the revenues generated by the channel. The product lines should be complementary and used by similar customers. For example, Hawaiian Kauai Kookie Kompany (HKKK) saw that Japanese tourists were stocking up on their product prior to returning home. In response, HKKK formed a piggyback arrangement with Japanese travel agents that allowed travelers to order cookies in Japan.[16]

### Indirect channels

Firms also employ indirect channels of resellers or middlemen to purchase products from the manufacturer, place the items in stock, and resell the products to customers when the need arises. These indirect channel resellers are categorized as wholesalers, distributors, and dealers. Indirect resellers supplement, rather than replace, the manufacturer's sales force. Since distributors take title to the goods, they are also customers of the manufacturer. Distributors work best as resellers under the following conditions:[17]

- Large potential customer base.
- Small sales quantities.
- Products stocked and serviced locally.
- Need for quick delivery and service.
- Lower level buyers that purchase basic products.

## SUPPLEMENTAL SALES METHODS

Firms also employ a number of methods that complement their sales efforts. One of the more ubiquitous supplemental sales methods today is *telemarketing*. Companies employ two methods of telemarketing – incoming and outgoing. *Incoming* telemarketing consists of toll-free numbers advertised by the company that allows buyers to order items that are shipped directly to them. Many firms also employ incoming telemarketing for smaller accounts that are not profitable enough to justify a personal sales call. This system permits customers to initiate a purchase when there are emergencies or when stock levels fall below anticipated levels. A number of office supply, computer supply, and consumer goods firms utilize incoming telemarketing systems to serve customers.

Telemarketing has also been expanded to serve the needs of a diverse marketplace. When customers call the toll-free number, their account records can be called up, providing information of previous dealings, and allowing the inside sales rep to add information to the customer relationship management (CRM) system. In effect the CRM system permits the firm to analyze business, determine the types of products purchased at specific intervals, and offers a venue for customer complaints. In addition, the CRM system provides telemarketing sales reps with specific information to initiate outgoing calls to customers in anticipation of needs and to offer specials on products the customer has ordered in the past.

*Administrative support* provides assistance to the sales force for such duties as prospecting, qualifying, expediting orders, and setting appointments. Basically, it is more economical to have someone within the firm provide these important services than to ask the salesperson to perform them. Also, sales support personnel that serve as telemarketers can make large amounts of sales to customers.[18]

*Technical Support*. When products are highly complex, it is important for firms to establish a technical support program to aid the sales force. Technically oriented firms provide web sites, brochures, product or application sheets, video tapes, and test equipment. It is also important to have technical support people who can be called upon for assistance at critical times during the sales cycle. For example, technical firms hire sales engineers to provide application and product expertise to technical buying center members. Team selling also incorporates technical support, as one of the team members should be an engineer or technical person who can answer questions posed by technical experts at the buyer organization.

## EVALUATING THE ORGANIZATION

On a continual basis, management evaluates the efficiency of the organization based upon its ability to service existing and potential customers. As long as sales personnel meet the needs of the customer base, it is not necessary to modify the sales force organizational structure. Managers monitor the variables discussed above in "Analyzing the environment" and refer to such metrics as customer feedback, number of lost customers, travel expense trends, sales force turnover, and competitive restructuring. Obviously, the metric(s) utilized depend(s) upon the objectives of the firm. When confronted with compelling evidence that the current structure is not working, the sales manager must adjust the sales organization to address shortcomings.

It is also important to understand that no one sales force organizational structure performs best in all situations. Since companies pursue different market segments, customers, competitors, strategies, and tactics, distinct organizational structures are adopted. And, as firms and markets mature, and strategies and customers change, modifications to the sales organization need to be made. Because the marketplace constantly fluctuates, sales managers must be able to both analyze and build effective sales organizations.

## CHAPTER SUMMARY

The organizational structure directly impacts the management of the sales force. The firm must decide, after conducting a thorough analysis of the internal and external environment, how to structure the sales force and whom to utilize as sales personnel. In this chapter, we have explained the company sales force, manufacturers' representatives, agents, and indirect and multiple channel partners. In the global marketplace, firms may use different sales organizations in closely located markets, based upon differences uncovered in socioeconomic, cultural, and legal analysis. The final sales force organization is also influenced by such managerial concepts as generalist versus specialist, centralization of decision making, span of control, line versus staff functions, and need for coordination. It is important to remember that the goal of sales force organizations is efficiency – providing superior service to current and potential customers at the lowest possible cost.

## DISCUSSION QUESTIONS

1   What areas are analyzed prior to designing a sales organization?

2   Since markets constantly change, what impact does this have on territory design?

3   When should a general salesperson be hired? What limitations do centralized organizations face?

4   What are the advantages and disadvantages of geographical, product, market, and functional sales organizations?

5   How might tradition, culture, language, and geography influence global sales territories?

6   What complaints have principals made against manufacturers' representatives?

7   What criteria or metrics might be monitored to assess organizational efficiency?

## REFERENCES

1   Cateora, Philip R., and John L. Graham (1999), *International Marketing*, Boston MA: Irwin McGraw-Hill.

2   Christensen, Clayton M. (1997), *The Innovator's Dilemma*, Boston MA: Harvard Business Press.

3   Wotruba, Thomas R., and Edwin K. Simpson (1992), *Sales Management*, Boston MA: PWS-Kent Publishing.

4   Wotruba and Simpson (1992).

5   Kotabe, Masaaki, and Kristiaan Helsen (1998), *Global Marketing Management*, New York: John Wiley & Sons.

6   Cateora and Graham (1999).

7   Johansson, Johny K., and Ikujiro Nonaka (1996), *Relentless: The Japanese Way of Marketing*, New York: Harper Business.

8   Hill, John S., and Richard R. Still (1990), "Organizing the Overseas Sales Force: How Multinationals Do It," *Journal of Personal Selling and Sales Management*, 10:2 (spring), 57–66.

9   Samli, A.C., R. Still, and J.S. Hill, (1993), *International Marketing*, New York: Macmillan.

10   Samli, Still, and Hill (1993).

11   Axtell, Roger E. (1990), *Do's and Taboos around the World*, New York: John Wiley & Sons.

12   Honeycutt, Earl D. Jr., and John B. Ford (1995), "Guidelines for Managing an International Sales Force," *Industrial Marketing Management*, 24, 135–44.

13   Wotruba and Simpson (1992).

14   Clark, Charles T. (1994), "Is Your Company Ready for Global Marketing?" *Sales and Marketing Management*, September, 42.

15  Birkinshaw, Julian, Omar Toulan, and David Arnold (2001), "Global Account Management in Multinational Corporations: Theory and Evidence," *Journal of International Business Studies*, 32:2, 231–48.

16  Keegan, Warren J., and Mark C. Green (1997), *Principles of Global Marketing*, Upper Saddle River NJ: Prentice Hall.

17  Hlavacek, James D., and Tommy J. McCuiston (1983), "Industrial Distributors: When, Who, and How?" *Harvard Business Review*, 61 (March–April), 96–101.

18  Blackwood, Francy (1995), "Did You Sell $5 Million Last Year?" *Selling*, October, 44–53.

## Chapter 7

# Selecting the global sales force

This chapter provides guidance for undertaking each of the four steps involved in finding, processing, interviewing, and hiring a sales force. Cross-cultural influences are also discussed.

## LEARNING OBJECTIVES

*After reading this chapter, you will be able to*:

- Explain the four steps that managers follow in the selection process and the outcome of not conducting an effective selection process.
- Discuss the advantages and disadvantages of the three categories of sales personnel.
- Understand why simply possessing several personal characteristics will not lead to sales success.
- Explain how to conduct a job analysis and write a job description.
- List internal and external sources of sales recruits.
- Discuss, in detail, each of the five stages of the selection process to include cultural influences on each stage.

## KEY TERMS

- Turnover.
- Expatriates, Local nationals, Third-country nationals.
- Job analysis and Job description.
- Structured, unstructured, and stress interviews.

## INTRODUCTION

Perhaps no decision made by the sales manager is as paramount as sales force selection. In today's global marketplace the diverse skills, knowledge, abilities, and relationships exercised and maintained by the sales force significantly impact the success of global operations. A survey of Canadian CEOs reported that attracting skilled employees was a major concern of 58 percent of the responding executives.[1] Perhaps this is because salespersons operate independently, often at great distances from management, in culturally distinct situations. To succeed, it is absolutely essential that highly skilled and competent people be hired for global sales positions. The hiring process consists of four steps:

- Determining the unique skills, knowledge, and attitudes required for the open position.
- Attracting sufficient applicants to assemble a pool of potential new hires.
- Conducting an interview process to assess the applicants' qualifications for the position.
- Making an offer to one or more applicants.

CASE VIGNETTE **CAN THE SELECTION PROCESS BE IMPROVED?**

Susanne Hoffman must hire three new salespersons for her industrial sales force based in Berlin. Previous hires have performed unevenly. That is, some have been very successful and exceeded annual goals. Others, however, left the firm after just a few months. Susanne wonders if hiring a salesperson is always a hit-or-miss proposition or if she can change the selection process to improve the probability of hiring the correct applicant.

## IMPORTANCE OF SELECTION DECISIONS

When poor selection decisions are made, newly hired sales personnel leave their job, the overall success of the firm decreases, and the costs to the firm are "staggering."[2] Total costs incurred in the selection process include: generating applicants, screening job applicant packages, interviewing and assessing potential candidates. These expenses, plus training costs and the salary of the new hire during the initiation period, are wasted when an incorrect selection decision is made. Total expense can reach 150 percent of the worker's annual salary.[3] To improve the probability of hiring success, and thereby lower salesperson turnover, a formalized selection process must be followed.[4]

### Cultural impact on selection process

A major complicating factor for sales managers is that culture and language are significant factors that must be considered when selecting a sales force. For example, firms that hire salespersons within mixed cultural societies like Malaysia or India consider cultural and religious criteria in the selection process. In India, Swedish Match decentralized sales force recruiting to insure that the salesperson speaks the correct dialect, that the individual is well respected in the community, and that personal contacts can be used to advantage.[5]

## Global sales force decisions

Global sales personnel and managers can be classified into three categories: *expatriates*, *local nationals*, and *third-country nationals*. Each category of salesperson, including both positive and negative aspects of their status, is discussed below.

### Expatriates

Expatriates are salespersons or managers who are transferred from the home country of the firm. For example, a British citizen transferred from London to Singapore for a three-year tour fits this category. Under certain conditions, such as when products are highly technical or application-oriented, firms prefer expatriates. This is because expatriates possess extensive technical experience, a broad range of successful application projects, and a seasoned understanding of the company and its policies. Expatriate sales personnel can add status to the global product and the home-country salesperson can take advantage of home office contacts.[6]

Conversely, expatriates can be difficult to recruit and expensive to maintain in the field. Expenses are increased significantly by cost of living benefits, moving expenses, taxes, and maintaining goods in storage. Also, many expatriates do not speak or understand the local language and/or culture of their assignment. Expatriates may decline global assignments because of family opposition, fear of loss of career momentum, and reduced visibility at the home office. Some firms make it known that, to advance, sales managers and executives must complete a global assignment.

### Local nationals

Local nationals, or personnel from the country of operations, are increasing in numbers because they understand the local marketplace and cultural ambiguities and are familiar with domestic distribution systems and referral systems. Qualified local workers can be found in numerous locales, since a number of European and Asian citizens have earned degrees in the United States and Great Britain and seek positions with global firms in their home country.[7]

There are also disadvantages when hiring local sales forces. First, headquarters personnel may ignore their inputs because of less assertive cultural behavior and limited English or other language skills possessed by local salespersons/managers. Well qualified local hires may also be difficult to find, for different reasons, in China and Japan. At least one study reported that there were ten openings in China for every qualified manager.[8] Finally in hierarchical societies, like Japan and Mexico, salespersons are viewed as at the bottom of the social ladder, which increases the difficulty of hiring the brightest college students for sales positions.

**111**

### Third-country nationals

Third-country nationals work for a global company in a third nation. An example is a Greek national who works in Saudi Arabia for a Japanese company. A number of third-country citizens work abroad for global firms, which has resulted in truly global citizens who work in a variety of countries for global sponsors. Many of these individuals speak several languages and understand specific industries or markets well. Global firms like third-country nationals and believe that these workers seek opportunity to exhibit their competence in the global marketplace. When one looks at global firms like Coca-Cola, General Motors, and Unilever, the executive ranks are composed of managers from diverse countries and cultures.

## CHARACTERISTICS OF SUCCESSFUL SALESPERSONS

Since the earliest days of modern sales activity, sales managers and business owners have sought to identify specific characteristics that predict the successful salesperson. Until now, no one characteristic has been identified that predicts success. What is difficult to know is: if and how specific traits contribute to sales success and, more important for sales selection, how specific attributes possessed by applicants can be identified during the sales selection process.

### What is known about successful salespersons

A tremendous amount of salesperson research has been conducted in an attempt to identify characteristics of sales success. Unfortunately, much of the research has contributed to confusion about the characteristics that determine success. That is, for a variety of reasons, inconsistent and conflicting results have been reported by researchers of sales success. Selecting salespersons for global customers is significantly more complicated than for one's domestic customers. Multinational companies (MNCs) use educational levels, interview skills, and previous experience to select global salespersons. However, personal interviews can lack reliability in hiring situations.[9] That is why it is important to identify needed skills or competences and to properly prepare and conduct the formal interview.

The myriad characteristics of success studies examined *aptitude* (mental abilities and personality traits), *personal characteristics* (education and lifestyle), *skill levels* (learned knowledge), *role perceptions* (perceptions of job demands and expectations of role partners), *motivation* (desire to devote time to job activities), and *organizational/environmental factors* (company position in market, territory potential, and salesperson autonomy).[10] Each of these areas is discussed below.

- *Aptitude*. Research has focused on intelligence, math ability, verbal ability and sales aptitude. The reasoning is that an applicant who possesses these abilities should be able to perform at a higher level than those not possessing these abilities.
- *Personal characteristics*. Past studies have investigated responsibility, dominance, sociability, self-esteem, creativity, need for achievement, and need for power.
- *Skill levels*. These learned proficiencies and attitudes encompass vocational skills, sales presentation abilities, interpersonal skills, general management skills, and vocational esteem skills.

- *Role perceptions*. It is important for the salesperson to accurately understand the expectations of both the firm and the customer. This requires open communication and a willingness by all parties to air concerns when they are not satisfied by the salesperson.
- *Motivation*. The salesperson must be motivated to devote the necessary time and energy to accomplish the job at hand, even when success is not guaranteed. Most firms utilize their compensation and management systems to motivate the sales force.
- *Organizational and environmental factors*. This variable recognizes that other forces, outside the control of the salesperson, affect the success of the salesperson. For example, a firm that is the market leader adds prestige and an ability to meet with a potential client. On the other hand, a relatively unknown company can negatively affect a salesperson's ability to gain a meeting with a potential purchaser.

In a landmark investigation, these characteristics were examined in a meta-analysis that combined large numbers of studies to identify which of the groups of characteristics contributed to salesperson success.[11] While none of the groups contributed significantly to success, the areas most responsible for success were skill levels and role perceptions. What this means is that sales managers can influence these variables through training and managing the sales force.

## Identifying successful characteristics

One way to determine the characteristics and skills needed for sales force positions is to conduct a thorough job analysis and then write a job description. Sales managers may not possess the technical expertise to conduct a job analysis, in which case a human resource specialist or consultant should be contacted for assistance.

### Job analysis

A job analysis provides the sales manager with a considerable amount of information about a sales position. This information includes how a salesperson currently spends their time and, more important, how – under ideal circumstances – the salesperson should spend their time. To gain this information, the person conducting the job analysis should talk to current salespersons, when available, and sales supervisors. In this way, the analyst obtains sources of information and perspectives from several vantage points.

Current salespersons should also be observed performing their job and interviewed to insure their actions are understood. This permits the person conducting the analysis to identify and analyze the duties and responsibilities, needed skills, and abilities of the salesperson. Often the analyst discovers that the salesperson is not prioritizing activities considered important by sales and upper management. These misunderstandings of role accuracy demonstrate the importance of accurate and detailed job analyses.

Sales managers can also provide valuable input about how the salesperson should conduct their job in an ideal market. Sales managers can identify ideal behavior by analyzing how the more successful members of the sales force prioritize their time. While it may be helpful to understand how successful salespersons allocate their time, it must be remembered that each sales territory will vary by customer size, product complexity, and travel time and that these influences will alter the ideal time derived from this type of study.

## Job description

After conducting a thorough job analysis, a written job description (see Exhibit 7.1) should address the following areas:

- The nature of the products/services sold.
- Customer type(s) and call frequency.
- The salesperson's specific tasks and responsibilities.
- Relationship(s) between the salesperson and others in the sales organization.
- Intellectual and physical demands of the job.
- Environmental factors affecting the sales position.

Once the job description has been written and agreed upon by management, the document can be utilized to develop a statement of job qualifications. With a statement of job qualifications, sales management can list the necessary qualifications of the applicants. It should be clear that without an accurate job analysis and description that contributes to a statement of job qualifications, it is difficult for a sales manager to select the correct person from a pool of applicants. This initial stage – determining the qualifications for a new hire – is the most difficult part of the sales selection process.[12] However, culture influences the adoption and use of job descriptions. In Japan, a written job description is employed less frequently because sales personnel are oriented for the position by utilizing on-the-job procedures.[13]

Firms attempt to minimize the costs of recruiting outstanding salespersons in the belief that training can correct individual weaknesses. However, such a strategy is fraught with danger because short-term training cannot correct such key competences as language

## EXHIBIT 7.1 JOB DESCRIPTION: ACCOUNT EXECUTIVE II

Responsible for acquiring new business. Develop partnerships between the firm and accounts by coordinating sales, contracts, technical support teams, and internal sales assistants. Perform long-range planning. Responsible for increasing account penetration, customer satisfaction, and sales growth for long-term results. Develop and plan account strategies and activities for specified accounts such as selecting accounts, selecting products for calls, identifying buyer influences, overcoming objections, introducing new products, making sales presentations and negotiating. Provide customer and competitor feedback to management. Attend and participate in industry sales conferences and trade shows. Must possess strong knowledge of industry products and sales tactics, demonstrated organizational and planning skills, and exceptional verbal and written communication skills. Required to operate remotely and/or travel 75 percent of the time. Prefer a Bachelor's degree or equivalent with a minimum of eight years of related sales experience.

fluency, maturity, and cross-cultural experience. If specific attributes are required of the new salesperson, then the sales manager must insure – through the interview process – that the individual hired possesses the requisite skills, knowledge, and attitudes.

## GENERATING APPLICANTS

Sales managers often encounter problems generating a substantial pool of highly qualified applicants from which to fill an open sales position. When sufficient applicants are not generated, there may be a problem with the process used to generate applicants. This section discusses a number of sources – both internal and external to the company – from which to attract sales force applicants.

### Internal applicants

Potential applicants for open sales positions may already work for the company as engineers, product managers, buyers, or manufacturing managers. When seeking well qualified sales position applicants one should not overlook outstanding candidates from within the company. Management has access to information about internal applicants, regardless of their current position, that includes: work habits, personality, and potential for assuming greater responsibility. This is critical information for sales managers who must make personnel decisions and it is more difficult to obtain such data about candidates who apply from outside the firm. However, internal candidates normally do not possess sales experience. Also, managers from other functional areas may view internal recruiting less positively than the sales department.

Current salespersons may also provide the names of friends or acquaintances that are seeking sales jobs. Since the salesperson would have to work with these applicants, they would be cautious in their recommendation. Also, members of the sales force may know competing salespersons that have expressed a desire to be considered for future openings with the firm. In some cultures, employees recommend their friends and relatives for openings. For example, referrals are extremely important and should be expected in high context cultures.[14] However, established policies and legal codes must be followed when seeking internal recommendations for open sales positions.

### External applicants

Often, internal sources alone do not produce either the quantity or the quality of applicants desired by the firm. In these cases a firm utilizes external sources to generate applicants for open sales positions.

#### Advertisements

One of the most common methods of generating sales applicants is by *advertising* in newspaper, magazine, and trade publication outlets. More technical and highly qualified applicants are reached through trade publications or in special issues of newspapers like the *European* or *Asian Wall Street Journal*. Advertisements assume many forms, as seen in Exhibit 7.2, but

## EXHIBIT 7.2 OPEN SALES ADVERTISEMENT

Sales – Consulting and Training Services

A leading consulting company devoted to improving quality systems and business practices worldwide, with headquarters in Ann Arbor MI, requires a seasoned sales representative to manage established territory in Midwest United States. Candidates with experience in selling consulting and training services – preferably with experience of ISO/QS-9000, Six Sigma and related systems and methodologies – desired. Automotive industry involvement preferred. Ability to develop opportunities and to close significant contracts a must. Related graduate degree or equivalent formal education desirable. To be considered, forward credentials and salary requirements to:

Sales Manager
3025 Boardwalk Drive, Suite 190
Ann Arbor, MI 48104

Equal Opportunity Employer

most follow a general format. Firms that seek professional salespersons communicate certain information in the advertisement:

- The title of the job opening.
- Minimum job qualifications.
- Preferred job qualifications.
- Location of the sales territory.
- Some discussion of pay and benefits
- Who to contact and how.

Firms that run blind advertisements, as seen in Exhibit 7.3, generate applicants of varied quality. Advertisements that generate a large pool of job seekers are not effective unless a significant number of applicants are qualified for a personal interview. Conversely, too large a pool of applicants results in costly screening activities. The goal of a sales force advertisement is to generate a sufficient number of *qualified* applicants for an open position so that managers can interview and then select highly qualified applicants. The more precisely the ad describes the minimum acceptable requirements, the greater the probability of attracting qualified applicants.

### Employment agencies

For complex sales positions, such as technical and global sales, career counselors or "headhunters" from private employment firms are utilized to contact and conduct the initial screening of applicants. Some career counselors specialize by industry or by company and maintain a pool of applicants who are looking to move to higher-paying and/or more challenging sales

## EXHIBIT 7.3 BLIND SALES ADVERTISEMENT

SALES

Firm expanding territory. Salary and commission opportunity for selling technical products to small businesses. Appointments furnished. Sales experience preferred. Call 555–4303.

positions. However, this avenue is criticized for being expensive and not producing long-term employees. Each of these concerns must be considered before contracting with an employment firm.

### Educational institutions

If entry-level salespersons are being sought, then colleges and universities are excellent sources of applicants. This is because college graduates have demonstrated – through degree completion and recommendations from professors – the ability to think soundly, manage their time, communicate, and remain focused on achieving a long-term goal. Many colleges and universities maintain well organized placement or career management centers that actively cooperate with potential employers about their organization's most important output: their students.

### Job fairs/career conferences

Job fairs and career conferences may be held in partnership with student organizations, universities, cities, or business consortiums. Job fairs occur when a group of firms that are seeking job applicants organize a date and location that is publicized in newspapers, television, radio, and at schools and universities. Firms that are seeking sales personnel are available at the job booth between a certain period of time – 10.00 a.m. until 5.00 p.m. – and job applicants simply walk up or stand in line until it is their turn to talk briefly with representatives of the firm. In effect job fairs provide an opportunity for firms to reach large numbers of potential applicants, to conduct initial screening interviews, and to consolidate a pool of individuals for formal interviews. All this is accomplished at a reasonable cost to the company.

### E-recruiting

It is now possible, thanks to the worldwide web (www), to run advertisements for job openings and to receive résumés from interested parties all over the world. This system requires potential applicants to go to a firm's web site, where job openings are posted on an electronic bulletin board. Also, job data banks can be found at www.monster.com; www.hire.com; www.careerpath.com; www.ecruiter.com; and www.careerbuilder.com. Firms find that recruiting electronically is economical for the breadth of coverage they receive from the job data banks.[15]

**117**

If the job seeker feels s/he meets the stated qualifications for the position(s), a résumé or application form is completed by the applicant and then electronically mailed to the appropriate person, who will review all applications. However, many firms conduct an electronic evaluation of e-mailed résumés that use key words, which reduces the amount of time managers must devote to screening applicant qualifications. Potential applicants can also learn about the firm, the job opening and gain other valuable insight by reading the firm's web page and hyperlinking to related web sites. The use of the Internet to match sales job seekers with open positions is expected to become more dominant over time.

### Creative external applicant sources

In certain cultures, where sales positions are viewed negatively, sales managers seek applicants through nontraditional means. Electrolux spends a significant amount of sales management time in Hong Kong, where it must interview 400 candidates in order to select ten applicants that will attend sales training.[16] In certain African countries, multinational corporations discovered that highly qualified applicants were military veterans who were completing their term of service. These former army veterans were: motivated to do a good job, organized and dependable, and accustomed to working in adverse situations.

It is the total cost of generating applicants – finding interested personnel and screening the applications – that managers must consider when computing the cost of generating applicants for open sales positions. Finally, the quality of the applicant pool is significantly more important than the quantity of the group of interested persons.

## SELECTION PROCEDURES

Once a pool of applicants has been identified for further consideration for the sales position, a formal interview process should be followed. The following five steps are followed to assess the qualification level of the applicants and to provide management with feedback that will permit the selection of the most qualified person for the job. These five steps, which are discussed in detail below, include: (1) application form, (2) tests, (3) personal interview, (4) references, and (5) physical exams.

## Application forms

Although applicants for sales positions normally submit a résumé, nearly all firms require an applicant to complete a standardized application form. There are a number of valid reasons for requiring applicants to complete this additional paperwork. First, completed application forms provide management with consistent information about all applicants. That is, résumés are the creation of the applicant and contain a variety of data, while application forms ask for specific information, such as dates, level of responsibility, and supervisors' names. Also, it may be required that the application form be signed, thereby granting legal permission for the interviewing firm to seek information about the applicant's qualifications from third parties.

Second, having to complete an application form requires the applicant to read and follow directions, respond to the questions, and demonstrate the ability to express themselves. While sales applicants should not perceive this requirement as a barrier to being hired, the application form provides the hiring firm with an initial impression of the applicant. Even when electronic recruiting procedures are employed, as discussed above, firms can check applications for misspellings and proper grammar usage.

Third, sales managers and other interviewers can use information submitted on application forms to plan the formal interview. For example, if managers want to delve into how well the applicant planned during their college or university days, a common question may be: "I see that you majored in English when you were a student at Cardiff. What made you choose English as a major for your undergraduate studies?" Likewise, application forms also provide managers with an opportunity to look for inconsistencies in dates or other questionable entries that can be probed during the personal interview. One example of areas that may need further exploration during the interview is why someone has frequently changed employers. Studies have shown that length of employment at one firm strongly influences how long the sales applicant will remain employed with a new firm.[17]

## Tests

Many firms test applicants and use the results as a confirmatory input to the interview process. First, and foremost, testing provides managers with another view of the applicant, but no one should be denied employment when all other indicators suggest an entirely different perspective of the applicant. There are a variety of tests available to managers that include personality tests, intelligence tests, and aptitude tests.

*Personality tests* can be used to evaluate numerous traits of an individual. These tests are lengthy, time-consuming, and may gather information not relevant to sales positions. There are more concise tests that predict specific sales positions (see Exhibit 7.4). Some tests measure traits such as empathy and ego drive to assess sales force applicants. Firms employ *intelligence tests* to assess whether applicants have the mental abilities to perform a job successfully. Intelligence tests are available to measure memory, reasoning, and verbal ability. *Aptitude tests* are designed to measure whether an applicant has an interest in or the ability to perform certain tasks and activities in comparison with current successful salespersons. Therefore, aptitude tests may not be appropriate for applicants without sales experience.

Firms that employ tests must insure their validity. That is, the tests must discriminate between applicants who will be successful and unsuccessful. If any test routinely discriminates between men, women, and/or minority members of society, then the test may be biased. There are statistical or psychometric procedures for validating human resource tests and, if challenged to defend tests in a legal venue of nations where there are nondiscrimination laws, the firm will be required to provide this information to the courts. Managers are often skeptical of using tests to predict future sales success, because past research has shown that no one personality or mental ability determines success as a salesperson.[18] This suggests that testing should be utilized as one factor in the selection process.

## Personal interview

The personal interview is often called the most important step in the hiring process. This is because the applicant appears before sales managers and other individuals where his/her responses to questions and directions will directly influence the interviewer to recommend

## EXHIBIT 7.4 CAN TESTING REDUCE RECRUITING RISKS?

Some firms utilize an employee profiling system to evaluate applicants for sales positions. Pioneered by a subsidiary of International Risk Management Institute (IRMI) of Dallas TX, the objective of the test is to identify and evaluate traits necessary for salesperson success. Early in the interview process, the applicant completes a fifteen to twenty-minute exam that identifies traits necessary for success in the sales field. The results of the test provide common traits about top and bottom percentage candidates, as well as "red flags" or concerns about the candidate. An IRMI spokesman says the exam goes beyond personality testing and determines if candidates have the "thinking orientation to be good in sales and like it." Managers like the system because, in addition to profiling candidates, questions are generated that allow sales managers to customize the interview process. Likewise, managers are provided with appropriate answers for each question. One user of the system claims testing prevents managers from hiring the wrong personality for an open sales position.

*Source.* Alana Harris, "Reduce the Recruiting Risks," *Sales and Marketing Management*, May 2000, 18.

or not recommend that they join the firm. In effect, in many sales interviews that are held in Western cultures, sales managers expect the applicant to "sell themselves." However, in certain cultures managers should not expect the sales applicant to demonstrate aggressiveness during the initial interview by asking for the job.

There are a variety of ways to conduct a personal interview. The following discussion focuses on three different interview approaches: structured, unstructured, and stress interviews. Each has its place in the selection process.

### Structured interview

A structured interview means that, before meeting with applicants, the sales manager or a company team prepares a list of questions along with a range of acceptable answers. For consistency, all applicants are asked the same questions. In effect, the sales manager prepares a long list of questions, as seen in Table 7.1, that cuts across areas of the applicants' background – work experiences, formal education, sales experience, and hobbies. An example of a structured question might be: "In your current job, how many hours must you work to be successful?" A sales manager looks for the applicant to correctly respond with a range of hours between forty-five and sixty. The acceptability of responses would vary across cultures.

Structured interviews have a number of advantages. First, if the sales manager is inexperienced in interviewing applicants, a structured interview provides confidence and "structure" to the process. Second, this approach insures that all areas are covered during the interview, since managers would have an outline of questions to ask. Finally, standard questions make it easier to compare applicant responses. Standardized forms allow the interviewer to record the applicant's response to questions. When multiple interviewers are used, recorded responses allow the interviewers to compare answers and discuss applicant responses. Structured interviews are twice as powerful a predictor of job performance as unstructured interviews.[19]

**Table 7.1** *Structured interview questions and answers*

| | Question | Listen for | Rate +/− |
|---|---|---|---|
| 1 | What number of hours do you think it takes to be a good salesperson? | 55–60 hours a week | |
| 2 | How would you feel if a coworker wanted to share a family concern with you? | Shows empathy – wants to listen/really cares | |
| 3 | Your sales manager is convinced that the best way to generate sales is by blanketing the marketplace with promotional materials. How do you feel about this? | Rejects in favor of qualifying according to need | |
| 4 | How do you persuade reluctant prospects to buy? | Finding and satisfying needs Can s/he persuade? | |
| 5 | Your manager has great ideas, but is a poor detail person. How do you best work with this person? | Perform detail work myself | |
| 6 | How do you feel about addressing a large audience? (Communication ability) | Enjoys, no qualifications | |
| 7 | Why do you want to work for this firm? | Can aid the growth of the company or serve the needs of the customer | |
| 8 | Some people feel it is better to do their best rather than win or lose. How do you feel about this? | Does not agree; must win | |
| 9 | If you had only three words to describe yourself, what would they be? | Honest, man of word, ethical | |

One criticism of structured interviews is that, if not experienced, the interviewer may fail to probe responses that deviate from the expected answers. That is, the interviewer may focus on reading the questions and marking the applicant's responses rather than critically evaluating those communications. It is important for sales managers to ask the question, evaluate the answer, probe when necessary, and take sufficient notes for future evaluation. Inexperienced sales managers may need to receive training, travel in the field with better performing sales representatives, and observe interviews conducted by more experienced colleagues before attempting a solo interview.

## Unstructured interview

An unstructured interview is the opposite of a structured interview. Basically, the interviewee is asked a general question and then allowed to address the subject. An example may be: "Tell me about your experiences as a salesperson." Then, once the interviewee begins to speak, the interview may interject: "Why do you enjoy travel?" The belief is that, by allowing the interviewee to speak freely, significant insight can be gained about the applicant. The interviewer must be skilled at redirecting the discussion and understand which areas require probing. Many sales managers are reluctant to employ unstructured interviews, because they have not received training, nor do they possess the experience necessary for successfully employing this interview approach. Research has concluded that unstructured interviews are a less effective selection tool.[20]

### Stress interview

Because salespersons find themselves in stressful situations, interviewers may place sales applicants into fluid situations to gain additional insight about their abilities and personalities. For example, during an interview, the applicant may be asked to sell the interviewer an item, like a pen, ashtray, or piece of furniture. The basic premise is that if the salesperson makes a good faith effort to sell whatever they are asked to sell, then there is a higher probability that potential clients will also be asked to buy something when they are called upon.

Sales managers who place an applicant into a stressful situation should have a predetermined range of acceptable behaviors in mind. That is, one can ignore the applicant, be rude and obnoxious, ask the applicant to sell an item, or sit in silence waiting for the applicant to react. All of these techniques are employed in an effort to gauge the experience of the applicant in handling potential customer situations. No matter, the sales manager must decide what the applicant can and cannot do to pass the stress interview. Firms that employ the stress interview do so in conjunction with the structured or unstructured interview. Managers must also understand that if the stress interview is too stressful, the applicant may seek employment elsewhere. Likewise, in many cultures a stress interview is an inappropriate means of interviewing sales candidates.

## References

One indicator of potential for success as a salesperson is performance in past activities. Therefore, sales managers normally call previous employers or supervisors and seek confirmation of how well the applicant performed in those positions. For example, if Ms. Kenyon-Jones worked for a sales firm in Birmingham, England, the sales manager at IBM in London would call the former sales manager to inquire about Ms. Kenyon-Jones. Sales managers seldom ask directly: "How would you rate her performance?" This is because this question is subjective in nature and is not factual. Instead, sales managers confirm the facts stated on the application form, such as: start and ending dates of employment, position held, accounts served, level of sales, ranking in the office, training completed and, where permissible, salary earned. If reference checks confirm the applicant has provided false information, then sales managers must question the basic honesty, trustworthiness, and reliability of the applicant.

Managers should contact those references listed by the applicant, but understand that the applicant has most likely listed individuals who will say only positive things about them. Where permitted, managers can ask former employers for other managers or individuals who could provide a meaningful reference. It is also helpful to require the applicant to provide different categories of references. That is, business references such as former clients or employers, financial references like banks and financial institutions, and educational references such as professors or counselors. In this way a more comprehensive examination of the applicant's background and previous experiences can be conducted.

## Physical exam

Performing a sales job is hard work! Salespersons may need to carry samples and products from their automobile to clients, which require physical stamina. Likewise, the salesperson must travel for extended periods, in diverse time zones, and unknown cultures. The responsibilities of a global salesperson require that they be healthy and capable of performing the sales job for which they are hired.

Firms may require that the salesperson, as a final condition of employment, undergo a complete physical to rule out serious medical conditions that would preclude them from successfully performing their duties. On occasions, physical defects are detected that are unknown to the applicant and if the condition precludes completion of the job, then the job offer is withdrawn. Firms may also want to detect potentially high cost physical ailments like HIV, cancer, and pre-existing conditions that would result in exorbitant medical costs for the hiring firm's insurance provider. In some countries it is illegal to discriminate based upon medical condition, so sales managers should seek legal guidance when hiring.

## MAKING THE JOB OFFER

Once all applicants have been interviewed, and their application packages considered, the sales manager or a team of interviewers normally rank each applicant in terms of their fit with the company and their potential for contributing to the firm. It is now time for the manager to contact the top applicant to discuss a job offer.

The sales manager should call the top applicant and ask if they are still interested in a sales position with the company. If the answer is "yes," then the sales manager should proceed with a description of the job responsibilities and make the job offer. Applicants may attempt to delay accepting the position, especially if the applicant is highly competent and has interviewed with several firms, in hopes that a better offer may be forthcoming.

After talking with the applicant on the phone, the sales manager should send a first-class letter to the finalist which is a formal offer of employment. The letter confirms the telephone conversation and states all pertinent information about job responsibilities, expectations, starting salary, moving expenses, formal training dates, time before the initial performance review, vacation days awarded, and the period of time before first consideration for salary increase. The letter should clearly state a deadline for accepting the position. Many firms allow one week or ten days for the applicant to formally accept the job offer. Finally, if necessary, the sales manager should be prepared to negotiate salary, benefits, and moving expense benefits with the job applicant in cultures where this is acceptable.

## CHAPTER SUMMARY

Hiring a salesperson is an extremely important decision for the firm. Because of cultural unknowns, the salesperson must be adaptive and able to perform in diverse and challenging situations. It is normally the sales manager's responsibility to determine the qualifications of new hires, to attract a sufficient pool of applicants, to interview and select the "best qualified" person for the job, and to make the job offer to the finalist. This chapter provides guidance for sales managers, along with cautions and potential cultural forces, that when followed will result in higher quality hiring decisions being made. By conducting job analyses and writing a job description, job qualifications can be determined. These job qualifications can then be employed to attract applicants, and to evaluate these applicants for potential success through the interview process. By following the process presented in this chapter, managers can reduce the likelihood of making incorrect decisions and improve the probability of hiring successful global salespersons. In effect, the extensive process is a means to a successful end.

## DISCUSSION QUESTIONS

1  In what ways is it costly for the firm when hiring mistakes are made?

2  What are the advantages and disadvantages of hiring expatriate, local and third-country salespersons?

3  Given that sales positions vary, will the success characteristics for each salesperson also deviate? Why?

4  What is the relationship between a job analysis and job description?

5  List and discuss five methods of attracting sales applicants.

6  Discuss the selection process and how each stage provides information and support for the decision to hire or not hire an applicant.

7  Why is the personal interview often called the most important step in the hiring process?

## REFERENCES

1  "Hiring: Love it or Leave it?" (1998), *Sales and Marketing Management*, December, 80.

2  Randall, E. James, and Cindy H. Randall (1990), "Review of Salesperson Selection Techniques and Criteria: a Managerial Approach," *International Journal of Research in Marketing*, December, 81–95.

3  Lawlor, Julia (1995), "Highly Classified: Hiring Top Salespeople may be a Manager's Most Important Responsibility," *Sales and Marketing Management*, March, 75.

4  Engle, Robert (1998), "Multi-step, Structured Interviews to Select Sales Representatives in Russia and Eastern Europe," *European Management Journal*, 16:4, 476–84.

5  Kirpalani, V.H. (1985), *International Marketing*, New York: Random House.

6  Honeycutt, Earl D., Jr., and John B. Ford (1995), "Guidelines for Managing an International Sales Force," *Industrial Marketing Management*, 24:2 (March), 135–44.

7  Cateora, Philip R., and John L. Graham (1999), *International Marketing*, Boston MA: Irwin McGraw-Hill.

8  Gross, Ames (1996), "Recruiting in Asia: Not an Easy Task," *Benefits and Compensation International*, 26:5 (December), 14–18.

9   Randall and Randall (1990).

10  Churchill, Gilbert A., Neil M. Ford, Orville C. Walker, Mark W. Johnston, and John F. Tanner (2000), *Sales Force Management*, Boston MA: Irwin McGraw-Hill.

11  Churchill, Gilbert A., Jr., Neil M. Ford, Steven W. Hartley, and Orville C. Walker, Jr. (1985), "The Determinants of Salesperson Performance: a Meta-analysis," *Journal of Marketing Research*, May, 103–18.

12  Churchill, Ford, Walker, Johnston, and Tanner (2000).

13  Samli, A. Coskun, and John S. Hill (1998), *Marketing Globally*, Lincolnwood IL: NTC.

14  Cateora and Graham (1999).

15  Piturro, Marlene (2000), "The Power of E-cruiting," *Management Review*, January, 33.

16  Terpstra, Vern, and Ravi Sarathy (1997), *International Marketing*, Fort Worth TX: Dryden Press.

17  Gable, Myron, Charles Hollon, and Frank Fangello (1992), "Increasing the Utility of the Application Blank: Relationship between Job Application Information and Subsequent Performance and Turnover of Salespeople," *Journal of Personal Selling and Sales Management*, summer, 39–55.

18  Churchill, Ford, Hartley, and Walker (1985).

19  Engle (1998).

20  Mak, C. (1995), "Successful People Selection in Action," *Health Manpower Management*, 21, 12–17.

# Chapter 8

# Sales training for a worldwide marketplace

This chapter discusses sales force training. The six-step sales training process and cultural influences on training are presented.

## INTRODUCTION

Global firms understand the importance of training their sales force because training provides numerous benefits for the sales force, the customer, and managers that include:

- Higher sales force performance.
- Improved customer relationships.
- More efficient time management.
- Less need for management supervision.
- Greater product and market knowledge.
- A more comprehensive understanding of company policies.

Sales force efficiency is a critical issue for firms worldwide because of the increasing cost of conducting personal sales calls. Given the huge cost of maintaining a sales force, it is imperative that sales activities be efficient. An equally important reason for providing relevant sales training relates to relationship marketing. If customers are not satisfied with the service provided by their salesperson, they will switch to higher performing competitors that better serve their needs.

In today's complex global marketplace, the salesperson must understand how to operate and succeed when dealing with clients from different cultures, may need to be fluent in a second language, and must be capable of performing as a company representative thousands of miles from headquarters in diverse situations with customers. Stated quite simply: sales techniques adopted and practiced in one country or culture – such as Great Britain – are not relevant when operating in Japan, the United States, or Southeast Asia. This chapter details how to provide the sales force with the necessary skills, knowledge, and attitudes to succeed in an ever-expanding global marketplace.

CASE VIGNETTE **MANAGEMENT'S VIEW OF SALES TRAINING**

Jim Cooper just completed a two-week formal sales training program in Seattle WA for a global computer manufacturer. When he returned to work, he ran into the regional sales manager, who curtly responded, "Forget all that theory you learned at training; remember we work in the 'real world'." Cooper was flabbergasted that his sales manager would make such a statement. He began to wonder if the training program, which he considered to be outstanding, had actually prepared him for a successful career with his new firm. More important, based upon the sales manager's negative attitude toward his company indoctrination, Cooper wondered if he had made a wrong decision when he accepted the position with the company.

## CULTURAL IMPACT ON SALES TRAINING

Culture directly influences the personal selling process and, as such, impacts all sales training activities. This means that national culture shapes the content and presentation styles of sales representatives and the way business is conducted. An excellent example of cultural influences on sales situations can be seen in Malaysia, a country comprised of three cultural subgroups: Malay, Chinese, and Indian. Due to tensions that exist between Chinese, who dominate commerce, and Malays, who are the political rulers, the government has mandated a 30 percent hiring quota for Malays. Malay businessmen also prefer more structured business situations where the status of each individual determines that person's role.[1] Global firms must insure training content and sales methods match local taste and culture. Decisions about whether to standardize or localize training blocks are made based upon the skills global companies want to transfer to trainees. "Soft skills," such as supervisory or communication skills, should be adapted to match local practices; however, more technical skills can be standardized.[2]

## THE NEED FOR SALES TRAINING

When an individual accepts a position or is transferred from another functional area within the firm to perform sales duties, they will need to be socialized about the work ethics, job expectations, and proper ways of conducting business. This means that the composition of trainees in any global sales training class will be diverse and may include: newly hired personnel without sales experience, new hires with sales experience, and in-house managers who may be familiar with the product line, but who are unfamiliar with sales activities. This learning situation is further complicated when trainees are also members of different races, creeds, or cultures. The growing diversity of the workplace, both domestically and globally, increases the importance of successful sales training. Sales training provides the firm with an opportunity to teach trainees *job accuracy* or the specific tasks they should perform on the job and set *job expectations* or the level of work expected by the company. In this way the salesperson is being "socialized" to the expectations of the firm.[3] Setting the correct expectations and providing the necessary skills to the sales force should result in a positive return on the firm's hiring and training investment. More importantly there is a higher probability that customers will be better satisfied in their interactions with the firm and this will result in long-term, profitable relationships.

## THE SALES TRAINING PROCESS

Sales training is a process, rather than a one-time event. The sales training process consists of six distinct stages: needs assessment, objective setting, planning the training program, conducting the training program, evaluating the training program, and follow-up training. As seen in Figure 8.1, these stages are interconnected and require successful completion of one stage in order to lead to success in subsequent stages. Let us now examine these six stages.

**129**

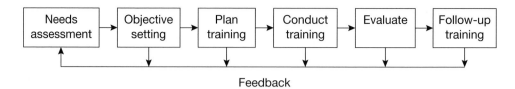

**Figure 8.1** *The sales training process*

## NEEDS ASSESSMENT

The purpose of the needs assessment stage is to determine the strengths and weaknesses of the sales force regarding their current skills, knowledge, and attitudes. A training need exists when there is a "gap" between the trainee's actual and desired levels of sales skills, knowledge of sales, product, market, and company information, and attitudes. The purpose of needs assessment is to identify areas that training can enhance. There are a number of specific methods for assessing sales training needs that fall into subjective, objective, and general categories.

### Subjective assessment methods

*Upper management judgment.* Upper management is aware of the role the sales force will play in achieving company goals. For example, a new product will be brought to market late this year and the firm's strategy will be to use the sales force to "push" the product through the distribution value chain. In this case, the sales force will require at least three training modules: new product training, advantages over competitor products, and customer applications of the new product. Such knowledge, gained through training, will greatly aid the sales force in introducing the new product to current and potential customers.

*Sales management judgment.* The sales manager, who makes calls with the sales force, may observe that the majority of local salespersons are weak in presentation skills. This observation needs to be taken into account for local training, but it may be difficult to generalize to the entire sales force based upon the judgment of one or a few sales managers. Since sales managers are often consumed by day-to-day business activities, they may be less familiar with the level of training needed to support corporate goals.

*Training department judgment.* Because sales training is their primary focus, training departments play a significant role in assessing sales training needs. This is because the training department is aware of the topical and skill areas that have caused problems for trainees during previous training sessions. Based upon in-class observations, trainers allocate additional emphasis to perceived areas of weakness in future training programs.

### Objective assessment methods

*Interviews.* Personal interviews or focus group interviews can be conducted with current salespeople, former salespeople, and customers. These interviews provide feedback and lead to a more comprehensive understanding of perceived sales training needs.

**130**

*Surveys.* Surveys can be utilized to assess training needs. First, the sales force can be asked to identify areas that require additional training. Second, sales managers can be surveyed to gather inputs about needed sales training. Third, clients can be mailed surveys in which they are asked to compare the firm's sales force in relationship to the best in the marketplace. Because of differing views and perspectives, it is important to gather input about sales training program needs from sales managers, trainees, and trainers.[4]

*Performance measures.* Analysis of such internal data as sales volume, customer service feedback, number of sales calls to close, expense reports, customer complaints, and turnover, when contrasted with the desired performance, can identify areas that require additional training.

*End-of-course evaluations.* This method of assessment tells management how effective the current program is and identifies gap(s) between desired and actual skill and knowledge levels, which pinpoints where future training programs should place additional emphasis.

## General assessment methods

*Organizational and sales training objectives.* Sales training objectives should flow from the overall organizational objectives. That is, the corporation may adopt a goal of increasing market share by penetrating the current marketplace. This means that planned sales training must provide the sales force with the necessary skills to increase sales to new customers in existing markets.

*Competitors' sales training programs.* To insure competitiveness, many firms benchmark their training program against competitors'. This practice reduces the likelihood of firms overlooking important topical areas and provides a basis of comparison for existing sales training programs.

## TRAINING OBJECTIVES

After assessing training needs, management sets objectives that communicate the sales training program goal(s). Normally, the objectives address the "gaps" identified during the needs assessment phase. These objectives should be SMART: Specific, Measurable, Attainable, Realistic, and Timely.[5] When objectives meet these standards, training goals state realistically what training will accomplish, how the objectives will be assessed, and how long it will take for the training to become effective. A training objective that states, "Total sales revenue will increase by 10 percent for the Model XBS stereo component set over the next six months," meets the standards listed above for writing effective training objectives. A large number of firms do not set training objectives.[6] Even when training objectives are set they tend to be general, rather than specific, in nature.[7]

Objectives communicate to planners the outcome of the training program. Without written and shared training objectives there is no actual goal for the sales training program to work toward. Clearly communicated and agreed upon objectives increase the probability of successful sales training, since there is agreement between top management, trainers, and sales managers.

## PLANNING SALES TRAINING

Once the needs and objectives of the sales training program are agreed upon, management next determines the content of the training program and the instructional methods to employ to transfer these topical areas to the sales trainees.

## Methods

*Methods* refer to the theme, scope, coverage, length, instructor, location, media, and materials employed in the training program. Training program *content* focuses on the type of instruction, topics covered, budgets, and details about how and what specific skills and abilities are imparted to the trainees.[8]

Global companies utilize both on-the-job (OJT) and formal training programs. Sales managers appear to be divided into different camps about OJT. For smaller firms, with limited training budgets and few salespersons to train, OJT is imperative. A well planned OJT program can transfer the needed knowledge in the form of an apprentice approach where new hires work in one or more firm areas and receive instruction and oversight from experienced company technicians and managers. On-the-job training works well when the technicians and managers are carefully selected, are motivated to help the newcomer succeed, and can respond to the questions and misunderstandings that may arise when a novice salesperson deals with clients. Firms may also utilize OJT as a way to provide the sales neophyte an opportunity to "practice" sales techniques learned in a formal training program.

Culture significantly impacts sales training. For example, Japanese salespeople receive on-the-job training in a ritualistic formal setting that insures that constructive criticism does not result in "loss of face" for the trainee.[9] Likewise, sales managers must move cautiously when transferring sales training methods. Because languages vary so dramatically, sales trainers must exercise caution in translating training manuals, and must be aware of the role language plays on thought and behavior patterns.[10]

Formal training means that a firm's sales trainees attend a structured program, often at a central location. For example, newly hired personnel in Europe may travel to London to attend formal sales training provided by either headquarters staff or a combination of local and home office personnel. Formal training is an expensive undertaking, since each trainee is transported, housed, fed, and educated for a period of time. A secondary cost is the lost opportunity attributable to the trainees not being in their territories serving their customers. Exhibit 8.1 details actual planning problems encountered in an emerging nation.

### Training program length

Many sales training programs are one to two weeks in duration, but may last as long as a year. The formal classroom portion of the training program usually consumes six to eight hours per day and generates thirty to forty hours of training blocks or modules each week. When planning training dates, local managers must be consulted to insure religious or ethnic holidays do not fall within the tentative schedule. Likewise, in Moslem countries, planners should schedule prayer breaks for the trainees.

## EXHIBIT 8.1 TRAINING *FAUX PAS* IN EGYPT

A major Egyptian soft drink corporation hired a Middle Eastern training firm to plan and conduct a sales training program in Cairo for approximately seventy salespersons. Egypt is divided into three basic regions: Cairo, Alexandria, and Upper Egypt. Salesmen from Alexandria and Upper Egypt arrived and were eager to participate in the training program. The principal instructor noticed that trainees who were assigned to sales territories around Cairo appeared to be less motivated and were absent more frequently from training modules. An investigation by the trainer uncovered several problems with the original planning of the sales training program.

First, sales personnel from Alexandria and Upper Egypt were receiving expense money for their hotel and meals—including lunch—for the duration of the training program. Salespersons who were assigned to the greater Cairo area received no expense payments even though a number of the trainees had to travel 30 km daily each way. The Cairo trainees also were required to pay for their noon meal, even though all trainees ate at the same time and location. Second, trainees from Cairo were often notified that they were to miss training in order to address an urgent problem with one of their customers. By this last action, upper management demonstrated that the training program was not very important and that training would be undertaken when it was convenient.

The lead instructor and president of the training firm were not surprised when nearly all trainees from the Cairo region rated their reaction to numerous aspects of the training program significantly lower than other attendees. The training consultants also pondered the effects of these shortsighted management policies on future sales performance and sales force retention.

*Source.* Ashraf M. Attia, "Measuring and Evaluating Sales Force Training Effectiveness: A Proposed and Empirically Tested Model," unpublished Ph.D. dissertation, Old Dominion University, Norfolk VA.

Differences in training program length can be attributed to a number of variables: (1) industry type, (2) company size, (3) the adoption rate of high-tech training, (4) training budgets, and (5) corporate culture.[11] The final length of sales training programs is a compromise between the expected time required to transfer the skills, knowledge, and attitudes balanced against the time and expense that can be invested to develop these sales force assets.

Sales personnel in the global marketplace should be taught: how to sell (even when they possess extensive domestic selling experience), company policies and procedures, product line and performance information, and local market conditions. Trainees should also learn about their clients' culture.

### Participative and non-participative training methods

Participative training methods involve role playing, case methods, computer games, and OJT. Non-participative training methods include lecture, videos, and guest speakers. Each method contributes to successful sales training programs and should be considered in the planning stage.

## EXHIBIT 8.2 COMMONLY USED HIGH-TECH TRAINING METHODS

*Computer Based Training (CBT)* CBT is any training that employs the computer as the focal point of instructional delivery. The use of software and computer equipment is used to aid in teaching. CBT is related to Computer Assisted Instruction (CAI), Computer Assisted Learning (CAL), and Computer Assisted Training (CAT)

*Artificial intelligence (AI)* Computer programs that are associated with human intelligence. That is, AI reasons and optimizes through experience. In sales, the trainee would interact with the AI program to learn reasoning and decision making that optimizes performance

*Hypertext* The linking of related pieces of information by electronic connections. This refers to nonlinear writing that is followed through a world of text documents, normally on the Internet

*CD-ROM* An optional storage medium similar to the technology utilized in audio CDs. This training medium exhibits low-cost reproductive capabilities but short-term currency problems. CDs can also function interactively with the trainee

*Training videos* Audio and visual presentations transmitted on VHS tapes. Videos can provide the latest information on product development, sales techniques, and product applications. The currency of the information becomes dated quickly

*Video-streaming* Electronic meetings that enable participants at one site to interact with participants or instructors at a different location. With proper hardware and software, any computer can display video-streaming. Firms can also project video-streamed classes and meetings on to larger surfaces, such as screens

*Interactive multimedia* Computer-based training that includes video, audio, text graphics, and animation. By utilizing computer technology, the trainee can move through a course or module in a customized way that individually addresses his or her needs.

Source: Earl D. Honeycutt, Jr., Kiran Kirande, and M. Asri Jantan, "Sales Training in Malaysia: High- versus Low-tech Methods," *Industrial Marketing Management*, 31:7 (October), 581–7

*High-tech training methods.* The adoption of technology in sales training courses can be grouped into numerous categories: computer-based training, artificial intelligence, hypertext, CD-ROM, training videos, video-streaming, and interactive multimedia (See Exhibit 8.2). Cost is an important factor in selecting and integrating high-technology methods into sales training programs. Likewise, resistance to change and company commitment are barriers to the adoption of high-tech training methods. Sales reps also complain about the intrusiveness of high-technology training methods that must be completed at night or weekends.[12] However high-tech training methods, that can be conducted and communicated by experts via satellite or the worldwide web (www), will revolutionize sales training in the twenty-first century.[13]

*Training methods.* A wide variety of methods are employed in sales training programs:

- *Lecture mode* is employed by most sales training programs. Although cost-effective and used for information transfer, it is not an effective method for skills training. Experienced sales personnel like lectures, because they are able to engage in a two-way dialogue. Lecture methods are accepted in many cultures because a sage is providing guidance to the students.
- *Programmed instruction* employs a narrative of facts and examples which are followed by questions that reinforce learning, and have been shown to be effective for knowledge acquisition and retention. This form of training may be assigned prior to formal training sessions or can be completed in the evening hours.
- *Case studies* help improve trainee problem-solving skills. Trainees are presented with actual field problems and limited information that must be analyzed. This method permits trainees to present their solution and then be questioned about their method of analysis and problem-solving skills. Additional learning occurs by listening to the logic employed by colleagues and instructors.
- *Coaching* is a superior training method where the sales manager observes the trainee in an actual or training situation and then offers guidance for improving performance. For example, after a trainee calls upon a customer in the presence of the sales manager, the manager finds a quiet spot and asks the trainee specifically how one area could be improved. The manager should model the correct behavior and provide positive reinforcement for effective behavior.
- *Role playing* requires trainees to play the part of either a salesperson or a customer. In this way one trainee can assume the role of the salesperson and attempt to gather information or proceed through the sales process. Many companies include video-taping of role-playing exercises so that study and critiquing of trainee behavior can take place.
- *Business games* require the trainee to engage in activity that increases understanding of the product, company, or market. These games further one's ability to understand why products work as they do, why the company requires certain actions, and how competitors react in the marketplace. Firms may use "in basket" exercises to simulate a day in the office. This includes making appointments, completing requests for quotations (RFQ), answering phone calls, and making a formal sales presentation.
- *Discussions with experienced salespersons* permit the interchange of ideas and exchange of valuable information and experience. The participating salespersons must be carefully selected and portrayed as a role model.

## Training program location

This decision is influenced by the physical location and availability of training facilities. While it may be convenient for managers and trainers to conduct sales training sessions at headquarters, planners must select a training facility that is comfortable, adequate in regard to space and equipment, and private, so that trainees and managers are not distracted by normal work activities. For these reasons, training programs are often conducted off site or at special company training facilities that allow both instructors and trainees to focus on transferring skills, knowledge, and attitudes with the minimum of interruptions.

**135**

A number of global firms schedule the training location at centralized sites that are convenient for both trainees and managers. For example, one Asian company conducts all its training at a hotel conference center in Manila, in the Philippines. The location is centralized, travel costs are economical for its Asian sales forces, the facilities are comfortable, and the total cost is significantly less when compared to conducting the training sessions in more expensive Asian locations. Similarly, IBM has a European training center, and Bank of America manages its sales training from offices in three global cities – Tokyo, Caracas, and London.[14]

### Instructor selection

A critical question is: should the instructor(s) be internal or external to the firm? Larger companies have full-time sales trainers, assigned to a training department, that plan and conduct training seminars. These individuals possess successful sales experience, are formally educated in theories of adult learning, and are qualified to instruct sales trainees. Consultants, who are viewed as "outsiders," are perceived as being objective or less likely to support the firm's position. One concern about engaging training consultants is that they may be less familiar with the firm's products and their training program may be generic in content. Customization of a sales training program increases the consultant's preparation time and the firm's total training cost.

## Content

### Training topics

Based upon the objectives set, planners next select the training topics that are to be taught in order to attain those objectives. That is, the trainees must be exposed to specific amounts of product, market, and company information, sales techniques, and socialization of company attitudes. In the United States, companies devote the majority of their time transferring product information and sales techniques.[15] However, the composition of training programs varies by culture.[16] Whatever the mix of topics presented, trainees must understand the products and how to sell these products to their target customers. In effect, sales training planners must strike the correct balance between the topical areas. Time devoted to training topics will vary based upon industry market situation, and product line offered by the firm.

### Sales training program content

Program content revolves around four topical areas: product knowledge, market knowledge, company information, and sales techniques. On average, firms report that they provide about 35 percent of training program time to product knowledge, 30 percent to sales techniques, 15 percent to market information, and 10 percent to company information and 10 percent to "other" miscellaneous topics.[17]

Different firms emphasize disparate training content to meet the unique industry environment. That is, industrial firms report a higher percentage of product knowledge content, while consumer companies provide greater sales techniques. Also the content of higher performing firms differs from lower performing firms. Specifically, the training program content of top

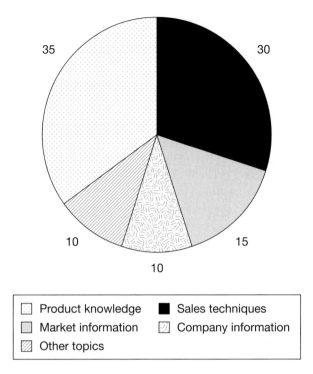

**Figure 8.2** *Sales training content (%)*

performing firms offers a broader range of topics that include: market knowledge, industry knowledge, listening techniques, communication skills, and complaint handling skills.[18]

Successful companies also train their sales force to pursue a market orientation, which leads to longer-term buyer–seller relationships.[19] The importance of customer-oriented selling was supported in a cross-cultural comparison of training programs in Saudi Arabia and the United States which concluded that, when contrasted with their Saudi counterparts, US salespersons spent significantly more time on customer-oriented sales techniques than on product-oriented selling activities.[20]

## CONDUCTING SALES TRAINING

When the sales training program is conducted, the planning stage is put into action. Although the best plans can go awry, it is important that sales managers work to implement the plan, but remain flexible should the plan obviously need on-the-spot modification. For example, a US firm sent a team to India to provide sales training that incorporated the latest computer technology and graphics. Shortly after the team leader welcomed everyone and started the high-tech training session, the electricity went out! Rather than adapting to the fact that power interruptions are common in many emerging nations, and remaining patient, the team leader began grumbling so loudly the trainees could hear his complaints about their "third-world" country being at fault for ruining the training program. Not only did the manager's comments dampen the training session, but they resulted in hard feelings that persisted among the trainees who attended the program.

## EVALUATING TRAINING

It is essential to evaluate sales training programs. In fact, when asked, US sales training executives stated that the evaluation of sales training programs was the most important area for future research.[21] Conversely, another group of sales managers reported that they would not evaluate their training programs even if sufficient time and resources were available[22] How can this dilemma be explained? The answer lies in the difficulties encountered in evaluating the effectiveness of training and because of the mixed results previously experienced by managers who attempted to evaluate their training programs. Numerous factors, shown in Exhibit 8.3, can impact sales training evaluations and are beyond the sales manager's control.

### EXHIBIT 8.3 SALES EVALUATION PROBLEMS ENCOUNTERED IN GLOBAL MARKETS

A number of problems have been identified that sales managers encounter in global markets when evaluating sales training programs. Any one of these business activities can complicate future sales training evaluation efforts. These activities include:

- Change in the size of sales territories
- Movement of sales reps and sales managers from territory to territory
- Promotion of sales reps to sales management without direct sales responsibilities
- Sales reps leaving the company for higher paying jobs
- Opening new territories, which requires the relocation of sales reps
- Decentralization of data – no central data base for evaluators
- Seasonality of the data
- Sensitivity or confidentiality of the data
- Burden on sales reps and management of collecting detailed data
- Changes in financial support by international division
- Changes in market strategy or product focus dictated by international division
- New competitors – either domestic or global – entering the market
- Sales managers being consumed by other responsibilities
- Sales managers canceling meeting(s) to address short-term emergencies

*Source.* Ashraf M. Attia, "Measuring and Evaluating Sales Force Training Effectiveness: A Proposed and Empirically Tested Model," unpublished Ph.D. dissertation, Old Dominion University, Norfolk VA

Even so, there remain ways to evaluate sales training programs that provide evidence of success for management and feedback for improving future training programs. A number of these methods are discussed below under the four evaluation levels of reaction, knowledge, attitudes, and results.

## Reaction

Reaction refers to trainee response to the training program. Trainees provide feedback about such pertinent areas as: the training location, meals, trainers, training methods, training content, and progress checks. Critics of this type of evaluation claim it is too "soft" to be reliable. However, the more important questions are: (1) what is the goal of obtaining feedback and (2) can the feedback be utilized to improve the training process? Trainee feedback can provide important information for managers to improve the process of future sales training programs.

In the global marketplace, there may be problems in gaining accurate reaction from trainees. In some cultures, and especially those in Asia, individuals are less likely to openly express dissatisfaction, particularly to their employers. Likewise, trainees may perceive and select scale numbers differently than citizens from the home country. For example, how would Vietnamese sales trainees respond to a Western European firm that asked them to rate its program using a scale of 1 (poor) to 10 (outstanding)? Since being rated a "10" in Vietnam is not a positive attribute, trainees might select 8 or 9 to communicate the training program met their needs. Finally, words and phrases have different meanings for sales trainees from different cultures. While these factors complicate reaction measures, managers of sales training programs must still insist that reaction feedback be gathered. For without feedback from the participants, how will trainers and managers become aware of potential problems – from the trainees' perspective – that exist in the training process?

## Knowledge

A trainee's knowledge level can be assessed by completing written or experiential examinations. That is, either at the end or during the training program, the trainee completes a written test or performance exercise that demonstrates they have acquired the knowledge or skill level sought by the training program. One way of improving the results of knowledge-based tests is to provide the trainees with learning objectives. In this way, the trainee is aware prior to each training session that: "At the conclusion of this training block, you will be able to correctly perform the six steps of a successful sales call." Learning objectives inform the sales trainee what is important and what they need to know to successfully complete the training program. Many training programs utilize progress checks at key junctures and then employ a comprehensive exercise at the end of the session that requires the trainees to integrate and apply their newly acquired knowledge. Trainers must also have the option to assist trainees who experience trouble during a training session, rather than waiting until the end to evaluate their performance. Early intervention is necessary in order to minimize the number of trainees who are unable to succeed in the training program. In many cultures this intervention requires confidentiality and private training away from normal group training sessions.

**139**

## Attitudes

Other indications of successful sales training outcomes are changes in attitudes. These include attitudes about the customer, the company, and the job itself. One way of determining attitudes is to take a "before" and then an "after" training measurement. However, this exercise may only result in the sales trainees providing socially acceptable answers about their beliefs. Therefore, many firms try to assess the trainees' attitudes through surveys completed by such third parties as managers and customers. This attitude measurement provides managers with a benchmark for how trainees are applying the approaches and techniques they have been taught in the training program.

There are some obvious concerns about assessing a salesperson's attitudes through a third party. These concerns include: accuracy, objectivity, and friendship. First, it is difficult for a customer or manager to be accurate in their assessment of a salesperson's attitudes. What is really being measured is an opinion about the salesperson's attitude based upon their overt behavior. Second, because of established attitudes toward the salesperson, it may be problematic for a third party to be objective. Instead of objective measures, preconceived attitudes will influence the evaluation of the salesperson. Finally, depending upon the level of friendship, managers and customers may bias their evaluation of the salesperson. This means that, in certain cultures, customers will rate the salesperson higher than deserved or simply rate them in the middle of the scale. Neither approach is helpful for managers who need accurate evaluations to improve the training process. One method of minimizing these potential cultural problems is to ask numerous managers and customers to evaluate the salesperson.

## Results

Measuring sales training results refers to utilizing objective measures – such as sales revenue, profits, number of new customers, and travel expenses – to assess the success of the training program. In effect, this evaluation stage attempts to create a cause-and-effect relationship. Accurate evaluation of results is the most useful of the four evaluation levels discussed here, but it is also the most difficult of the four stages to objectively accomplish. As discussed in the introduction to this chapter, many other variables – like the economy, the weather, competitor actions, inaccurate advertising messages for the culture or subculture, or changes in sales force compensation and motivation plans – can influence objective measures like sales revenue and profitability. That is because none of these variables can be controlled by sales force management. However, one study of Caterpillar in international markets reported that the results of sales training could be evaluated by matching and comparing locations that received training with other locations that had not received training.[23]

## OTHER EVALUATION METHODS

Another method available to sales managers for evaluating sales training is to compare the outcome of training against the objectives set for the training program. For example, a stated training objective might be to teach a new sales process for product C that will result in a sales increase of 10 percent over the next year. Sales managers need only look at the overall sales figure for product C at the completion of one year to see if the objective was reached. However, using objectives to determine sales training effectiveness requires the establishment of SMART objectives. Otherwise, it is not possible to compare actual performance against loosely stated objectives that were set many months (or even years?) earlier.

Human resource managers also utilize *utility analysis* to assess the value of sales training. Utility analysis requires managers to estimate costs and gains and then compute an outcome utility. The greater the positive number, the higher the probability the training program made a positive contribution. Basically, if the monetary benefits of the training program exceed the monetary costs, the training program was worth implementing.[24] Sales managers should be aware of the existence and basic use of utility analysis to evaluate sales training programs, but a detailed discussion is beyond the scope of this text. Because utility analysis requires sales managers to estimate certain inputs, there has been criticism of the methodology.[25]

## FOLLOW-UP TRAINING

Sales training is a continual rather than a one-time event. This is because salespersons require repetitive training in order to maintain current skills, knowledge, and attitudes. Because of this necessity, firms offer myriad types of follow-up training. Most firms have initial sales training programs that are required of all newly hired personnel. Then additional formal sales training is provided after a time in the field. Additional training may also be required before salespersons move to specific assignments. However, global firms realize the importance of reinforcing important concepts and maintaining salesperson proficiency between formal training sessions. These follow-up training programs are provided as needed at centralized locations, by sales managers in the field, by correspondence courses, by traveling training teams, or through high-tech methods. Firms continue to experiment with technology so that the field salesperson remains current in the skills, knowledge, and attitudes that lead to first-class service for customers. By establishing a well trained and competent sales force, firms realize there is a higher probability of establishing and maintaining long-term, profitable relationships with the customers in the global marketplace.

Continual training is especially important in the global marketplace, where salespeople may cling to practices that are reinforced by local culture. For example, in the former controlled markets of Russia and China, merit performance was not rewarded under the economic system. In these situations, it is necessary to modify such deeply held attitudes during training sessions. Likewise, expatriates may be captive of their own ethnocentric habits and patterns learned in their home culture, which calls for continual follow-up training.[26]

## CHAPTER SUMMARY

Training provides numerous benefits for the company, the salesperson, and the customer. Perhaps the most important contribution made by sales training is that it results in higher salesperson performance, greater customer satisfaction, and longer-term buyer–seller relationships. Because of this importance, most firms invest large sums of time and money training their sales forces.

The sales training process consists of six stages: needs assessment, objective setting, planning, conducting, evaluating results, and providing follow-up sessions that maintain and enhance sales skill proficiency. Each stage of sales training is interconnected and dependent upon the other five stages. Because of this, managers must insure all sales training stages are conducted effectively so that trainees are provided with timely and pertinent skills, knowledge, and attitudes.

The role of culture, whether encountered within or between countries, is making an increasingly larger impact upon sales training programs. For example, culture complicates all stages of the training process. Sales trainees in a worldwide marketplace must be trained differently, to match the expectations of their customers. Although the salesperson may be thoroughly grounded in product knowledge, they must also be able to behave and communicate in a manner that is acceptable to the client. Also, trainees from dissimilar cultures perceive the training process differently. This is true of scales and questions utilized in needs assessment and evaluation, as well as the instructor's method of presenting training topics. The large influence of culture must always be considered when planning, conducting, and evaluating sales training programs.

Sales training evaluation is extremely important, because this step provides management with evidence of the training success. Because firms in the global marketplace invest large sums, it is imperative to validate the success of the training effort. As the world enters the twenty-first century, with attendant technology advances, managers must focus on continually improving the sales training process. However, it will be difficult for continual improvement to occur in sales training programs without an objective evaluation process being in place.

## DISCUSSION QUESTIONS

1. Provide specific examples of each of the six benefits that are gained from sales training.
2. Are any sales training stages within the process more important than another? Why or why not?
3. Write a SMART objective for a software company that wants to increase profits in the Scandinavian marketplace by 10 percent by the end of next year.
4. Why are some training programs shorter or longer than other training programs?
5. List as many reasons as possible why it is difficult to objectively evaluate sales training.
6. Of the four evaluation stages, which is easiest to conduct? Which is most valuable?

## REFERENCES

1. Honeycutt, Earl D., Jr., and John B. Ford (1995), "Guidelines for Managing an International Sales Force," *Industrial Marketing Management*, 24, 135–44.
2. Selmer, Jan (2000), "A Quantitative Needs Assessment Technique for Cross-cultural Work Adjustment," *Human Resources Quarterly*, 11:3 (fall), 269–81.

3  Dubinsky, Alan J., Roy D. Howell, Thomas N. Ingram, and Danny N. Bellenger (1986), "Salesforce Socialization," *Journal of Marketing*, 50:4 (October), 192–207.

4  Honeycutt, Earl D., Jr., John B. Ford, and John Tanner (1994), "Who Trains Salespeople?" *Industrial Marketing Management*, 23:1 (February), 65–70.

5  Honeycutt, Earl D., Jr. (1996), "Conducting a Sales Training Audit," *Industrial Marketing Management*, 25:2 (March), 105–13.

6  Dubinsky, Alan J., and Thomas E. Barry (1982), "A Survey of Sales Management Practices," *Industrial Marketing Management*, 11, 133–41.

7  Honeycutt, Earl D., Jr., Clyde Harris, and Stephen Castleberry (1987), "Sales Training: A Status Report," *Training and Development Journal*, 41:5, 42–5.

8  Newstrom, John W. (1975), "Selecting Training Methodologies: A Contingencies Approach," *Training and Development Journal*, 29 (October), 12–16.

9  Hill, John S., Richard R. Still, and Unal O. Boya (1991), "Managing the International Sales Force," *International Marketing Review*, 8:1, 19–31.

10 Honeycutt, Earl D., Jr., John B. Ford, and Lew Kurtzman (1996), "Potential Problems and Solutions when Hiring and Training a Worldwide Sales Team," *Journal of Business and Industrial Marketing*, 11:1 (winter), 42–53.

11 Jantan, Mohammed Asri (2000), "Sales Training Practices in Malaysia: Comparisons of Domestic and Multinational Companies," unpublished Ph.D. dissertation, Old Dominion University, Norfolk VA.

12 Shellenbarger, Sue (2001), "New Training Methods Allow Jobs to Intrude Further into Off Hours," *Wall Street Journal*, July 11, B1.

13 Honeycutt, Earl D., Jr., Kiran Karande, and M. Asri Jantan (2002), "Sales Training in Malaysia: High- versus Low-tech Methods," *Industrial Marketing Management*, 31:7 (October), 581–7.

14 Terpstra, Vern, and Ravi Sarathy (1997), *International Marketing*, Fort Worth TX: The Dryden Press.

15 Honeycutt, Harris, and Castleberry (1987).

16 Erffmeyer, Robert, Jamal A. Al-Khatib, Mohammed I. Al-Habib, and Joseph F. Hair, Jr. (1993), "Sales Training Practices: A Cross-national Comparison," *International Marketing Review*, 10:1, 45–59.

17 Honeycutt, Harris, and Castleberry (1987).

18 El-Ansary, Abdel I. (1993), "Sales Force Effectiveness Research Reveals New Insights and Reward–Penalty Patterns in Sales Force Training," *Journal of Personal Selling and Sales Management*, 13:2 (spring), 83–90.

19 Siguaw, Judy A., Gene Brown, and Robert E. Widing (1994), "The Influence of Market Orientation of the Firm on Sales Force Behavior and Attitude," *Journal of Marketing Research*, February, 106–16.

20 Erffmeyer *et al.* (1993).

21 Honeycutt, Earl D., Jr., John B. Ford, and C.P. Rao (1995), "Sales Training: Executives' Research Needs," *Journal of Personal Selling and Sales Management*, 15:4, 67–71.

22 Honeycutt, Earl D., Jr., and Thomas Stevenson (1989), "Evaluating Sales Training Programs," *Industrial Marketing Management*, 18:3, 215–22.

**143**

23  Cavusgil, S. Tamer (1990), "The Importance of Distributor Training at Caterpillar," *Industrial Marketing Management*, 19, 1–9.

24  Wexley, K.N., and Latham, G.P. (1981), *Developing and Training Human Resources in Organizations*, Glenview, IL: Scott, Foresman.

25  Honeycutt, Earl D., Jr., Kiran Karande, Ashraf Attia, and Steven Maurer (2001), "A Utility-based Framework for evaluating the Financial Impact of Sales Force Training Programs," *Journal of Personal Selling and Sales Management*, 21:3 (summer), 229–38.

26  Cateora, Philip R., and John L. Graham (1999), *International Marketing*, Boston MA: Irwin McGraw-Hill.

# Chapter 9

# Managing the global sales territory

This chapter presents methods for determining sales force size, composition, and criteria for ethically selecting partners in a sales territory.

## LEARNING OBJECTIVES

*After reading this chapter, you will be able to*:

- Compare and contrast the advantages and disadvantages of a company salesperson and sales agent.
- Explain the positive and negative aspects of using expatriates, host-country, and third-country salespersons.
- Compute a break-even analysis to determine the economic switchover point between a company sales force and a sales agent.
- Discuss the four criteria for selecting partners.
- Compute a breakdown and composite methodology to determine sales force size.
- Explain cultural influences on sales control and administration.
- Discuss ethical dilemmas encountered in territory management.

## KEY TERMS

- Expatriate, host-country, and third-country salespersons.
- Break-even analysis.
- Value chain.
- Marginal cost and Marginal revenue.
- Breakdown and Composite methods.

## INTRODUCTION

Sales managers that oversee sales territories face constantly changing environments. With change, a number of managerial decisions about the sales territory should be revisited. First, sales managers must consider the option of a company sales force or sales agents. To assist, a computational formula for determining the switchover point between agents and a company sales force is provided. In addition to cost, however, this decision is influenced by desired service level and degree of relationship. Second, criteria for selecting partners in the global marketplace are reviewed. It is essential that partners share similar goals and business philosophies if commercial unions are to work. Third, managers are presented with three ways to compute sales force size by utilizing economic, breakdown, and composite sales force methodologies. Finally, a discussion of ethical dilemmas faced in global sales territories is presented.

CASE VIGNETTE **AGENT OR SALESPERSON AT TRW**

Jamie Cooper is a sales manager for TRW, and manages a sales force that sells electronic components to OEMs, or original equipment manufacturers. Several territories currently utilize sales agents to service customers, but sales growth raises the issue of converting to a company sales force. Ian Fujimora, the firm's national sales manager, has asked Cooper to determine whether it is economically advantageous to change from sales agents to a company sales force within the territories. If the decision is to switch to a company sales force, Cooper must also determine the appropriate number of company sales personnel to hire for the territories.

## COMPANY SALES FORCE OR SALES AGENTS?

### Pros and cons

In the sales/channels area, the firm can use either independent sales agents or company sales-people. An extensive study of industrial and consumer goods companies reported that 72 percent of global firms outside the United States employ independent sales representatives.[1] Typically, companies use agents when they enter developing markets with low sales volume. This makes sense, because agents are often paid higher, incentive-oriented commission, but when sales are not forthcoming, agents receive no remuneration for their efforts.[2] Sales agents are also expected to possess a competent knowledge of the respective market's supply/demand situation and customer base. This means that global firms engage agents when:

- Markets are geographically dispersed.
- There are few customers in the marketplace.
- The firm is inexperienced in global marketing.

- The product is new and demand is uncertain.
- The firm wants to simplify business activities.[3]

While agents are cost-effective, there may be problems ensuring company loyalty, especially when the agent also represents local firms.

There are several options available should the sales manager determine that a company sales force is more advantageous. First, sales managers must determine who should be hired for the positions. As discussed in some detail in Chapter 6 global salespeople can be expatriates, local or host-country nationals, or third-country nationals. A managerial summary of the advantages and disadvantages of each salesperson category is presented in Table 9.1.

Firms often choose a company sales force when there is a need to control their activities. This need translates into the company sales force exclusively selling the firm's products and services. With a company sales force, sales managers can both direct and expect the company salesperson to work toward achieving the goals set by the firm's management team. Agents, on the other hand, almost always represent a number of non-competing firms, which means that any one manufacturer can receive only a limited portion of the sales agent's attention during customer sales calls. So, from a firm's perspective, having a company sales force provides control and increased focus on finding and servicing customers. When a firm has large numbers of established customers located in close proximity, it is almost certain a company sales force will be maintained.

Firms engage sales agents to act on their behalf in markets that are not economically sufficient to hire and staff a company sales force. That is, company salespersons must receive a salary and benefits even if sales do not justify these expenses. Conversely, sales agents receive commission only after a sale is made. In global markets, sales agents are also hired because of their knowledge of the local marketplace and as a result of their established

**Table 9.1** Advantages and disadvantages of salesperson types

| Category | Advantages | Disadvantages |
|---|---|---|
| Expatriate | Product knowledge<br>High service levels<br>Train for promotion<br>Greater home control | Highest costs<br>High turnover<br>High training costs |
| Host-country | Economical<br>High market knowledge<br>Language skills<br>Cultural knowledge<br>Implement actions sooner | Needs product training<br>Held in low esteem<br>Language skills importance declining<br>Loyalty assurance |
| Third-country | Cultural sensitivity<br>Language skills<br>Economical<br>Allows regional sales coverage | Identity problems<br>Blocked promotions<br>Income gaps<br>Needs product/company training<br>Loyalty assurance |

contacts with decision makers or business leaders. Both of these reasons explain why global firms partner with local businesses to represent their product line in unfamiliar markets rather than establishing their own sales force.

Firms wonder whether they should hire their own sales force or contract with another organization to serve as their agent or representative in the marketplace. In the global marketplace there are no simple answers to this conundrum. In fact, a wide array of issues must be explored before making the decision.

## Breakeven analysis

From an economic perspective, a sales manager can compute when it is advantageous to hire an agent over a company salesperson. To complete this computation, the sales manager must know the selling price, fixed costs, variable costs, and forecasted sales by the agents to determine the breakeven or switchover point. The process is described below by the formula:

$$Q* = \frac{\text{Fixed costs}}{CM_{sp} - rCM_a}$$

where: $Q*$ = point of indifference where salesperson and agent costs are equal, Fixed costs = costs that are obligated whether the salesperson works or not, $CMsp$ = contribution margin (sales price – variable expenses) of salesperson, $CMa$ = contribution margin of sales agent, $r$ = percent of time an agent focuses on product line versus salesperson. If we assume that monthly fixed costs for the territory are $2,000 and that the contribution margins for the salesperson and sales agent are $60 and $50 × 50 percent focus, respectively, $Q*$ is 2,000/(60–0.5 × 50) = 57 units per month. Total forecasted sales for the territory are 100 units.

Once $Q*$ is computed, the forecasted sales in units are compared to the point of indifference. Since the forecasted sales figure (100) is greater than computed $Q*$ (57), the most economical sales party to service the territory is the company salesperson. If, on the other hand, forecasted sales are less than $Q*$ (any number less than fifty-seven units), the sales manager should hire or continue to employ a sales agent. A practical example of computing the point of indifference is provided in Figure 9.1.

## SELECTING PARTNERS

In global markets it is important to carefully select and build relationships with business partners. As discussed by Porter, value chains are comprised of all functions performed by the firm, including the sales function.[4] Therefore, global firms must decide if it is more economical and efficient to maintain their own sales force or to select a partner that can perform this function. In most markets, whether domestic or global, firms that select partners expect them to possess the following attributes:

- *Knowledge of the marketplace*. In global markets, firms select partners that possess a cultural and economic understanding of the local market. That is, the local partner

**148**

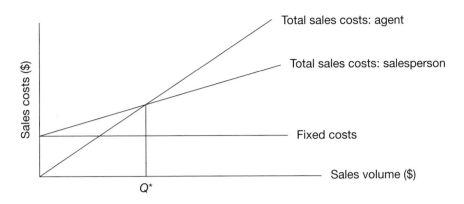

**Figure 9.1** *Breakeven graph and practical example*

Sales costs begin at zero for sales agents and increase quickly as revenues increase. At *Q** agent sales costs equal those of the company sales force, then begin to increase more rapidly.

Computations and practical example:

$$\text{Contribution margin} = \frac{\text{Sales price}}{\text{Variable costs}}$$

|  | Agent | Salesperson |
|---|---|---|
| Sales price | $200 | $200 |
| Cost of goods sold | (120) | (120) |
| Commission | (30) | (10) |
| Travel expenses | (0) | (10) |
| Contribution margin | $50 | $60 |

The fixed costs of the salesperson are $2,000 per month, less salary $1,500, plus auto $500. Agents are predicted to devote 50 percent of their time to selling product (r = 0.5). Given these figures,

$$Q^* = FC/CMsp - rCma \text{ or } \$2,000/60 - 50 \times 0.5$$

or fifty-seven units to break even each month. If the forecast of sales for the territory is 100 units, the forecast exceeds *Q** as shown and it is more economical for the firm to hire its own salesperson to serve the territory.

more accurately understands the cultural aspects of conducting business and is familiar with local business companies and their leaders. The knowledge possessed by local partners greatly reduces the time global firms would need to master the culture and gain credibility with local businesses using a company sales force.

■ *Marketplace status.* Partners should be known in the marketplace. This means the local partner's sales force is familiar to customers, has a positive reputation, and is adequately trained and qualified to provide outstanding customer service. This attribute reduces the amount of sales promotion effort and necessary time to form and enhance relationships. In certain circumstances, the global partner will need to provide technical and product application training to the local partner's sales force.

■ *Possess similar goals and values.* Partners should hold similar goals and values regarding how business is conducted. It is extremely important for both partners to share similar long or short-term goals, such as market growth, high profits, customer service levels, and market leadership. Attempting to partner with firms that hold dissimilar values can lead only to frustration and disappointment for both partners.

■ *Partnering should be a win–win situation.* Partnerships should be a win–win situation for both parties. A partnership allows the global firm to sell its products at a profit in a new marketplace. Conversely the local partner that represents the global firm in the marketplace must make a reasonable profit and perhaps also have its product line represented elsewhere by the global partner. If both partners are not winners, the partnership will not prevail.

## DETERMINING SALES FORCE SIZE

Another important decision made by the sales manager is determining the appropriate sales force size. That is, how many salespersons are necessary to perform current or forecasted sales activity? As markets expand, firms may slowly add additional salespersons to serve new customers. Sales managers may not sit down, however, and assess whether the sales force is either too large or too small. There are at least three distinct methods of determining sales force size: the economic method, the breakdown method and the sales force composite method. Each method is discussed below.

### Three methods of determining

*Economic method*

Economically, it is viable to hire a salesperson as long as marginal revenues (*MR*) generated by that salesperson exceed their marginal costs (*MC*). This means that as long as the next salesperson makes a positive financial contribution to the firm, then an additional salesperson should be hired. Based upon economic theory, the sales manager is guided by the following relationships:

■ When $MR > MC$, additional salespersons should be hired.
■ When $MR = MC$, the ideal number of salespersons has been hired.
■ When $MC > MR$, additional salespersons should *not* be hired.

An example of this relationship would be:

| Salesperson No. | MR | MC | Difference |
|---|---|---|---|
| 35 | 100 | 60 | +40 |
| 36 | 85 | 65 | +20 |
| 37 | 70 | 70 | 0 |
| 38 | 60 | 75 | −15 |

**150**

As shown above, the sales manager should hire exactly thirty-seven salespersons, because at this point marginal revenue and marginal costs are in equilibrium. However, while this method provides sales managers with hiring guidance – one should hire additional salespersons as long as they positively impact the firm – it is difficult to accurately perform this analysis in the "real world"! This is because sales managers do not know the precise impact (revenue or costs) of hiring an additional salesperson. While a sales manager can estimate the revenue and cost figures of hiring an additional person, in reality the analysis is seldom practiced.

In some industries or companies, sales managers are willing to hire additional salespersons on a straight commission basis. This is because the marginal revenue of salespersons compensated exclusively by commission will always exceed marginal costs. Therefore, straight commission salespersons are economically advantageous to the firm. For example, insurance salespersons in China are paid in the form of commission on actual sales. This results in the insurance firms operating in China believing that it is better to have more, rather than fewer, salespeople.[5] What this situation omits, however, is that the economic relationship may not be advantageous to the salesperson or partner and may lead to higher than normal sales force turnover rates! Additionally, other factors influence the size of a sales force than profit, which leads sales managers to consider other computational methods.

## Breakdown method

The breakdown method of determining sales force size is relatively easy to understand and conduct. To perform the calculation, the sales manager need only have access to forecasted sales in dollars or units for the year and the average sales revenue or units per salesperson. This allows the sales manager to compute the size of the sales force in the following way:

$$\text{Sales force size} = \frac{\text{Forecasted sales (euros or units)}}{\text{Average sales (euros or units) per salesperson}}$$

An example of this computation is presented for a firm forecasting €250 million in sales, where the average salesperson sells €20 million per year. If we substitute these figures into the formula, the results are:

Sales force size ($) = €250 million/€20 million or 12.5 salespersons

Using forecasted units, where a firm expects to sell 120,000 units total and the average salesperson sells 10,000 units, the following practical example is provided:

Sales force size (units) = 120,000 units/10,000 units = 12 salespersons

There are concerns about the precision derived from the breakdown method. First, it is simplistic. Only two figures are utilized in the computation and one is forecasted, while the other is an average. There is no consideration given to travel time, number of visits, or the importance of accounts. Also, managers often inflate sales revenue expectations in an effort to motivate the sales force toward greater achievement. Second, there are seldom "average" salespersons. In most firms 20 percent of their salespersons generate the majority of the firm's sales, while the remaining 80 percent struggle to reach average sales figures. There are also real differences in territory potential, routing, and customer location. However, the breakdown method can be useful in approximating the size of the sales force as long as these limitations are taken into consideration.

## Composite method

A third way to determine the appropriate size of the sales force is to compute a composite or "build-up" method. The computation takes a number of important variables into account and managers must make decisions about allocating sales force assets. First, firm accounts are prioritized into categories from most to least important. Managers may categorize customer accounts based upon current or potential sales revenue or profitability. This means that A accounts are the most important, B accounts the next most important, and C accounts the least important in regard to sales/profits/future business. Second, the sales manager determines how frequently each account category will be visited or called upon. Generally, A accounts are called upon the most frequently and C accounts the least frequently. To compute the total number of calls that are necessary to service the existing accounts, the sales manager multiplies the number of accounts placed into each category by the number of visits per year allocated to each category. As shown in Figure 9.2, this computes to 4,210 annual sales calls.

Once the total number of sales calls is computed, the second step of this process ascertains the total number of calls an average salesperson will conduct annually. This step also requires the sales manager to make a number of decisions. First, work level or the average number of calls per day must be set. Then the number of days each week the salesperson will call upon customers must be decided. Finally, the total number of weeks per year the salesperson works must be recorded. As an example, let us say a salesperson averages four industrial sales calls per day, works in the field four days each week, and after accounting for training/vacation/holidays determines the salesperson works forty-five weeks per year. When these numbers are multiplied, this computes to four calls per day, times four days per week, times forty-five weeks, or a total of 720 calls per year.

Now that the sales manager has arrived at the total number of calls that are needed to service existing customers and the total number of calls a salesperson can make, the third step is to divide the total number of calls by the total calls made by a salesperson. In this example, it works out to be 4,210 total calls divided by 720 calls per salesperson. This equates to (4,210/720) approximately 5.85 salespersons. However, if the salesperson is expected to perform cold calls, market research, or other types of service calls, this final number must be further adjusted. To account for additional time devoted to cold calling or other such activities, the sales manager must allocate a percentage to the activity. For example, the expectation might be that 10 percent of salesperson time is to be devoted to cold calling and market research activities. To factor in these responsibilities, the sales manager takes the final number (5.85 salespersons) and divides this number by 0.9 (1–0.1). The final number of salespersons needed to service existing accounts and perform additional sales calls in the field works out to be (5.85/0.9) 6.5. The sales manager then decides, after

⇨ Step 1. Compute the total number of sales calls needed to service existing accounts.

| Account category | No. of accounts | Yearly calls | Total calls |
|---|---|---|---|
| A | 60 | 15 | 900 |
| B | 145 | 10 | 1,450 |
| C | 310 | 6 | 1,860 |
| | | Annual calls | 4,210 |

⇨ Step 2. Compute the total number of calls made annually by sales representative.
Assumptions:

| | |
|---|---|
| (a) Number of sales calls made per day | 4 |
| (b) Number of days per week on the road | 4 |
| (c) Weeks available per year | 45 |

Multiply a × b × c or 4 × 4 × 45 = 720 sales calls per year by salesperson.

⇨ Step 3. Arrive at number of salespersons needed to satisfy basic account servicing. Divide total annual calls/annual calls made or 4,210/720 = 5.847.

If the sales force must make cold calls, conduct market research or undertake other activities, this must be computed into the final number of sales representatives needed in the following manner. Assumption: sales force expected to utilize 10% of field time making cold calls and conducting market research

Basic activity requires 5.847 salespersons. Correct this number for "other" activities by dividing by the reciprocal (1–0.1) = 0.9 or 5.847/0.9 = 6.5 salespersons needed. The sales manager can utilize this final figure to better understand how many salespersons are needed to service accounts and conduct other forms of business activities.

**Figure 9.2** *Composite sales force size method*

reviewing factors such as expected sales growth and competitive activity, whether to hire six or seven salespersons to cover the required salesperson duties.

## Sales administration

Administering the sales force represents another set of challenges for the global sales manager. What types of activities – office hours, reports, cold calls, and travel frequency – should the sales manager require of a global sales force? Salesperson requirements will differ depending upon cultural expectations. In the name of efficiency, and as is common in the United States, an American manager directed his Japanese sales force not to report to the home office each morning, as is customary in Japan. The sales force was directed to begin calling upon customers early in the morning to increase the total amount of time devoted to daily meeting with potential customers. The net result of this change was that sales levels decreased significantly. In reassessing his decision, the manager determined that the Japanese sales force needed the administrative meeting requirement in order to bestow group identity on the

Japanese sales force. Upon reflection, the sales manager re-instituted the morning sales meeting and sales increased.[6]

As more companies enter China, the trend has been to hire and train local salespersons instead of moving expatriates from the United States, Japan, and Europe. But in a Confucian-oriented society like China the firm is expected to play a parental role and provide high levels of supervision and inspiration. Salespersons in China prefer *guan xi*, or personal relationships, rather than the Western concept of "management."[7]

A number of global firms have established decision support systems in order to maintain comprehensive information about their customers. A decision support system allows global salespersons to understand the importance of their global customers so that proper resources are devoted to major accounts, regardless of the location.[8] Global salespersons must understand that a firm's importance is determined by its total purchase level, rather than single territory sales. Without appropriate information, salespersons in distant locations may fail to realize the overall importance of their accounts to the company.

Sales automation is also becoming imperative for success in the competitive global arena. Despite the myriad efficiency benefits generated by automation, sales managers should know that phone systems remain unreliable in most countries, e-mail addresses may be unavailable, a few nations may frown upon possessing laptop computers, and in some countries answers to technical questions are unavailable.[9]

## Sales management control

Another area of concern involves the level of sales force control. US managerial thinking is one of a "master of destiny" philosophy.[10] That is, many US sales managers believe that sales force members are in control of their destinies and responsible for their own resources. This philosophy suggests that reward decisions in the United States are objective and based upon merit. However, such a philosophy is missing in many other cultures that are more "fatalistic" in their world-views. In some countries, like Saudi Arabia, managers believe that uncontrollable higher-order forces – rather than the individual – influence future outcomes.[11] Given this diversity, what criteria should sales managers identify and track as being important?

Likewise, managers that operate cross-culturally must understand that in some parts of the world, like Southeast Asia, the concept of nonconfrontation conflicts with an objective evaluation of salesperson performance. In effect a "totally honest" review of the salesperson's performance could cause "loss of face" and the breaking of a societal norm.[12] While in highly individualistic countries the sales force is perceived to individually be responsible for their performance. But this is not true in collectivist countries that exist in many parts of the world; therefore, managing a global sales group will require different human resource systems.

A second question is: how much authority should be delegated to overseas managers and salespeople to make decisions? The level of corporate control varies across cultures. US firms attempt to maximize profits, which equates to a bottom line or quantitative orientation. Other cultures – especially Japan – tend to deemphasize numbers for control purposes. Most Asian countries also have less formal planning systems and use fewer quantitative measures than US companies. However, firms conducting business in highly competitive markets tend to employ increased levels of control.[13]

Firms that rely upon local management teams for contracts and cultural expertise must understand the importance of delegating negotiation and decision authority to global teams. One study concluded that local managers in global companies have significant inputs into planning, administration, and control decisions.[14] To do otherwise results in decisions being made at headquarters that are inappropriate for the local situation. Stratus Computer, a US company, hired local managers and gave them the authority to negotiate agreements without input from headquarters. Motorola Asia Pacific Semiconductor Division allows its Asian managers to formulate strategy for their markets.[15] Both companies have been very successful.

The type of managerial control mechanisms used must also reflect sensitivity to the local needs and conditions within each global target market. These control mechanisms must be carefully assessed from the standpoint of whether expatriates, host-country nationals, or third-country nationals are employed. The control mechanisms for expatriates may be similar to those expected at home, but the same control requirements may be viewed by local and third-country salespersons as being totally constricting and culturally inappropriate.

## Salesperson travel planning

Since travel can consume a significant portion of the salesperson's time, it is essential for the sales manager to monitor this activity. Some firms require the salesperson to submit a travel plan for management approval prior to undertaking the travel. Other companies permit their sales force to travel at will within their territories. Common sense suggests that excess time spent traveling reduces the amount of time the salesperson can allocate to the customer. Therefore, the salesperson must minimize the time spent traveling between accounts.

There are several methods of planning sales calls. These include driving to the most distant point and working back toward the office, planning a circuitous routing that reduces backtracking, and utilizing a computer program to plan the most efficient routing for the sales force. Sales personnel that travel inefficiently often do so unconsciously. This means the salesperson is not always aware of their wasteful work habits. When one of the authors first began working in sales, a senior sales manager related the following story.

One of the best salespersons in Boston had gone from the highest sales position in the district to a spot near the bottom of the list. His sales manager flew into Boston to ride the territory with the salesperson and hopefully identify "why" this change had occurred to one of his star salespersons. The salesperson and manager met at the hotel and drove for an hour outside of Boston and made two sales calls. At 11:00 a.m. the salesperson informed the manager that he normally met with other company salespersons for lunch at a favorite restaurant. To reach the restaurant required a forty-five minute drive in the direction of Boston. After a leisurely lunch, the salesperson again drove outside of Boston for nearly an hour and made three additional sales calls. At about 4:30 p.m., the salesperson told the manager he normally met friends for "Happy Hour" beginning at 5:00. This meant the salesperson quit work early and drove back to Boston. The result was nearly four hours' driving time and only four or five sales calls being made each day. The sales manager was relieved to discover why his star salesman had stopped performing. The hard part was convincing the salesperson to modify his work behavior!

## ETHICAL ISSUES OF TERRITORY DESIGN

A number of ethical issues arise when making decisions about territory design, customer assignment, and securing partners in the global marketplace. These concerns include:

- *Equitable opportunity*. Are the sales territories equitable in their division? That is, to the greatest extent possible, has the sales manager divided the territories so that each salesperson has an opportunity to succeed in their territory of assignment? Sales managers may claim that a salesperson has sufficient territory potential to succeed, when this is not the case. Perhaps the correct question is: does an average salesperson have a chance to succeed under normal work conditions?

- *Territory assignment*. How are territories assigned? Does the sales manager assign territories based upon seniority or as a reward? Does the sales force understand how this process works? Most important, are assignments made fairly to all salespersons? Obviously, fairness is a culturally bound attitude and perceptions will vary around the world.

- *Account service levels*. Sales managers must decide the level of service provided to each account category. This means that A or "major" accounts receive the highest level of service and C accounts the lowest level of service. Likewise, the firm may charge different fee levels for services provided or have small accounts order through distributors or by phone. Smaller firms may feel that it is unethical to be charged higher prices than larger customers, but it is essential for suppliers to make a reasonable profit on all transactions. By charging higher prices to small customers, the supplier is able to provide service to the less profitable account.

- *Partner relations*. In the past large multinational or global firms attempted to coerce their partners into doing things their way. This was accomplished through threats of loss of future business or other intimidation. Partners do not appreciate being threatened or coerced to perform a certain way, regardless of their size or reputation. This is certainly questionable ethical behavior.

- *Switching from agents to salespersons*. It is standard practice for a firm to enter a new market with a sales agent and then, once the market has grown, to switch to a company salesperson. While this practice is understood by the sales agent(s), communication about future plans between both partners must be open and frequent. Often the parties discuss the eventual switchover, prior to the partnership being established. The understanding should include how the switchover will occur, the responsibilities of each party in such an event, and the financial responsibilities of both the agent and the principal. Such an agreement helps minimize potential problems should a switchover occur.

- *Treatment of local and third-country hires*. Global sales managers must also determine the pay, benefits, and expectations of local and third-country employees. Managers must insure the benefits and compensation meet local standards and comply with national legal requirements. For example, many European countries require generous benefits be extended to local hires of global firms.[16]

As can be seen, there are a number of ethical concerns associated with territory management. To insure that partnerships work, it is important that all relationships are ethical and, as stated before, every endeavor should be made to make the relationship a "win–win" one.

## DISTRIBUTORS AND CHANNEL PARTNERS

Because of rising costs, industrial firms have had to refer smaller customers or accounts to distributors. Distributors act as a wholesaler/retailer for accounts that buy in quantities that are considered too small by the manufacturer. For example, if a small manufacturer of microcomputers wanted to purchase fifteen Intel® Pentium IV® processors, chances are the Pentium® factory may have a minimum purchase quantity of fifty or 100 units. Any order less than the minimum set by the factory would have to be purchased from an electronics distributor. While the distributor charges a higher price, per unit, than the manufacturer, the customer is paying for the utility of buying in small quantities and being able to receive the purchase quickly.

A sales manager must coordinate activity with distributors that service customers in the territory. Distributor salespersons must be trained about new products and their applications and sales activity coordinated so that both organizations pursue a coherent sales strategy toward the marketplace. This partnership works because the distributor services smaller accounts that are willing to pay for the utilities they receive, while the manufacturer serves larger accounts that purchase in significant quantities. The two organizations improve service to the market by complementing, rather than competing against, one another.

## CHAPTER SUMMARY

Territory management in the global marketplace is an important responsibility of the sales manager. First, some firms employ a company sales force to insure control and increase emphasis on the company product line. Agents, on the other hand, are preferred when the market is small, slow account growth is expected, and local market expertise is needed. Second, an example of how a sales manager can make the economic decision between hiring a company sales representative and sales agent was explained. This quantitative reasoning was followed by a discussion of important qualitative criteria that companies should also consider when selecting a sales partner. Third, three different methods of determining sales force size were presented. These include the economic approach, the breakdown method, and the composite or "build-up" computational methods. Fourth, sales force administration and control areas were discussed. Managers must set expectations for their global sales offices and determine how much authority to delegate to them. The chapter concluded with an examination of ethical issues that face sales managers when managing territories in the global marketplace.

## DISCUSSION QUESTIONS

1   Under what conditions are company salespersons preferable for covering a territory? Why are agents utilized in new territories?

2   If a firm decides to expand into a new territory with a high-tech product, which form of salesperson – expatriate, host-, or third-country – would be appropriate? For a consumer good, such as clothing?

3   What other factors would influence your decision to switch from an agent to a salesperson?

4   List and discuss the four criteria necessary for sound partner selection.

5   How familiar must the sales manager be with culture to manage a sales force? Why?

6   In what ways is the management of the sales territory impacted by ethics?

## REFERENCES

1   Hill, John S., and Richard R. Still (1990), "Organizing the Overseas Sales Force: How Multinationals Do It," *Journal of Personal Selling and Sales Management*, 10:2 (spring), 57–66.

2   Cheng, Maria, and Jiang Xueqin (2000), "Let's Talk Insurance," *Asiaweek*, August 11, 55–6.

3   Onkvisit, Sak, and John J. Shaw (1993), *International Marketing*, New York: Macmillan.

4   Porter, Michael E. (1985), *Competitive Advantage: Creating and Sustaining Superior Performance*, New York: Free Press.

5   Cheng and Jiang (2000).

6   Prestowitz, Clyde V., Jr. (1988), *Trading Places*, New York: Basic Books.

7   Wong, Yim Yu, and Maher, Thomas E. (1997), "New Key Success Factors for China's Growing Market," *Business Horizons*, 40:3, 43–52.

8   Eisenhart, Tom (1990), "Computer-aided Marketing: After Ten Years of Marketing Decision Support Systems Where's the Payoff?" *Business Marketing*, 75:6, 46–51.

9   Adams, Eric J. (1991), "Stalking the Global Sale," *World Trade*, June–July, 34–6.

10   Cateora, Philip R. (1993), *International Marketing*, Homewood IL: Irwin.

11   Usunier, Jean Claude (1996), *Marketing across Cultures*, London: Prentice Hall.

12   Redding, S.G. (1982), "Cultural Effects on the Marketing Process in Southeast Asia," *Journal of the Market Research Society*, 24:2, 98–114.

13   Hill, John S., and Arthur W. Allaway (1993), "How US-based Companies Manage Sales in Foreign Countries," *Industrial Marketing Management*, 22, 7–16.

14   Hill, John S., Richard R. Still, and Unal O. Boya (1991), "Managing the Multinational Sales Force," *International Marketing Review*, 8:1, 19–31.

**158**

15  Batson, Bryan (1992), "The Road Less Traveled," *Sales and Marketing Management*, December, 46–53.

16  Harzing, Anne-Wil, and Joris Van Ruysseveldt (1995), *International Human Resource Management*, London: Sage Publications.

## Chapter 10

# Motivating the sales force

This chapter presents several theories pertaining to sales force motivation and discusses the issues involved with the motivation of an international sales force.

**LEARNING OBJECTIVES**

*After reading this chapter, you will be able to*:

■ Understand the importance of motivation.
■ Identify the factors influencing salespeople's motivation.
■ Appreciate the complexity of the motivational process and explain the theories of motivation.
■ Understand the impact of cultural differences on motivation.
■ Explain various tools available for motivating the global sales force.
■ Discuss the relationship between motivation and job satisfaction.

**KEY TERMS**

■ Needs, Values and Goals.
■ Reinforcement.
■ Job satisfaction.

## INTRODUCTION

As the market becomes increasingly global, many firms are venturing into foreign markets. Some companies are tremendously successful in international sales. Their salespeople are tireless in striking deals with distributors and customers and establishing strong and lasting relationships. Other companies are less successful, whilst others often fail in their sales efforts. Although the potential for international sales can be infinite, companies need a skilful and highly motivated sales force capable of taking advantage of the emerging opportunities.

By understanding what motivates salespeople and knowing how to motivate them, sales managers can help 'average' salespeople transform to 'super' salespeople. Generally speaking, the main benefits of having a highly motivated sales force are that they do a superior job (more sales) and get the job done better (more satisfied customers). However, one of the sales manager's most difficult tasks is to motivate their salespeople and help them achieve success. Often, it requires more than sales managers' constant attention, care and effort to keep salespeople focused and move them toward achievement and fulfillment.[1] It is the purpose of this chapter to discuss such difficulties by providing information on the nature and process of motivation and identifying the tools available for motivating salespeople. In addition, the chapter examines the influence of cross-cultural individual differences on motivation, along with the relationship between motivation, job satisfaction and productivity.

CASE VIGNETTE **THE PERFECT COMPANY**

In the last five years, Harry Bern was by far the most productive salesperson in his company. He loved his job and was advocating "This is the perfect company and job for me." During the last two months his performance dropped to record low levels. Two months ago, the sales manager announced to him the company's decision to reject his request concerning financial assistance to attend an evening part-time MBA. The sales manager told him that he and the company could not see how an MBA could help him to improve his otherwise excellent interpersonal and selling skills. Harry disagreed with this explanation. In the past, the manager had turned down some of his other requests but now he feels different. Since that happened, Harry finds it very hard to forget and is unwilling to work as before.

## MOTIVATION DEFINED

The study of sales force motivation is concerned with the search for explanations and underlying principles that help sales managers understand why salespeople initiate, choose, and persist in specific actions under specific circumstances. For example, why has Harry's motivation changed this time but not before? What has an MBA to do with the motivation and performance of a salesperson? What could be done to motivate Harry again? Would acceptance of his request now put things in order? To what extent is motivation of salespeople controllable? Several concepts and theories exist which shed light on a plethora of issues on motivation, but before we go any further let us define motivation.

*Motivation* is the inner force that guides behavior and it is concerned with the causation of specific actions. For example, when we ask questions such as "Why did the sales manager reject Harry's request?" or "Why has Harry decided to change his behavior in the last two months?" we are asking about the actors' motivation. Motivation is a three-dimensional construct consisting of the following:

- The magnitude of mental activity and physical effort expended towards a certain action, or *intensity*.
- The extension of the mental activity and physical effort over time, or *persistence*.
- The choice of specific actions in specific circumstances, or *direction*.[2]

In our example, the magnitude of Harry's mental activity and physical effort this time has been of considerable *intensity*, as revealed by his record lower levels of performance than in any previous circumstances when his requests had also been turned down. Harry finds it very difficult to cope with this rejection and his thoughts *persistently* act as a barrier to change his recent attitude to work. The choice or *direction* not to work as before has been extended over a relatively long period of time.

Motivation can have a significant impact on the behavior of salespeople. It is imperative that sales managers, who have the responsibility of sustaining and directing the sales effort within their organizations, fully understand its nature and acquire the skills that are necessary for positively influencing the motivation of their salespeople. Knowledge and skills on motivation will also help sales managers avoid practices that can adversely affect the motivation of the sales force.

## MOTIVATION: THE DETERMINANTS OF ACTION AND INACTION

From a managerial perspective, motivation needs to be understood at two fundamental levels. Namely: the motivational content and its process. The following two questions represent the issues addressed by each level respectively:

- What motivates salespeople?
- How do salespeople choose their actions?

When sales managers know what motivates their salespeople they will be more equipped to satisfy or generate conditions that facilitate the satisfaction of their needs, as in Harry's case. Furthermore, when sales managers know how salespeople choose their actions then they may be able to intervene in the process and influence their behavior. For instance, the manager could have intervened in the process by offering alternative rewards or changing the beliefs of the salesperson concerning the value of the alternative rewards that could compensate for the rejection. The main theories that explain the determinants of motivation and describe its process are briefly discussed next.

## What motivates salespeople?

The *content* theories of motivation focus on the "what" motivates individuals and are concerned with the factors that arouse and initiate motivational behavior. These theories consider human needs as the primary mechanism of motivation. Needs can be physiological, security, belongingness, self-esteem and self-actualization, according to need hierarchy theory[3] (Maslow, 1943), motivating or hygienic, according to two-factor theory[4] (Herzberg, 1966) and existence, relatedness and growth, according to ERG theory[5] (Alderfer, 1972).

### Hierarchy of needs

The need hierarchy theory postulates that the needs of individuals are arranged in a hierarchical order, from low to high level needs (see Figure 10.1) and influence behavior as follows. Unsatisfied needs act as motivators, whereas satisfied needs do not, and that individuals advance to higher level of needs only when the lower level needs have been at least minimally satisfied.

The need hierarchy theory provides a very useful framework for identifying the variety of needs that salespeople may experience at work and understanding the ways in which

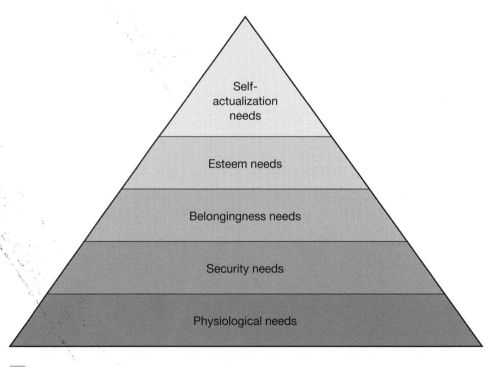

**Figure 10.1** *Maslow's hierarchy of needs and organizational examples*
*Physiological needs, e.g., basic salary. Security needs, e.g., pension plan. Belongingness needs, e.g., friends in work group. Esteem needs, e.g., job title. Self-actualization needs, e.g., challenging job.*
*Source: A.H. Maslow, "A Theory of Human Motivation,"* Psychological Review, *50 (1943), 374–96*

their motivation is caused. However, the universal applicability of the theory can be questioned on the grounds of (1) the five levels of needs are not always present among people in the world, (2) the ways people arrange their hierarchies do not always conform to Maslow's model, and (3) the need structures are more unstable and variable than the theory postulates.[6] For example, the hierarchy of needs of a Japanese salesperson may be different from the hierarchy of needs of an American salesperson. Cultural differences may cause salespeople from the collectivist culture (Japan) to place their needs for love and affiliation somewhat higher than some of their safety needs.

## Two factor theory

The two factor theory argues that in any work situation a manager can distinguish between the following two factors:

- *Motivation* factors, or motivators (achievement, recognition, the work itself, responsibility, advancement and growth) as primary causes of satisfaction and motivation.
- *Hygiene* factors (supervision, working conditions, interpersonal relationships, pay and job security, and company policies) as factors that cannot be turned into satisfying or motivating factors.

More specifically, by satisfying the hygiene factors, the best a sales manager can achieve is a state of neutrality; these factors cannot be turned into motivators. The hygiene factors are necessary conditions of successful motivation and they deal with the question 'Why work here?', whereas the motivators, that are capable of causing motivated behavior, deal with the 'Why work harder?' question.[7] As the need hierarchy theory, the two factor theory also fails to account for individual differences. For example, in Arabic cultures, salespeople may be motivated by such hygiene factors as interpersonal relationships where friendships are very important, sought after and personalized.

## Existence, relatedness and growth

The ERG theory also considers needs to be structured in a hierarchical order (starting with existence to relatedness and then growth) and argues that the lower the level of satisfaction in a need, the more it will be desired. It also postulates that the higher the satisfaction in a lower level need, the greater the desire to satisfy a higher level need, and the lower the satisfaction in a higher level need the greater the desire for satisfying lower level needs. Alderfer has suggested that more than one kind of need may motivate an individual at any given time.

In summary, the above theories are based on the fundamental principle that needs – a form of deprivation – cause an inner drive that leads to some form of action – goal-directed behavior – for the fulfillment or reduction of the felt need.

Needs vary considerably between salespeople across the world and change over time. For example, the English are more inclined toward their free time and have the reputation of being less motivated by money than the Americans.[8] Furthermore, needs change along the career stages of salespeople. For salespeople in the early stages of their career, needs such as peer acceptance, achievement, autonomy, and competitiveness are more important, as opposed to reduced competitiveness, security, and helping younger colleagues, that are valued more by salespeople in the late stages of their career.[9]

Although there is little doubt that the range of needs as specified by the above theories explains sufficiently the "what" motivates salespeople, these theories do not provide any explanation concerning the particular action that salespeople will take to satisfy their needs. For instance, the content theories can adequately explain the "what" in Harry's case. Harry wanted to pursue an MBA in order to satisfy his need for self-actualization, a psychological or a growth need. The theories, however, fail to explain how and why he chose this particular action. In other words the action and outcome components as depicted by the diagrammatic model (Figure 10.2) have not been adequately addressed by the content theories. Questions such as "Why did he not choose to work as hard as before while trying to persuade his manager to agree with and support his request?" and "How would this action help him satisfy his need?" cannot be answered. The process theories of motivation that are described in the next section attempt to provide answers to these questions.

## How do salespeople choose their actions?

The choice of a particular behavior of salespeople has been the focus of the *process* theories of motivation. These theories provide an explanation of "how" and "why" salespeople choose a particular behavior and are being discussed next.

### Equity theory

Equity theory[10] is based on the premise that people want to be treated fairly. Equity is defined as the belief that one is treated *fairly* in relation to others and inequity as the belief that one is treated *unfairly* in relation to others. The theory explains motivation by proposing that an individual's *choice of effort* to be expended at the workplace is a result of a comparison between his outcome–input ratio and the outcome–input ratios of others. Inputs are contributions of individuals to the company such as effort and loyalty and outcomes are the received rewards such as pay and recognition. Salespeople use these "outcome–input" ratios to determine relative equity, and when the compared ratios are not in balance the individual is motivated to reduce the perceived inequity.

The individual who perceives himself to be inequitably treated can change his inputs, change his outcomes, alter the perceptions of self and/or others, change comparisons, or leave the situation. Most research on equity theory focuses on one ratio only – outcome (quantity or quality) to payment (overpayment or underpayment). Although findings support the predictions made by the theory, other research has indicated that some people are more sensitive than others to perceptions of inequity.[11] This is particularly true when it is seen in a multicultural context. For example, according to a study of values based on respondents' self-image, Americans ranked equality first, whereas no other cultural group (Japanese, French, Arabs, and Malaysians) ranked equality as important.[12]

### Expectancy theory

Expectancy theory[13] attempts to explain how individuals choose between different alternative behaviors. More specifically, the theory suggests that motivation is a function of a per-

Motivation = *f* (Expectancy × Instrumentality × Valence)

**Figure 10.2** *The expectancy theory of motivation*
*Effort (or motivation) is a function of Expectancy × Instrumentality × Valence,*
*Where:*
**Expectancy** *= the salesperson's perception that effort will lead to performance,*
**Instrumentality** *= the salesperson's perception of the probability that performance will lead to certain outcomes, and*
**Valence** *= the salesperson's perception of the attractiveness or unattractiveness of an outcome. (× = denotes the multiplicative nature of the relationship).*

son's anticipation that a particular behavior will lead to outcomes that s/he values, and explains the motivation process as follows. First, individuals develop beliefs concerning the likelihood that a certain amount of effort will lead to successful performance. In other words they ask the question "Can I do it?" Then, they try to establish the link between the performance and given outcome or reward. At this stage, they address the question "What do I get for doing it?" Finally, they assess the strength of preference that is associated with each of the possible outcomes or rewards by asking, "How much do I value the reward?" Consequently, if a salesperson can perform a task and knows the kind of reward that is attached to performing the task, s/he will be motivated provided that s/he values the reward.

The theory's components are effort, performance, and outcome (see Figure 10.2). Effort is the result of motivation, performance is a joint function of effort, environment and ability, and the outcome is anything that might possibly result from performance. For example, a salesperson will be motivated when s/he values the expected rewards (e.g., promotion), believes that her/his efforts will lead to performance (e.g., can successfully engage on-the-job training of new salespeople), and the performance will result in the desired rewards (e.g., if new salespeople are trained properly and meet sales quotas s/he will be promoted). A study examining the ranking of alternative rewards in two manufacturing companies indicated that the value placed on rewards such as more pay, sense of accomplishment, and opportunities for personal growth was different among each company's salespeople.[14] The difference in value systems between cultures leads to the conclusion that the values placed on rewards by salespeople internationally are far from universal.

## Attribution theory

Attribution theory[15] considers motivation to be a function of a person's observation of his/her behavior and his/her decision and whether that behavior is a response to some factors. Consequently, it argues that different behaviors can be attributed to various factors and is concerned with the "why" question posed by individuals. For example, individuals try to attribute success or failure as the outcome of their behavior to some causes by posing the question "Why did this happen?"

The theory provides a classification or taxonomy of causes based on the similarities and differences of their underlying properties. For instance, causes that are within or outside the individual, i.e., internal–external (or "locus of control" dimension), stable–unstable (or stability dimension), controllable–uncontrollable (or control dimension). Although these dimensions do not exhaust the taxonomy of causality that the theory provides, they can advance a structured explanation of Salespeople's behavior based on the inferences made by them.

Cultural differences of salespeople globally necessitate the understanding of the impact of various causal attributions on their motivation. For example, promotion in Japanese firms is based more on seniority than on individual performance, whilst in American companies individual performance is often used as a measure for promotion.[16] As a result, a new and high performing Japanese salesperson who is not being promoted may attribute this event to different causes than a similarly successful but not promoted American counterpart working for the same company in Japan.

### Goal-setting theory

Goal-setting theory[17] assumes that behavior is the result of conscious goals and intentions and stresses the relationship between goals and job performance. The theory starts from the point that an individual has determined to engage in an activity and argues that a person's inclination to act in a particular way is influenced by the:

- Anticipated result (goal),
- Intention (will), which implies:
- Effort (will–act) and
- Strategy to reach the goal (object-oriented content).

Goal difficulty – the extent to which a goal is challenging and requires considerable effort – and goal specificity – the precise definition of the target for performance – are two important aspects that shape performance. When managers of an international sales force try to influence their job-related goals they must be aware of the complexities of goal comparability among culturally diverse salespeople in the organization. For instance, it is hard to establish similar goals among salespeople from the European Union and the United States, since there is a fundamental difference of cultural priorities. The priorities of a European salesperson are company, individual, and job, whereas for an American sales representative these are individual, job, and company.[18]

The major drawback of the process theories of motivation is that although they are value-based theories they do not provide any specification of particular values. In addition, these theories do not seem to be able to overcome methodological problems such as perceptual bias, and difficulties in establishing the validity of the measures for some of their components.[19] In summary, the theories attempt to explain how and why individuals engage in certain behaviors, and, although the explanation advanced by each is somewhat different, they are all based on the principle of the value of expected outcomes and the relationship between effort, performance, and outcomes.

## Reinforcement theory

In addition to the content and process theories of motivation described above, there is another approach that offers an alternative explanation of motivated behavior. The theory is known as *reinforcement theory*,[20] or *operant conditioning*, and suggests that behavior is a function of its consequence and explains how the consequences of past action influence future action in a cyclical manner.

The theory is based on the "law of effects," stating that a behavior that leads to a rewarding consequence is likely to be repeated. Consequently future behaviors are dependent on the immediate consequences of similar previous behaviors. Therefore, an individual's behavior (response) to a situation (stimulus) is caused by the specific consequences of a similar preceding response. Diagrammatically, the basic process of operant conditioning can be expressed as in Figure 10.3.

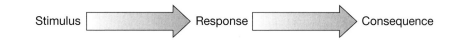

Stimulus ⟹ Response ⟹ Consequence

**Figure 10.3** *Operant conditioning*

The consequences can lead to the repetition of the response (positive reinforcement), avoidance of the response (negative reinforcement), extinction (decrease the frequency of the response), or punishment (an aversive consequence that eliminates the repetition of the response). A sales manager may provide positive reinforcement for desired responses or other types of reinforcement for undesirable responses. Reinforcement can be continual, when behavior is rewarded every time that it occurs, fixed-term, when behavior is reinforced on a fixed-time schedule, or variable interval, when the time interval for reinforcing behavior is variable.

The above discussion has provided a brief analysis and explanation of some well known theories of motivation. The theories are not mutually exclusive. Instead, they complement one another, especially when they are considered in the light of the complexity of human behavior. In the next part of the chapter, some ways in which sales managers can apply effectively the knowledge provided by these theories will be discussed.

## MOTIVATING THE GLOBAL SALES FORCE

All human behaviors are complex and all kinds of complex behaviors are possible. Sales force motivation is caused, shaped and maintained by the needs, values, and goals of the individuals, their relations with the situation, and the consequences of their actions. Salespeople are free agents causing effects in their own right, and their cultural background dictates to a certain extent what their needs, values, and goals will be and the type of action that is appropriate in certain circumstances. The following section describes cultural diversity and discusses ways in which such differences impact on the motivation of salespeople.

## Cultural differences and motivation

The challenges a sales manager faces when motivating international salespeople are related to the identification of their culturally bound needs, values, goals, and behaviors. The differences in needs, values, and behaviors of culturally dissimilar salespeople are much greater than those of culturally similar salespersons. Research pertaining to cultures has found that cultures differ on at least six bipolar dimensions.[21]

| | | |
|---|---|---|
| 1 | Universalism | Particularism |
| | Rules, codes, laws and generalizations | Exceptions, special circumstances, unique relations |
| 2 | Individualism | Communitarianism |
| | Personal freedom, human rights, competitiveness | Social responsibility, harmonious relations, cooperation |
| 3 | Specificity | Diffusion |
| | Atomistic, reductive analytic, objective | Holistic, elaborative synthetic, relational |
| 4 | Achieved status | Ascribed status |
| | What you have done, your track record | Who you are, your potential, and connections |
| 5 | Inner direction | Outer direction |
| | Conscience and convictions are located inside | Examples and influences are located outside |
| 6 | Sequential time | Synchronous time |
| | Time is a race along a set course | Time is a dance of fine coordination |

The range of different cultural values above dictate, to a certain extent, the work-related needs and values of salespeople and regulate their behavior. For example, American salespeople are guided by cultural values such as "Take pride in accomplishment," "Put freedom and initiative first," and "Forgive mistakes." Their European counterparts, however, are driven by values such as "Take pride in yourself and your group," "Put duty and obedience first," and "Avoid mistakes."[22] Based on these values, a goal based on the need of "becoming someone by doing things" will be more easily accepted by an American than by a European salesperson.

Similarly, different cultures associate a sales job with varying degrees of social status. In Greece, for example, a sales job is not regarded as a prestigious job and companies which compensate their salespeople on commission only find it hard to recruit new salespeople. In motivating an international sales force, one challenge is to find out the mix of physical rewards or incentives such as salary, commission, and company car and psychological rewards or incentives such as status, responsibility, and praise appropriate for each international salesperson.

A study published in *Psychology Today* in 1984 reported that a range of different needs motivate top salespeople. These needs were found to be as follows:

- Need for status (need for recognition and promotion).
- Need for control (need to be in control and influence others).
- Need for respect (need to be seen as experts who can give advice).
- Need for routine (need to follow a routine that must not be interrupted).
- Need for accomplishment (need more money and challenges).
- Need for stimulation (need to seek outside stimulation and challenges).
- Need for honesty (need to believe in the rightness of their practices).[23]

The above needs will vary between individual salespeople globally. For instance, financial rewards, which have long been considered to be one of the primary motivators,[24] will not motivate every salesperson. However, such rewards are expected to have a significant motivational impact on those who have a high need for accomplishment. If managers are to successfully motivate their salespeople, they must have a multifacet motivational program that accounts for the complexity of needs, values, and behaviors of salespeople internationally.

Recognizing the needs and values of salespeople and providing them with appropriate incentives or rewards are significant steps in the right direction for the successful motivation of salespeople. As part of a global motivational program, it is necessary, however, that sales managers engage in activities aimed at determining the level and direction of effort (setting sales quotas), giving them a sense of purpose and providing appropriate training.

Sales quotas are quantitative objectives or targets to be achieved by salespeople in a specific period of time. They provide an indication of the level of effort that is expected, point out the types of activities that this effort should be directed toward, and provide standards for performance evaluation at the end of the period. Internationally, even this very basic task becomes complicated. For example, in cultures such as the Japanese, individuals' targets are seen more in the context of a "team approach" to business. Furthermore, differences in national cultures require a careful examination of the amount of effort required to achieve sales quotas. In Malaysia, for instance, only five demonstrations on average are required to make a sale, as opposed to twenty demonstrations that are required in the Philippines.[25] Consequently, setting challenging yet attainable goals for the international sales force is absolutely crucial. In turn, rewarding salespeople's achievement in such a way that their needs and values are satisfied is the best way to maintain their efforts and job satisfaction at the highest possible level. The rewards that a sales manager can use to motivate a global sales force are discussed next.

## Motivational tools

Although knowing the needs and wants of salespeople may not tell sales managers how to motivate their global salespeople, it is arguably a vital input for determining what motivational tools are more appropriate.

A motivational tool should satisfy two criteria. First it should generate extra effort that will help the company achieve its objectives and second it must increase job satisfaction among salespeople. The most widely known motivational tools are: (1) *sales meetings*, (2) *incentive programs*: sales contests and competitions, (3) *recognition programs*: special titles, praise, promotion, extra responsibilities.

*Sales meetings,* which can be *ad hoc* or regular, with local, national, and/or international salespeople, can have a strong impact on motivation. In these meetings, issues such as the company's plans, promotional support, ways of delivering value to customers, training needs, and the launch of new products or the introduction of a sales contest can be discussed. Salespeople are asked to share their ideas to the issue under discussion and contribute to their company's decision-making process. It is important to remember that in all these meetings sales managers reinforce the notion that what salespeople are doing is important and worthy and helps them to connect with each other and build relationships well beyond the meeting's context. The sales meeting, therefore, is an important motivational tool because it brings salespeople together and encourages them to discuss with each other issues of mutual interest.

*Incentive programs* such as sales contests and competitions provide incentives geared at motivating salespeople to achieve short-term objectives. Contests and competitions can be *ad hoc* or recurring and must provide an equal opportunity to every salesperson to win a prize. The prize will vary according to the duration of the program and the additional amount of effort that the contest requires. Sales contests and competitions can help managers improve the motivation of their salespeople and achieve objectives such as, for example, to increase sales volume, secure more orders, revive dead accounts, and introduce new products.

Sales contests and competitions should have clearly stated objectives, attractive themes, written sets of procedures and eligibility for participation, attractive prizes, adequate duration, and be widely publicized. Sales managers, however, should be aware of the negative impact that is associated with sales contests and competitions. If a sales contest is not carefully planned and implemented it may damage the morale of salespeople and adversely affect their motivation. Unattainable goals, repetition of the same prizes over time, and predictability as to who is going to be the winner are aspects that may render the sales contest and competition ineffective and perhaps damaging.

*Recognition programs* are similar to incentive programs. The main difference is that the recognition programs aim at rewarding an overall high performance over a long period of time as opposed to incentive programs that provide rewards for the accomplishment of short-term sales objectives. By rewarding salespeople with highly sought responsibilities, special titles, pay raises, promotion, and praise, a sales manager can keep salespeople motivated throughout their careers.

The recognition of salespeople's high performance over time helps them to develop positive emotional reaction to their performance. This, in turn, leads to positive job attitudes and subsequent high performance.[26] Recognition programs assist in the development of positive attitudes to high performance and reinforce motivated behavior while inhibiting undesirable attitudes and behaviors such as job dissatisfaction and low productivity. Well administered recognition programs can create a virtuous circle for maintaining the continuation of their motivated behavior.

The purpose of the motivational tools is to strengthen desirable behaviors and weaken undesirable behaviors. However, the problem with some rewards is that, like punishment, they attempt to control the behavior of salespeople. They are aiming to "do things to people" as opposed to "working with people" and, in the long term, managers may not be able to get what they want by using them. For example, when salespeople are trying to get a reward, they may become less interested in whatever they have to do to get it. Rewards may turn enjoyment into work, and work into drudgery, so that, if salespeople are less committed to and excited by their job as a result of chasing rewards, they cannot be expected to sustain high motivational levels.[27] None the less when rewards, as part of a motivational tool, are appropriate and applied effectively they can become powerful motivators.

## MOTIVATION, JOB SATISFACTION, AND PERFORMANCE

Motivation and job satisfaction are closely related. Job satisfaction refers to all characteristics of the job itself and the work environment which salespeople find rewarding, fulfilling, and satisfying, or frustrating and unsatisfying.[28] The relationship between job satisfaction and motivation is positive in that satisfied salespersons will work harder than those who are not satisfied. Consequently, by replacing the aspects of the job and work environment that produce frustration and dissatisfaction with those that are capable of satisfying salespeople, sales managers can increase both job satisfaction and motivation. To this end, sales managers should regularly monitor the job satisfaction of their salespeople.

The relationship between job satisfaction and performance is more complex, and its direction has not yet been established. More specifically, what is not known is whether job satisfaction causes performance or performance causes job satisfaction. What is clear, however, is that sales managers should be concerned with the satisfaction of their salespeople and the important relationship between motivation, job satisfaction, and performance. High motivation of salespeople is a prerequisite for achieving high performance, and high job satisfaction is required for high motivation. Therefore, the interplay of these three very important components must be fully appreciated by sales managers who are responsible for motivating the global sales force.

## CHAPTER SUMMARY

Effective motivation of the sales force in today's global environment is one of the key success factors for every company. Motivation, which is the inner drive that energizes and directs the behavior of individuals, can be caused by the needs, values, and goals of salespeople. Motivation can also be caused by the consequences of a response. The theories that exist offer significant insights, although each theory examines motivated behavior from a different perspective. It is important that sales managers understand them and try to apply this knowledge effectively when attempting to motivate their sales force.

Motivating a global sales force successfully also requires a deep knowledge of the cultural differences of salespeople. Cultural differences dictate salespersons' needs, values, and goals and regulate, to a large extent, their behavior. These differences make the choice of an appropriate motivational tool a complex task. The range of different motivational tools allows sales managers the flexibility to design motivational programs that best fit the needs and goals of their global force. The job satisfaction of salespeople, as an important factor that is linked to motivation and performance, should also be understood and monitored by sales managers.

**173**

## DISCUSSION QUESTIONS

1 Define the three-dimensional construct of motivation and explain why it is important to sales managers.

2 Discuss the need theories of motivation and assess their explanation of motivated behavior.

3 Identify and explain the process theories of motivation. What question have these theories addressed?

4 What does the reinforcement theory postulate and how does it differ from the content and process theories?

5 What are the main motivational tools and how can cultural differences in a global sales force impact their effectiveness?

6 Explain job satisfaction and attempt to establish ways in which motivational tools can contribute to the job satisfaction or dissatisfaction of culturally diverse salespeople.

## REFERENCES

1 Farber, B.J. (1995), "Success Stories for Salespeople," *Sales and Marketing Management,* 147:5 (May), 30.

2 Weiner, Bernard (1980), *Human Motivation,* New York: Holt Rinehart & Winston.

3 Maslow, H.A. (1954), *Motivation and Personality,* New York: Harper & Row.

4 Herzberg, F. (1966), *Work and the Nature of Man,* Cleveland OH: World.

5 Alderfer, P.C. (1972), *Existence, Relatedness and Growth,* New York: Free Press.

6 Wahba, M.A., and L.G. Bridwell (1976), "Maslow Reconsidered: A Review of Research on the Need Hierarchy Theory," *Organisational Behaviour and Human Performance,* April, 212–40.

7 Handy, C.B. (1981), *Understanding Organisations,* second edition, London: Penguin Books.

8 Burt, N.D. (1984), "The Nuances of Negotiating Overseas," *Journal of Purchasing and Materials Management,* winter, 2–8.

9 Cron, L.W., J.A. Dubinsky, and E.R. Michaels (1988), "The Influence of Career Stages on Components of Salesforce Motivation," *Journal of Marketing,* January, 79–92.

10 Adams, J.S. (1963), "Toward an Understanding of Inequity," *Journal of Abnormal and Social Psychology,* November, 422–36.

11 Greenberg, G. (1989), "Cognitive Re-evaluation of Outcomes in Response to Underpayment Inequity," *Academy of Management Journal,* March, 174–84.

12 Elashmawi, F., and P.S. Harris (1998), *Multicultural Management 2000: Essential Cultural Insights for Global Business Success.* Houston TX: Gulf.

13 Vroom, V. (1964), *Work and Motivation,* New York: John Wiley & Sons.

14 Churchill, A.G., Jr, M. N. Ford, and C.O. Walker, Jr., (1976), "Motivating the Industrial Salesforce: The Alternative Rewards," Report No. 76–115, Cambridge, MA: Marketing Science Institute, p. 14.

 **174**

15 Kelley, H.H. (1971), *Attribution in Social Interaction*, Morristown NJ: General Learning Press.

16 Hoecklin, L. (1995), *Managing Cultural Differences: Strategies for Competitive Advantage*, EIU series, Reading MA: Addison Wesley.

17 Locke, A.E. (1968), "Toward a Theory of Task Performance and Incentives," *Organisation Behaviour and Human Performance*, 3, 157–89.

18 Garrison, T. (2001), *International Business Culture*, third edition, ELM Publications.

19 Campell, P.J., and D.R. Pritchard, (1976), "Motivation Theory in Industrial and Organisational Psychology," in D.M. Dunnette (ed.), *Handbook of Industrial and Organisational Psychology*, Chicago: Rand McNally, 63–130.

20 Skinner, F.B. (1953), *Science and Human Behavior*, New York: Macmillan.

21 Hampden-Turner, C., and F. Trompenaars (2000), *Building Cross-cultural Competence: How to Create Wealth from Conflicting Values*, New York: John Wiley & Sons, 11.

22 Simmons, F.G., Vasquez, C., and Harris, P. (1993), *Transcultural Leadership: Empowering the Diverse Workforce*, MCD series, Houston TX: Gulf.

23 Smyth, R.C., and M.J. Murphy (1969), *Compensating and Motivating Salesmen*, New York: American Management Association.

24 Anonymous (1984), "What Motivates Top Salespeople", *Psychology Today*, March, 6.

25 Terpstra V., and R. Sarathy (1994), *International Marketing*, sixth edition, Fort Worth TX: Dryden Press.

26 Brown, S., W. Cron, and T. Leigh (1993), "Do Feelings of Success Mediate Sales Performance–Work Related Attitude Relationships?" *Journal of the Academy of Marketing Science*, 21 (spring), 91–100.

27 Vogl, A.J. (1994), "Carrots, Sticks, and Self-deception", *Across the Board*, 31:1, 39.

28 Churchill, G.A., N.M. Ford, and O.C. Walker, Jr. (1974), "Measuring the Job Satisfaction of Industrial Salesmen," *Journal of Marketing Research*, 11 (August), 254–60.

## Chapter 11

# Compensating the global sales force

This chapter discusses compensation plans in the global marketplace and includes pay structures, sales contests, nonfinancial rewards, and expense plans.

## LEARNING OBJECTIVES

*After reading this chapter, you will be able to*:

- Explain why compensation is such an important determinant of sales force quality and performance.
- Compare and contrast the three types of compensation plans.
- Understand how ethical compensation issues impact the sales force.
- Explain how to design and manage a sales contest.
- Discuss how nonfinancial rewards can be merged with compensation plans to increase sales force job satisfaction.
- Compare and contrast the three types of sales expense plans.

## KEY TERMS

- Straight salary.
- Straight commission.
- Combination pay plan.
- Pay caps.
- Unlimited expense account.
- *Per diem* expense account.
- Limited expense account.

Compensating the sales force in the global marketplace is important for a number of reasons. This is because a compensation plan:

- Helps attract potential salespersons.
- Impacts a salesperson's motivation.
- Is a determinant of status and how the firm values the salesperson.
- Determines the lifestyle and purchasing power of a salesperson.

Thus compensation in the global marketplace is complex and affected by multiple forces. In response, most global compensation plans are a balance between company-specific policies, on one hand, and country-specific elements for salespersons working in different nations, on the other.[1]

Global firms offer total incentive packages to their global sales force, which includes financial and nonfinancial incentives. Financial incentives include salary, commission, bonus, stock options, and benefits. Financial incentives can also be earned through sales contests. Nonfinancial incentives relate to awards, recognition, vacation, and promotion or reassignment. In fact, interesting work and good career prospects may influence a person to accept a global sales position even when the compensation package is lower than expected.[2]

CASE VIGNETTE **DETERMINING A COMPENSATION PACKAGE**

Rajiv Mehta has worked as a salesperson for an Indian computer manufacturer for the past ten years. A global firm recently offered him a position as sales manager for ten countries in Southeast Asia. Given this new responsibility, he must move to the regional sales office in Singapore with his wife and three children. Rajiv is unsure about the compensation plan he has been offered. Does the plan pay him enough money to live on an equal level in Singapore as he can live in New Delhi? He also wonders about the cost of rental housing and international schooling for his children in Singapore. Mehta is very close to his family and wants to travel back to India regularly to check on their health and welfare. He would like to know where an individual can gain access to important compensation information.

## COMPENSATION PLANS

A wide range of compensation is paid for similar jobs in different countries (see Table 11.1). Because of disparate cultures, political and economic systems, traditions, and stages of development, it is difficult to accurately compare compensation levels across countries. The challenge for sales managers is to find the correct combination of financial and nonfinancial rewards for each locale.[3]

**Table 11.1** *District sales managers' compensation in selected global economies ($)*

| Country | 25th percentile | Median | 75th percentile | Bonus % pay | Benefits/ perks |
|---|---|---|---|---|---|
| Japan | 79,275 | 99,000 | 120,000 | 11.0 | 9.5 |
| Germany | 75,300 | 87,150 | 102,500 | 11.6 | 13.4 |
| UK | 60,800 | 69,200 | 79,300 | 9.4 | 20.3 |
| Hungary | 16,550 | 20,565 | 25,000 | 13.7 | 14.4 |
| Russia | 32,366 | 38,940 | 44,675 | 21.3 | 18.4 |
| Saudi Arabia | 45,900 | 51,075 | 57,000 | 11.7 | 25.9 |
| Brazil | 30,450 | 40,500 | 50,280 | 17.0 | 15.0 |
| US | 58,800 | 80,500 | 102,200 | 20.0 | 12.7 |

Watson Wyatt & Co., Washington DC, as of July 1, 1999. Reprinted by permission.

In some countries a salesperson receives a lower salary, but higher deferred income in the form of insurance and retirement funds. Since cultural practices and expectations vary greatly around the world, as discussed in Chapter 2, it is imprudent to simply transfer a compensation plan from one culture to another. Should a compensation plan be transferred directly among countries, without considering the cultural implications of such an action, the result would be quite different than intended. As constantly stated in this book: what works in one culture may be totally unacceptable in another culture.

A principal purpose of all compensation plans is to motivate employees to accomplish the managerial set goals. The first step is to determine the sales objectives of the company. Next, sales managers must assess how the sales force spends its time and how this behavior contributes to the achievement of the firm's sales objectives. If current sales activities do not support the firm's sales objectives, management has the ability and obligation to reconfigure pay plans to direct the sales force toward the goals set by management.

Organizations can select between three different types of compensation plans: *straight salary*, *straight commission*, and *combination plans* that include salary and commission/bonus components. Any pay plan can be appropriate, depending upon the specific marketplace situation and goals set by the firm and the sales manager. However, most US and European firms compensate their sales force through a combination pay plan. In this way, the firm leverages the positive aspects of each compensation plan to produce a more effective pay system than either the straight salary or straight commission systems are capable of individually. Now, let us look individually at each pay plan.

## Straight salary

A straight salary compensation system is time-related since the salesperson is paid a set amount of money for working a specific time frame. For example, a salesperson is paid a set amount every week, two weeks, or once a month for working set hours on the job. A straight salary compensation system may be adopted when the sales force must devote time to customer service, market research projects, and management and administrative duties rather than sales volume. It can also be appropriate to compensate a salesperson by straight salary when the salesperson is new or when selling is a team effort that makes it difficult to determine individual contribution.

A principal advantage of straight salary compensation plans is simplicity. It is easier for sales managers to budget and manage straight salary compensation plans. Also, when the sales force receives a straight salary, it is easier to reassign salespersons to a different sales territory, since their level of compensation remains constant.

The major shortcoming of all straight salary compensation systems is the lack of a direct link between salesperson contribution and the level of pay. Two salespersons could receive the same pay per period, even though one makes a more significant contribution to the firm. For this reason, many sales managers do not favor straight salary compensation plans.

However, national culture may dictate that senior employees are paid higher salaries than junior employees, even when they are less productive. Straight salary compensation systems are more prevalent in the European countries of the Netherlands, Italy, and France. While the employment of straight salary compensation plans may vary by country, industry, and position within the firm, pay practices are dictated by culture and tradition, which may be difficult for global managers to ignore[4] (see Exhibit 11.1).

## Straight commission

Firms that adopt straight commission pay plans are performance-oriented, because the salesperson is paid for sales results. The pay plan is very simple – each salesperson receives a percentage of what is sold. If the salesperson sells $100,000 in goods a month and receives a commission of 5 percent, then the salesperson's monthly pay is $5,000. Conversely, if

### EXHIBIT 11.1 MERIT PAY AROUND THE GLOBE

In some cultures sales personnel are compensated based upon their ability to produce for the firm. In other words, sales personnel are paid a commission or bonus based upon their ability to close the sale and produce revenue and profit for their company. In other cultures, however, compensation is influenced by other, less specific, variables. For example, in Korea, workers are compensated based upon their position or seniority in the firm. Korean workers rebel at the idea of performance-related pay. Workers in Korea regard their job title as a status symbol and find it unacceptable to be paid less than people who have been with the firm less time or who occupy lower positions in the firm's hierarchy. As might be expected, this type of worker mentality and bureaucratic pay system complicates the role of global firms who may prefer the Western practice of linking compensation to worker productivity.

*Source.* "Marrying an Alien: South Korean Restructuring," *Economist*, July 3–9, 1999, 56–7.

the salesperson is on vacation or is ill and sells $30,000 for the month, then the monthly compensation is $1,500. It is easy for sales managers and salespersons to observe the direct link between earned sales results and compensation. With a straight commission pay plan, management and the salesperson can both evaluate performance. Should a salesperson's salary not be as high as they would like, the solution is simple – the salesperson is told to work smarter or harder to increase their sales level and sales commission!

However, commission pay plans encompass an element of insecurity. In cultures that rank low on uncertainty avoidance – like most English-speaking countries – commission pay plans are more readily accepted than in cultures that seek to reduce uncertainty. Germany is an excellent example of a culture that tries to reduce uncertainty, and performance pay plans are less popular there. In Italy, where citizens are more accepting of different social and economic levels within the culture, a wider range of pay will be evident between executives and lower level workers. Conversely in Scandinavian countries, where egalitarianism is interwoven within the culture, compensation packages are more uniform between workers and management. One incentive scheme proposed by a company in Denmark was withdrawn because a group within the firm was favored and this was in contrast to the Danes' sense of egalitarianism.[5]

Japan is another country where commission selling has traditionally been viewed with skepticism. When NCR pioneered commission selling in Japan, many viewed the firm's attempts with astonishment. However, after more than a decade, NCR's sales have quadrupled in Japan and sales force acceptance of this pay system has improved. Now other Japanese firms are adopting commission compensation plans.[6] Perhaps, with proper planning, communication, and implementation, it is feasible to employ different compensation plans in other cultures.

There are also a number of potential disadvantages inherent in straight commission pay plans. First, since the salesperson is rewarded for closing sales the salesperson may be reluctant to engage in nonselling activities. Second, some salespersons may try to sell unneeded products at the end of the reporting period when sales goals have not been met. Third, salespersons may concentrate on existing customers – who can purchase more immediately – than taking the time to cultivate new accounts. Fourth, straight commission pay plans make it more difficult to predict monthly compensation, since pay can vary significantly from month to month. Perhaps the biggest shortcoming of straight commission compensation plans is that salespersons are responsible for generating their salary even though they have little or no control over pricing, the quality of the product, delivery, or competitor actions.

## Combination plans

Combination pay plans appear to be the most popular of the three presented in this chapter. For example, in the US printing industry more than 80 percent of sales professionals receive some level of commission as part of their compensation plan.[7] Most US industries employ similar levels of combination pay plans (see Table 11.2).

With a combination pay plan, a salesperson receives a base or straight salary component that is dependable and received regularly – weekly, biweekly, or monthly. In addition to base

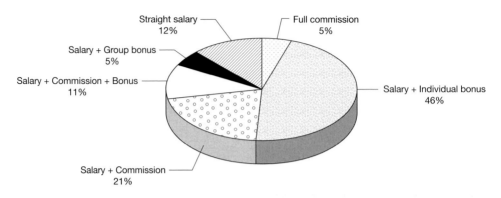

**Figure 11.1** *Firms' use of compensation plans*
*Source:* Alexander Group 1986/7 Sales Personnel Report, *New York, 1988*

**Table 11.2** *The world's most expensive cities*

| | |
|---|---|
| Tokyo, Japan | 164.9 |
| Osaka, Japan | 143.6 |
| Hong Kong, China | 141.5 |
| Beijing, China | 138.3 |
| Moscow, Russia | 136.1 |
| Shanghai, China | 128.0 |
| Seoul, South Korea | 111.1 |
| St. Petersburg, Russia | 109.7 |
| Guangzhou, China | 107.9 |
| London, England | 106.9 |
| Taipei, Taiwan | 102.8 |
| New York, USA | 100.0 |
| Hanoi, Vietnam | 94.9 |
| Singapore | 94.7 |

Source: William M. Mercer Cos., in *Virginian Pilot*, June 27, 2002, D1–D2

Note: The survey calculated the relative cost of living using more than 200 food, clothing, entertainment, and housing cost items

pay the salesperson can earn a commission or bonus that is based upon sales performance. One advantage of a combination pay plan is that it allows sales managers more flexibility with their sales force. For example, since the salesperson receives a base salary, the sales manager can assign salespersons to nonselling activities. Also, the combination pay plan provides financial security for salespersons because a basic level of pay will be received each pay period.

Combination pay plans assume many forms since commission can be paid on different products, total sales, new accounts opened, and reduced sales expenses. Higher rates of commission can also be paid as sales revenue or profitability increases. For example, commission of 5 percent may be paid on sales up to 100 percent of quota and of 6 percent for 101–10 percent; and 7 percent for all sales above 111 percent of quota. In this way, the salesperson is motivated to exceed forecasted sales levels. Firms can also add a bonus on top of commission when certain conditions are met, such as customer satisfaction levels or when a specified percentage increase in business occurs at major accounts. To earn both the commission and the bonus, the salesperson should have an exceptional year in which he or she satisfies the goals of both their firm and their customer base. However, combination pay plans can be more complex and difficult for the sales force to understand. Likewise, combination pay plans are more time-consuming for the sales manager to oversee.

## ETHICAL COMPENSATION ISSUES

There is a major dilemma when firms establish a compensation plan, because the firm attempts to hire the best salesperson at the lowest possible salary. In effect, this dilemma can cause a number of problems that are discussed below.

*Pay at, below, or above market salaries?* Most firms attempt to pay the going market salary. This practice may necessitate that the firm conduct surveys of the local marketplace and then offers the average pay level for that market. However, what should a firm pay a salesperson with the potential for sales performance that is either significantly above or slightly below average? A properly designed pay plan that provides avenues for earning additional compensation based upon commission may resolve this equity issue.

*Setting a cap on total pay.* A few firms set a cap or ceiling on sales compensation plans to prevent a salesperson from earning more than the sales manager or other senior managers. While in theory this approach may seem appropriate, the policy creates potential problems. First, why is the salesperson not being compensated for his or her contribution to the success of the firm? Second, at what level of work will the salesperson perform late in the year when they have maximized their pay? Is it ethical for the salesperson to be forced to work at the end of the year without having the ability to earn compensation? A maximum pay policy suggests that the compensation plan is not properly constructed. Pay caps also erode trust between management and the sale force.[8]

*Assigning territories.* If a firm pays a significant portion of compensation based upon commission, then salespersons must be assigned to territories that have adequate sales potential. Said differently, it is unethical to assign better territories to one salesperson rather than another unless there is a company policy that higher-potential territories are to be assigned to senior sales representatives. Otherwise, the salesperson will have little chance of reaching the goals set by the firm, regardless of the effort put forth.

*Team versus individual incentives.* In some cultures, like the United States, salespersons are viewed as individuals who alone are in control of their destiny in accomplishing sales goals. This cultural expectation has resulted in US compensation being based upon individual accomplishment. More and more today, compensation plans are viewed as team effort that requires group cooperation. Team incentives are employed more often in Asian cultures, while being utilized less in individualistic countries.

*Frequency of paying commissions.* The interval or frequency of being paid sales commission varies by firm. Guidance, from a behavioral standpoint, suggests that the sooner a salesperson is rewarded for the desired behavior the greater the probability of repeat behavior. When a long period elapses between the time the sale was made and the time the salesperson receives payment for this accomplishment, positive reinforcement is withheld.

*Pay discrimination*. In some cultures, firms pay certain members of society less. For example, in the United States, women may receive a lower starting salary than an equally qualified man. Numerous explanations are offered for this disparity, but global sales firms understand that pay discrimination that is based upon sex, race, or age is morally difficult to defend. Pay should be based upon an individual's contribution to the firm and sales careers provide opportunities for individuals to earn a salary based upon their ability to succeed. If the management of the company is unwise and fails to recognize the contribution being made by a successful salesperson, it is relatively easy for that salesperson to secure a higher paying position elsewhere!

## SALES CONTESTS

Sales contests are short-term incentive programs that are implemented to motivate salespersons to accomplish specific sales goals or activities. In effect, sales contests provide the sales force with an opportunity to gain additional financial resources in the form of cash, prizes, or trips, while receiving nonfinancial recognition awards.

For sales contests to be successful, a number of things must occur:

- Objectives must be specific and clearly defined.
- The contest theme must be exciting and well communicated.
- Each salesperson must perceive they have an opportunity to be a winner.
- The list of awards must be attractive to the participants.
- The contest must be promoted and managed properly.

### Contest objectives

Before implementing a sales contest, managers must set contest objectives. The two most frequent sales contest objectives are increase sales revenue and increase specific product sales.[9] Less popular contest objectives include increased market penetration, increased market share, new product introduction, focusing on higher profit accounts, and overcoming seasonal sales slumps. No matter, sales contest objective(s), should be specific and clearly defined for the sales force.

Also, the length of the sales contest should be sufficient to allow the sales force to contact customers and have a reasonable period to reach the objective(s) of the contest. For most firms this means the sales contest will last approximately three months. It is imperative that all rules, exceptions, and other information about the contest be clearly stated to the sales force prior to the start of the competition.

### Contest theme

Most sales contests receive a theme, in an effort to create enthusiasm for the competition and to promote the event. Themes may be sports-related such as "World Cup" or location-related such as "Spanish Holiday." The sports themes suggest competition and the location topic implies the grand prize of the contest.

## Chance of winning

It is important that every salesperson perceive that they have a fair chance of winning the sales contest. Otherwise salespersons will not be motivated to actively participate. Firms must structure the sales contest to insure maximum participation and effort. Therefore, participants must be able to win something if they achieve the objectives set by management.

Sales contests assume one of three forms. The first is *competing against yourself*, in which the salesperson works to increase total sales revenue or total product sales over the amount that was sold during a previous time period. For example, management may set a quota of increasing total sales by 10 percent over the previous quarter. The second contest form is *team competition*. In this scenario, the sales force is divided equally into a number of teams that compete to see which team can make the greatest contribution toward achieving or exceeding the objective set by management. A team structure creates peer pressure among members and motivates individuals to increase their sales efforts so as not to disappoint fellow team members. Team competition appears to work best in collectivist societies. The final category of sales contests occurs when *all salespersons compete against one another*. Managers may set individual goals depending upon past performance and territory potential or simply look for the largest contributors toward reaching the contest's objective(s). It is this last scenario, where it is vitally important that managers structure the contest to insure each salesperson has a reasonable chance to be a contest winner. Most firms insure there is ample opportunity for a number of salespersons to win a prize for their efforts. One US study found that the average salesperson had a 30–40 percent chance of being a winner in a sales contest.[10]

## Types of rewards

Sales contests offer participants rewards in the form of cash, prizes, or travel. More than three-quarters (77 percent) of companies utilize cash prizes, 61 percent offer prizes, and 60 percent provide travel awards.[11] The key is to select rewards that are valued by the sales force. For example travel to desirable locations, such as Disneyland, in southern California, may be viewed as a valued reward by a Japanese salesperson. But this would not be the case for a salesperson based in Los Angeles. Cash rewards are easy to administer, but the salesperson may spend the money paying debts or meals. Thus the cash has little long-term significance. Because of this, firms award televisions, VCRs, cellular phones, and other items that remind the salesperson of their success in previous sales contests. A final aspect of reward is the perceived value. That is, the prize must be of sufficient value to motivate the salesperson to expend additional effort toward winning the reward.

## Promotion and management of contests

Firms normally launch sales contests with a highly publicized special event. An example might be that a meeting room at a local hotel is decorated in the theme of the contest – "The World

Cup." All sales team members are required to attend the event, where they find managers and workers dressed in soccer and referee uniforms. The contest rules are explained to everyone over a meal and drinks, perhaps served similarly to refreshments sold in the soccer stadium. Then the sales team is presented with reminders of the prizes available for winners of the contest in the form of notebooks, soccer ball key chains, posters, and scorecards. In this way, the sales contest is promoted and the sales team learns the rules and becomes motivated to participate in and win the contest.

Large scorecards for each sales team are posted in sales offices to show the progressing sales scores until the end of the contest. Additional promotion during the contest can take the form of newsletter articles and smaller prizes being awarded at the end of each discrete event period. It is also important for participants to receive feedback about their ranking in the contest. At the conclusion of the contest, it is imperative for winners to be recognized and for awards to be presented as soon as possible. For example, if the top five salespersons win a trip to the World Cup championship game, this should be publicized in both local and firm newspapers.

## Sales contest concerns

While sales managers believe that sales contests are a great way to motivate the sales team and increase sales productivity, there are also a number of concerns about this process. Most concerns fall into the categories of poor design and implementation, impact on sales team morale, and the shifting of sales from one period to another.

It is important that sales managers effectively design and implement sales contests; otherwise, the sales contest will consume a tremendous amount of time, energy, and expense and will not result in the achievement of contest objectives. To increase the probability of success, a number of private firms can be hired to manage sales contests for organizations.

When firms fail to follow contest rules or have a "winner take all" contest, this can result in reduced morale among those who are not contest winners. As one manager remarked: "Our sales contest produced one winner and ninety-nine losers!" To prevent this from happening, everyone who participates in the contest may be eligible to win a prize or reward even if it is of nominal value. A sales contest should be a motivating, rather than demotivating activity.

There is also some question of sales contests being able to generate significant additional sales revenue. Sales contests suggest that the sales force simply needs to work harder or smarter to sell its products to existing customers. Some critics state that sales contests result in the sales force withholding orders until the contest begins, customers placing orders that are returned at the conclusion of the contest, and unneeded pressure being placed on customers to "help" their friendly salesperson. When a customer obliges and stocks up during the contest, sales may be lower during the next sales period. Therefore, an important question is: do sales contests result in sales revenue being shifted from one sales period to another?

Finally, compensation experts warn that a firm that depends upon sales contests to reach sales goals violates a number of principles. First, when sales contests are employed, the sales force is being paid twice for doing the same job. Second, if sales contests are short-term incentive programs, then why are they employed continually? Firms that engage in perpetual sales contests may need to conduct a compensation audit to examine their entire compensation and incentive program.[12]

## NONFINANCIAL INCENTIVES

The sales job requires sales managers to address different levels of human needs. Sales managers agree that salary is an important incentive; however, the nonfinancial compensation aspects discussed below can contribute to the success of the salesperson.

### Ability to grow

Many global salespersons today are looking for positions that offer both financial and career growth. For example, a company may hire the new salesperson as a Territory Manager. After completing all training requirements, attending certain elective classes, and satisfying stated performance conditions, the salesperson is promoted to Senior Territory Manager. Then, after a specified time period, more training, and meeting other agreed upon accomplishments, the salesperson can be promoted to Executive Account Manager. In this way, a company can have two career tracks for sales personnel – one within the sales path and the other a managerial track. Each time the salesperson is promoted, they receive higher pay and additional responsibility within the firm.

### Recognition programs

Recognition programs often take the form of letters of appreciation, salesperson of the month, quarter and year awards. Salespersons can also be elected to select groups, such as the "Million Dollar Club," "President's Circle," and "Platinum Group." Recognition programs are established to raise the status of the salesperson within the organization and motivate effort to gain and retain this status. These recognition programs should be difficult to attain for the majority of salespersons, but they should not be so difficult that only a few salespersons can gain membership in the programs.

A letter of appreciation demonstrates that the salesperson's efforts are recognized and appreciated. For example, the salesperson may have worked over the weekend to complete a large request for quotation (RFQ) for a major customer. Depending upon cultural practices, the letter may or may not be presented at a formal meeting of the sales force. However, the letter should be placed in the salesperson's file and discussed at the time of the next performance review.

Firms may recognize their highest performer by designating a "Salesperson of the Month." Then, at the end of three months, one of the monthly winners is selected as the "Salesperson of the Quarter." Likewise, each of the quarterly winners is eligible to be accorded the title "Salesperson of the Year." Sales personnel must understand the criteria utilized by the sales manager in making these selections. In this way, salespersons have the ability to earn such recognition. In some cultures, recognition programs must acknowledge the accomplishments of the entire sales team rather than singling out an individual salesperson[13]

**187**

Many companies, particularly in Western societies, recognize select groups – such as the top 10 percent of all sales personnel. A salesperson who earns a title such as "Member of the Round Table" has concluded a significant amount of sales activity and has been recommended by management for this award. With the award, the salesperson and spouse receive an all-expenses-paid trip to a holiday location where they are formally recognized and presented with tangible signs of the award, such as rings, lapel pins, pen and pencil sets, and plaques. Additional recognition is provided by pictures and stories in the company newsletter/magazine/web site and on the recipient's business cards.

## Opportunity to travel

Global firms are able to compensate their top sales force performers by providing international travel to them. It may be difficult for salespersons to afford the time or expense of a trip to Europe, Japan, or the United States on their own resources. Global firms can send their best salespersons for a trip to headquarters in Paris and then provide tickets and other perquisites for EuroDisney. Companies may offer incentive trips for the entire sales team that has performed well during a specific period of time.

## Educational assistance

Many firms today provide educational or tuition assistance to their sales personnel. In this way, the firm pays either all or a portion (e.g. 75 percent) of the tuition charged for legitimate undergraduate or graduate college level courses. Some firms reimburse differently, based upon performance in a class. Additional formal education is important for today's global salespersons and firms believe this benefit is greatly appreciated by the salesperson. However, as salespersons attain additional formal education, the probability that they will seek a different type of position also increases.

## SALES EXPENSE PLANS

While paying for a global salesperson's expenses is different from salary plans, this area is linked with individual compensation in many ways. For example, when a global salesperson is posted in another country the firm must pay for numerous incidental expenses generated by the new assignment. These expenses, for expatriates and third country salespersons, include: family travel, children's education at international schools, spousal employment, housing, auto leasing or shipment, servants or household assistance when entertaining, membership fees at clubs, entertainment accounts, and storing assets in the home or third country. This may explain why global firms attempt to maximize the number of global sales force members that are local hires.

Sales expense plans can assume one of three forms: unlimited expense plan, *per diem* or per day plan, or limited expense plan. The primary goal of every expense plan is to reimburse the sales force for legitimate expenses. Properly constructed expense plans should result in the salesperson receiving exact reimbursement for what was expended on behalf of the firm. In other words, reimbursement should be expense neutral – the salesperson should neither lose, nor gain, from the reimbursement process. Each expense plan is discussed in detail below:

## Unlimited expense plan

An unlimited expense plan means that all legitimate expenses incurred by the global salesperson are reimbursed 100 percent. This plan has a number of advantages. First, the plan communicates that the sales force is trusted to spend necessary company resources to gain business. This means that the salesperson can spend sums, within reason, to secure business from existing and potential clients. Second, it is not necessary to quibble about every expense with the sales force, which allows the sales manager to focus on more important duties. Third, the salesperson is unable to complain that business could have been secured if only another trip or dinner had been invested in the relationship.

Obviously, global salespersons must spend the firm's money like it was their own. This means that the salesperson should be ethical and prudent in their sales activities. A global salesperson can spend large amounts of money entertaining clients in Tokyo, Paris, London, or Johannesburg. However, the salesperson must limit these activities to a frequency that maintains relationships within the comfort zone. Likewise, salespersons must be ethical with their personal expenses and not pad or exaggerate expense reports in order to earn extra money. Sales managers must oversee unlimited sales force expense plans, while not being too restrictive on the sales force. Some firms provide guidelines for entertaining and spending company funds. For example, companies may refuse to pay for alcohol, female escorts or hostesses, or other activities. The level of expenses and expected levels and forms of entertainment will vary by culture. In Japan, businessmen spend large amounts of money entertaining business associates from other countries. This may include thousands of dollars that are spent at sushi restaurants and at karaoke parlors. In other cultures these types of expenses are not reimbursable.

## *Per diem* expense plan

A *per diem* expense plan means the salesperson is provided a set amount of money for each day they are in the field on behalf of the firm. For example, a firm in the global marketplace may allocate $250 per day for business expenses when the salesperson is calling on current or potential customers. The *per diem* plan has advantages for the firm, because the amount of sales force expenses can be approximately computed by multiplying the actual or anticipated number of selling days in the field times the approved *per diem* rate. This means if the sales force is expected to call upon customers 500 days next year, the expense will be (500 times $250) $125,000 a year for the sales force.

However, setting a single *per diem* rate will not work in the myriad places salespersons must travel. As seen in Table 11.3, larger cities in Japan and China are rated the most expensive for travelers. Given the wide disparity in travel expenses around the globe, some multinational firms annually set different *per diem* rates for all their business locations. This system permits the firm to tailor the sales force expense plan to the cities visited. But this type of system is more complicated and expensive to keep current and accurate. Firms like

**189**

**Table 11.3** *Average salesperson expenses (Can. $$^a$)* *(Montreal, Canada)*

| Lodging | | |
| --- | --- | --- |
| Expense | Average | Range |
| Single rack | 193.50 | 167.50 – 234.00 |
| US $ | 125.00 | 108.00 – 151.00 |
| Double rack | 195.50 | 176.50 – 236.00 |
| US $ | 126.00 | 114.00 – 152.00 |
| Single corporate | 173.00 | 153.50 – 200.50 |
| US $ | 111.50 | 99.00 – 129.50 |
| *Meals* | | |
| Breakfast | 15.10 | 12.30 – 18.45 |
| US $ | 9.75 | 7.95 – 11.90 |
| Lunch | 15.05 | 13.00 – 17.40 |
| US $ | 9.70 | 8.40 – 11.20 |
| Dinner | 30.30 | 25.95 – 38.00 |
| US $ | 19.55 | 16.75 – 24.50 |
| *Three meal total* | 60.45 | |
| US $ | 39.00 | |
| *Total per diem$^b$* | 253.95 | |
| US $ | 164.00 | |

Source: Permission granted by Runzheimer International, *Guide to Daily Travel Prices,* © 2002

Notes: *a* US$ = 1.5507 (August 2002) *b* Single rack lodging and three meals

Runzheimer International report *per diem* rates for major cities annually, which permits firms in the global marketplace to set or adjust *per diem* rates.

## Limited expense plan

When limited expense plans are utilized, the firm sets a specific maximum or limit on each major expense category that will be covered daily. For example, $125 for hotel lodging, $50 for meals, $30 for a rental auto, and $20 for miscellaneous items such as taking a client to lunch or for laundry services. Limited expense plans allow the firm to compute the upper limit for sales force travel expenses.

Like *per diem* rates, limited expense plans must be constantly updated and they should vary based upon the city or area visited. The major complaint with limited expense plans is that the salesperson must spend time insuring that the daily limit set for each category is not exceeded. Some salespeople try to compensate for inadequate upper limits in one category by borrowing money from another category. For example, if the hotel room costs $135 per day or $10 above the maximum for that expense, the salesperson may eat at lower cost restaurants and then claim a higher than actual expense for food. In effect, the salesperson's attention is diverted away from providing satisfactory service to or solving problems for the customer to compensate for a faulty expense plan.

Expense plans are important and the global sales manager must maintain constant oversight of how the firm's money is being expended. This is because of the basic business equation of: revenues – expenses = profits. This means that every dollar, pound, or yen of expense money saved is profit for the global sales firm. The sales manager should demand that the global salesperson put forth every legitimate effort to secure business from profitable accounts. And, when the salesperson travels on official business, it is normal for all *bona fide* expenses to be paid. Problems arise when the sales force is not aware of or does not understand what is an allowable expense. Sales managers can reduce these misunderstandings through sales training seminars, information sheets that provide company policy and guidance, and through personal counseling of the sales force.

## CHAPTER SUMMARY

Compensation of the sales force determines the quality of salesperson the global firm can hire, as well as the motivation of the salesperson once out in the field. The global firm can choose between three types of salary plans – straight salary, straight commission, and combination pay plan – to compensate its salespersons. Each of these pay plans has advantages and disadvantages and may be appropriate for given market conditions. Many firms find the combination pay plan to work best, because the salesperson receives the security of base pay with provision for earning additional amounts through incentives and bonuses.

In some countries compensation is culturally or legally influenced and components may vary significantly to avoid taxes. This makes it difficult to directly compare salaries paid between countries and firms. What is important is the *total* compensation package received by the global salesperson.

Firms utilize sales contests to motivate the sales force in the short term. To be successful, sales contests must address a number of details to increase the probability of success. Contests generally focus on increasing an aspect of sales revenue and reward participants with cash, prizes, or travel. Some experts question whether sales contests are truly effective and whether sales generated by contests are borrowed from future sales periods.

Salespersons are also compensated through nonfinancial incentives such as recognition, opportunity to travel to exotic locations, the ability to grow, and the job itself. Recognition, through such means as letters of appreciation, salesperson or sales team of the quarter, or being elected to elite sales clubs can all be used to compensate the salesperson for a job well done.

Salespersons work in the field conducting business for the global firm. Most firms reimburse the salesperson for legitimate and acceptable expenses incurred on behalf of the firm. In this chapter three types of expense plans are discussed that include: unlimited, *per diem*, and limited. The question that sales managers must ask themselves is what should the

**191**

salesperson spend time on – working with the customer or trying to balance activities to minimize travel expenses. The optimal answer is that the salesperson should be able to do both, but it is management's responsibility to make travel rules simple enough that the salesperson is not consumed trying to comply with the policies of the firm.

## DISCUSSION QUESTIONS

1 How do compensation systems affect the type of people that are attracted to a sales position and, more important, why they remain with the firm?
2 What are the advantages of each pay plan? The disadvantages?
3 Which pay plan would work best for a software firm that is the market leader?
4 Is there a connection between the ethical practices of management, regarding pay matters, and the ethical behavior of the sales force? What is it?
5 How would you design a sales contest to increase the number of new customers for your firm? What actions are necessary to increase the success rate of contests?
6 How might you use nonfinancial incentives to compensate the sales force?
7 What is the purpose of expense plans? Compare and contrast the advantages and disadvantages of the three expense plans covered in this chapter.

## REFERENCES

1 Logger, Ed, Rob Vinke, and Frits Kluytmans (1995), "Compensation and Appraisal in an International Perspective," in Anne-Wil Harzing and Joris Van Ruysseveldt (eds), *International Human Resource Management*, London: Sage Publications, 144–55.

2 Vinke, R.H.W. (1993), *Handboek belonen*, Deventer: Kluwer.

3 Terpsra, Vern, and Ravi Sarathy (1997), *International Marketing*, Fort Worth TX: Dryden Press.

4 Vinke, R.H.W., and Thierry, H. (1985), *Flexible belonen: van cafetariaplan naar praktijk*, Deventer: Kluwer.

5 Schneider, S.C. (1988), "National versus Corporate Culture: Implications for Human Resource Management," *Human Resource Management*, 27:2, 231–46.

6 Terpsra and Sarathy (1997).

7 Anonymous (1998), "Salespeople and Compensation," Chicago: American Printer.

8 Strout, Erin (2000), "What's Your Sales Superstar Worth?" *Sales and Marketing Management*, January, 71.

9 *Current Practices in Sales Incentives* (1988), New York: Alexander Group.

10 *Current Practices in Sales Incentives* (1988).

11 *Current Practices in Sales Incentives* (1988).

12  Wildt, Albert R., James D. Parker, and Clyde E. Harris, Jr. (1987), "Assessing the Impact of Sales Force Contests: An Application," *Journal of Business Research*, 15, 145–55.

13  Honeycutt, Earl D., Jr., John B. Ford, and Lew Kurtzman (1996), "Potential Problems and Solutions when Hiring and Training a Worldwide Sales Team," *Journal of Business and Industrial Marketing*, 11:1 (May), 42–54.

## Chapter 12

# Evaluation in the global marketplace

This chapter presents ways to evaluate the sales force and individual salespersons.

## LEARNING OBJECTIVES

*After reading this chapter, you will be able to*:

- Provide reasons for evaluating the sales force and individual salespersons.
- Discuss differences that exist in local and global evaluation efforts.
- List the advantages and disadvantages of sales, cost, and profitability analysis.
- Understand the relationship of the four areas assessed in performance appraisals.
- Compute sales volume per call, order per call, and average cost per call ratios.
- Detail the different evaluation techniques utilized to rate the sales force.
- Explain why "informal" evaluation is harmful to the sales force.
- Discuss the impact and importance of minimizing assessment bias.

## KEY TERMS

- Sales, cost, and profit analysis.
- Informal and formal evaluation.
- Activities, outcomes, profitability, and professional development criteria.
- Management by Objectives (MBO).
- Behaviorally anchored rating scales (BARS).

## INTRODUCTION

Sales managers plan, implement, and control sales activities. In order to control activities that lead to the attainment of planned goals, evaluation must occur. For example, if a sales force goal is to increase the number of new customers by 10 percent in six months, the sales manager must monitor progress toward that goal. Without evaluation, it is difficult to know what has worked, what has not, and why. When evaluating, the sales manager must pause, reflect on what has happened, and learn from this experience. Since market and competitor conditions change rapidly, managers must monitor past decisions to identify ways to improve future performance.

The purpose of evaluation is to improve salesperson and ultimately firm performance. Without accurate sales force information, control decisions tend to be weak and haphazard.[1] Therefore, through evaluation and assessment efforts, sales managers can gain important information and more effectively control the sales force by:

- Identifying recruiting criteria.
- Determining training and counseling needs.
- Providing information for human resource planning.
- Motivating salespersons.
- Setting work expectations.
- Tying compensation/rewards to actual salesperson performance.
- Identifying individuals for promotion or termination.
- Helping salespersons set career goals.
- Identifying firm and individual deviations from targeted goals.
- Determining the cause of identified deviations.

Comprehensive evaluations investigate whether identified deviations are attributable to incorrectly set goals or weak performance in reaching those goals. That is, did the sales force fail or were inappropriate goals set?[2] Evaluations differ, and vary in form and content, depending upon their purpose. For example, if the goal of the evaluation is to reward the salesperson, then the focus should be on such salesperson activities and results as sales revenue, new business, or profitability. Conversely, if the purpose of assessment is to identify promotion potential, then evaluation criteria should examine factors related to success as a sales manager.

Firms may already assess such marketing activities as sales training and advertising. Even so, it is important to evaluate the sales force in order to spotlight situations that are less transparent in specific evaluation efforts. The purpose of this chapter is to explain sales force evaluation in the global marketplace. First, a short discussion of evaluation in the global marketplace is provided. Second, directions for evaluating sales force activities and outcomes, with the goal of identifying deviations from standard or expected performance, are presented. Finally performance appraisal, that involves four areas of individual salesperson assessment, is discussed.

CASE VIGNETTE **SHOULD EVALUATIONS DIFFER IN ASIA?**

Ferdinand Roxas, a Filipino-American sales manager for Logicom in San Francisco, has five salespersons that report to him in Southeast Asia. That is, a Logicom salesperson resides in Singapore, the Philippines, Taiwan, Vietnam, and Thailand. Roxas must decide if the company's US evaluation system should be employed in Asia. Although all five current salespersons were formally educated at US universities, Roxas wonders if a customized assessment process would be more appropriate for the firm's Southeast Asian sales force?

## GLOBAL EVALUATION GUIDANCE

Evaluation is important in global sales operations because management can identify markets that are performing below expectations and adjust training, compensation, or strategy to improve performance.[3] Assessing sales personnel in the global marketplace is a more complex undertaking than the process in the home country, because individual ability to adjust to local conditions and culture differs significantly.[4] For example, in collectivist societies, teamwork is favored over individual accomplishment. In these cultures evaluation involves close observation and inputs from customers, colleagues, and managers, whereas individual performance is perceived to be less important.[5] In Japan, salespersons receive a greater sense of performance from the group than what occurs in individualistic cultures.[6] Global evaluation criteria most often include technical ability, cultural empathy, adaptability, flexibility, diplomacy, and language ability.[7] However, in the global marketplace, cultural skills appear to be more relevant than technical and managerial capabilities.[8]

Global assessment requires a system that is accessible, easy to understand, equitable, and motivating for salespersons, regardless of culture or nationality. Also, since global firms employ internal transfer pricing and assign each division a specific role that maximizes total firm profits, financial evaluation metrics may be less appropriate evaluation criteria. Second, when global salespersons reside distant from headquarters, evaluations must be conducted from afar. Even with advances in information technology, the field behavior of salespersons may be unknown to the evaluator. Finally, local and third-country salespersons may view their role with the firm to be temporary; thus their efforts are short-term in nature.[9]

## EVALUATING SALES FORCE PERFORMANCE

In general, sales managers evaluate overall sales force performance by analyzing sales, cost, and profit data. Different evaluations are necessary because no one measure of sales force effectiveness exists. That is, since firms set myriad goals, multiple measures must be employed to assess company objectives. The three most common forms of analysis are discussed below.

## Sales analysis

Sales analysis consists of gathering, sorting, assessing, and making decisions based upon company sales data. Firms routinely gather sales information for accounting purposes, which means that the data are not organized in a form that is amenable to sales analysis. No matter, as shown in Table 12.1, the sales manager must insure the data are organized so that market and salesperson deviations are evident. In global markets, it is important to know how markets are performing in comparison with last year, but also in contrast to one another.[10] Sales analysis examines products, customers, markets, areas, organizational units, order size, method of sale, terms of sale, selling strategy employed, and time period. Sources of information include company records, sales reports, managers' field reports, and customer feedback.[11]

Sales data are generally the most readily available, since firms collect and record this type of information with each purchase. To analyze the information, companies need only attach customer and salesperson numbers to the products sold. Sales data are also deemed to be an important area to track, since the sales force is responsible for increasing customer demand and reaching sales goals set by management. Because of this, sales analysis provides important feedback for managers to gauge sales force performance.

Managers must insure that two points related to sales are standardized. First, it is important to consistently define the term "sold." That is, some firms define "sold" as when the item is ordered, others when the product is shipped, and still others when the customer actually pays for the product. Second, when conducting sales analysis, it is significant to examine sales in the local currency – dollars, pounds, yen, or euros – and units sold. In times of inflation or stagnant sales, firms can increase sales revenue but actually sell fewer items. By analyzing both sales revenue and units sold, a sales manager can more clearly understand the market situation.

## Cost analysis

The second area of sales force evaluation is cost analysis, which focuses on the relationship between costs incurred and sales generated. As seen in Table 12.2, cost analysis allows the sales manager to calculate the variance between actual and budgeted expenses for sales regions. Those regions where the actual costs far exceed budgeted costs should be set aside for further analysis. This does not mean that variations are either good or bad, only that they should be investigated to understand the differences uncovered. Sales costs are often stated as a percentage of sales, which permits managers to assess whether the sales–cost relationship has been preserved. For example, if sales expenses were 5 percent of sales revenue this year, this method makes it easy to tell if the ratio of expense to sales remained the same in subsequent time periods.

Cost data allow a firm to set pricing levels, budgets, and sales commission rates. This type of analysis also permits a firm to determine which products cost more to sell, whether the cost of a sales call is increasing, and when it is time to modify commission rates for product classes. Because of the availability of data, sales and cost analyses are the two most frequently used methods of evaluating sales force effectiveness. When firm orientation shifts from sales volume to profitability, cost analysis becomes even more important.

**Table 12.1a**

*Sales analysis (a): by region ($)*

| Region | Quota | Actual | Difference | Performance (%) |
|---|---|---|---|---|
| North America | 4,861,500 | 4,948,920 | 87,420 | 102.0 |
| Europe | 5,093,000 | 5,209,880 | 116,880 | 102.0 |
| Asia/Australia | 4,167,000 | 4,147400 | −19,600 | 99.5 |
| South America | 3,588,250 | 3,425,100 | −163,150 | 95.0 |
| Middle East/Africa | 3,472,500 | 3,698,875 | 226,375 | 107.0 |
| Total | 21,182,250 | 21,430,175 | 247,925 | 101.0 |

*Sales analysis (b): South America, by salesperson ($)*

| Salesperson | Quota | Actual | Difference | Performance (%) |
|---|---|---|---|---|
| Alberto (Peru) | 804,000 | 810,000 | +6,000 | 101 |
| Xavier (Brazil) | 868,000 | 851,000 | −17,000 | 98 |
| Claudia (Venezuela) | 609,000 | 631,000 | +22,000 | 104 |
| Juan (Paraguay) | 592,000 | 416,000 | −176,000 | 70 |
| Julio (Colombia) | 345,000 | 345,000 | 0 | 100 |
| Maria (Argentina) | 370,000 | 372,000 | +2,000 | 103 |
| Total | 3,588,000 | 3,425,000 | −163,000 | 95 |

*Sales analysis (c): Juan Valdes, by product ($)*

| Product | Quota | Actual | Difference | Performance (%) |
|---|---|---|---|---|
| A | 143,000 | 149,000 | 6,000 | 104 |
| B | 244,000 | 160,000 | −84,000 | 66 |
| C | 118,000 | 42,000 | −76,000 | 36 |
| D | 87,000 | 65,000 | −22,000 | 75 |
| Total | 592,000 | 416,000 | −176,000 | 70 |

## Profit analysis

When firms combine sales and cost data, it is possible to compute profitability. The equation sales − costs = profits confirms that lower costs result in higher profits. Profit analysis permits the sales manager to identify unprofitable territories and customer segments, evaluate territory and product performance, and calculate year-end bonuses for the sales force. Profitability analysis is easier to conduct with advanced information technology and has become more important as firms follow a relationship marketing approach to business. However, fewer firms analyze sales force profitability than sales and cost analyses.

**199**

**Table 12.2** Cost analysis for sales force compensation and training

| Region | Compensation costs | | | Training costs | | |
|---|---|---|---|---|---|---|
| | Budgeted ($) | Actual ($) | Variance | Budgeted ($) | Actual ($) | Variance |
| | | | *Dollar cost* | | | |
| North America | 429,000 | 472,500 | 43,500 | 237,600 | 263,250 | 25,650 |
| Europe | 396,000 | 411,750 | 15,750 | 113,300 | 110,812 | (2,488) |
| Asia/Australia | 407,000 | 393,750 | (13,250) | 224,400 | 237,375 | 12,975 |
| South America | 374,000 | 354,375 | (19,625) | 116,600 | 93,375 | (23,225) |
| Middle East/ Africa | 308,550 | 301,218 | (7,332) | 96,195 | 79,368 | (16,827) |
| Total | 1,914,550 | 1,933,593 | 19,043 | 788,095 | 784,180 | (3,915) |
| | | | *As percent of sales* | | | |
| North America | 9.5 | 8.7 | | 5.3 | 4.8 | |
| Europe | 7.9 | 7.6 | | 2.1 | 2.2 | |
| Asia/Australia | 9.5 | 9.8 | | 5.7 | 5.4 | |
| South America | 10.3 | 10.9 | | 2.7 | 3.4 | |
| Middle East/Africa | 8.1 | 8.3 | | 2.1 | 2.6 | |
| Total | 9.0 | 8.9 | | 3.7 | 3.7 | |

## Conducting sales, cost, and profit analyses

Analyzing sales, cost, and profit information consists of a three-step process:

- *Identify the needed information.* Management conducts analyses that provide information deemed to be important. This means that the sales manager must clearly identify the decision at hand. Within this decision, the manager must also decide how to subdivide sales, cost, and profit data to reveal the origin of sales force deviation(s).
- *Establish procedures.* This next step includes identifying the sources of data and compiling the results into useful reports. Firms collect data from either the accounting or the information systems functional areas and sales managers must clearly communicate their need for specific information to these functional areas. In some firms, sales managers can directly access needed information contained in existing decision support or customer relationship management (CRM) systems.
- *Analyze the results.* Sales, cost, and profit analyses are performed to identify areas that require further investigation. This means that identified deviations from forecasts or expectations, either positive or negative, are set aside for further examination. Once identified management must conduct additional research to determine whether goals

**200**

were incorrectly set or sales force performance was below expectation. Customer relationship management systems also provide managers with an ability to perform "what if" analyses to see how outcomes might have differed based upon alternative price changes or reassigned sales effort. Sales managers can also employ spreadsheets and software available in the marketplace to better understand the situation.

## PERFORMANCE APPRAISAL

The second area of evaluation is the assessment of individual sales force members. Most firms conduct individual performance appraisal on a regular schedule. For example, salespersons receive evaluations at the end of the calendar or the fiscal year. A few companies assess sales personnel two or more times a year, while some firms do not formally evaluate their sales force at all!

The following evaluation practices have been reported:

- Most firms examine both quantitative and qualitative input and output criteria. However, greater emphasis is placed upon output measures like sales revenue.
- Salesperson input is sought, to varying degrees, when setting quotas or standards.
- Sales objectives receive different weights based upon activities and territories.
- Companies gather multiple sources of information to perform evaluations.
- Field sales managers, who supervise the salesperson, conduct most evaluations.
- Most salespersons receive a written evaluation conducted in an office setting.[12]

Salesperson appraisals should cover a wide range of areas, since the salesperson's responsibilities are so diverse. This can result in four separate appraisal areas being assessed: *activities*, *outcomes*, *profitability*, and *personal development*. In combination, these four areas comprise a comprehensive evaluation process. That is, each set of criteria provides management with different insights about how the salesperson is performing and how they can be more effectively directed or controlled.

## Activities

Formal evaluation efforts should include quantitative data that result in the same figures being calculated regardless of who compiles them. The first group of data the sales manager investigates is salesperson *activities*. For example, when assessing salesperson *activities*, the sales managers may compute the number of:

- Sales calls per period.
- Required reports completed.
- Customer complaints.
- Customer training meetings conducted.
- Letters or phone calls to customers.
- Product demonstrations.
- Service calls.

**201**

- Sales calls per customer.
- Dealer meetings held.
- Advertising displays set up.

Sales managers may also subdivide types of sales calls into:

- Existing versus potential customers.
- Planned versus cold sales calls.
- Sales versus service calls.
- Telephone versus in-person sales calls.

One reason to separate call activities into distinct categories is that different probabilities of success apply. That is, cold sales calls have a lower likelihood of success than planned sales calls. Likewise, most firms set minimum activity standards like four sales calls per day. If a sales manager discovers that one of his salespersons is completing only three calls daily, but makes higher than average phone calls to customers, this may indicate that: (1) the salesperson is not conducting enough in-person calls or (2) the territory is too large to maintain the expected sales call work load. Only more detailed analysis can solve this dilemma.

Managers may also examine the way a salesperson devotes their time and how the sales call is spent. Time analysis provides managers with insight that allows the setting of standards based upon the activities of top sales performers. Time analysis permits the sales manager to compare average or less productive sales members' time allocation with that of top performers. Deviations between high and low performing groups may demonstrate how time can be spent more efficiently. How the salesperson spends their time on the sales call allows the manager to improve the effectiveness of the sales call. For example, managers can review the sales approach utilized and the type(s) of questions posed to the buyer.

When sales management evaluate sales force effort, they signal concern about the strategy used to close sales. This means that relationship-oriented companies expect a number of sales calls to be made and rapport to be developed with the client prior to a sale being made. Otherwise, the salesperson is not devoting adequate time to build a relationship with the customer. Finally, managers discover that all sales effort is not the same. This is evident when two salespersons conduct the same number of customer calls, but one salesperson closes significantly higher levels of sales dollars. The perceptive manager will realize that training can help the marginal salesperson achieve higher quality and more effective sales calls.

Sales managers also need to be familiar with effort–result ratios. These include *sales volume per call*, which measures productivity. Low sales volume per call infers the salesperson is spending too much time on small accounts or is not devoting enough attention to larger accounts. This suggests that the salesperson's strategy is to generate greater numbers of small sales rather than smaller numbers of large sales. A commonly used ratio is *order per call ratio* or "batting average." This is computed by dividing the number of successful sales calls by the total number of sales calls made. For example, if a salesperson is successful twenty-five times out of 100 sales calls, then the batting average is 0.250 (25/100). All other things being equal, the higher the batting average, the greater the salesperson's sales efficiency. A third ratio is *average cost per call*, which is total sales expense divided by the total number of calls made by the salesperson. A low cost per call ratio, given that all other measures are satisfactory, signals efficiency. However, if a salesperson is not making sufficient sales calls to establish a long-term relationship with customers, both sales volume and cost per call ratios will be low.

Additional ratios that can be employed by sales managers to evaluate salespersons include:

$$\text{Strike rate} = \frac{\text{Number of orders}}{\text{Number of quotations}}$$

$$\text{Profit per call} = \frac{\text{Total profit}}{\text{Number of calls made}}$$

These measures are clearly diagnostic and provide insight about why a salesperson is not reaching their goals. Ratios also indicate where additional investigations need to look – for example, poor call effectiveness points to sales skill problems.[13]

Performance efforts, as shown in Table 12.3, focus on the activities and behaviors of US salespeople, and similar evaluation practices are performed in the United Kingdom.[14] Since

**Table 12.3** *Output measures US firms use to evaluate the sales force*

| Performance measure | Percentage |
| --- | --- |
| Sales | |
| Sales volume | 79 |
| Sales volume/Previous year's sales | 76 |
| Sales to quota | 65 |
| Sales growth | 55 |
| Accounts | |
| Number of new accounts | 69 |
| Number of lost accounts | 33 |
| Profit | |
| Net profit | 69 |
| Gross margin | 34 |
| Return on investment | 33 |
| Orders | |
| Number of orders | 47 |
| Average order size | 22 |
| Order per call ratio | 14 |

Source: John C. Mowen, Janet E. Keith, Stephen W. Brown, and Donald W. Jackson, "Utilizing Effort and Task Difficulty Information in Evaluating Salespeople," *Journal of Marketing Research*, 22 (May 1985), 185–91

Note: *a* Percentage of firms that use this measure to assess sales force performance.

salesperson effort – like number of calls made and type of customer called upon – greatly influences performance, sales managers monitor these areas. Also, since sales effort is more controllable than results and defines the strategy that is being followed, it may be a more valid indicator of performance than results.[15] This may be true because economic conditions and product quality are beyond the control of the salesperson. But a salesperson has direct control over days worked, number of sales calls made, type of customer called upon, and products offered for sale.

## Outcome measures

Managers should also examine *outcome measures* that are impacted as a result of salesperson activities and include:

- Sales revenue generated.
- Profits achieved.
- Sales per account.
- Sales revenue as a percentage of potential.
- Number of orders.
- Number of new customers.
- Sales to new customers.

The belief is that output measures are more successful when the salesperson devotes sufficient time and quality to input activities. This is supported by a study conducted in Singapore that found that working hard was as important as working smart.[16]

## Profitability measures

Firms are now placing increased emphasis on such *profitability* measures as:

- Net profit as a percentage of sales.
- Net profit contribution.
- Net profit dollars.
- Return on investment.
- Gross margin.

The salesperson can impact profitability in two ways: (1) through the specific products sold and (2) through the final prices negotiated. This means that two salespersons can sell the same sales revenue levels and meet the exact quota requirement. However, based upon the type of product sold and price charged, one salesperson would produce higher gross margins. Likewise, salespersons impact profitability through the expenses they accumulate in their sales roles. This is because the salesperson has control over travel and entertainment expenses. Profitability criteria are increasingly being incorporated into salesperson assessments and have a direct impact on quota and bonuses. Profitability is especially important to firms during times of slow growth and increased competition.

## Qualitative measures

Sales managers also examine qualitative performance measures, which are judgments by the salesperson's supervisor. Within this area, a salesperson's *professional development* is assessed. For example, Asian managers report evaluating a salesperson's company, product, and market knowledge, personal appearance, and motivation.[17] Basically, the manager assesses to what degree the salesperson's knowledge and behavior compare with those of an ideal salesperson. To minimize bias, sales managers should follow a systematic assessment process where evaluations are complete, consistent over time, and comparable in scope.[18] A systematic appraisal includes a three-step process: (1) the setting of objectives, (2) the choice of rating techniques appropriate for the objective(s), and (3) the selection of individual behavior items to judge.

### Objectives

The principal purpose of conducting appraisal evaluations is to improve the sales organization. However, the more immediate impetus for evaluating sales force efforts includes counseling and developing salespersons, providing a basis for compensation and raises, promotion, termination, and validation of selection and training procedures. The specific purpose must be clearly defined, since each goal requires different evaluation techniques and measures.

### Techniques

A number of techniques are available to satisfy the various objectives of the evaluation:

- *Essay technique* is a brief statement written by the sales manager to describe salesperson performance. Since there is no standardization of style or focus, salesperson evaluations are difficult to compare.
- *Rating scales* utilize phrases or terms that describe the salesperson's personal characteristics or performance. A variety of rating scales can be used to evaluate the sales force, such as graphic rating/checklist methods. An example of this type of scale is shown below:

  Delivers what he or she promises on time
  Almost never 1 2 3 4 5 Almost always

- *Ranking* occurs when each salesperson is ordered within a district or region based upon performance. The rater bases his or her final ranking on all characteristics relevant to performance, though the specific factors used to rank may not be written. This technique provides little feedback information, but is useful in selecting persons for promotion. General Electric and Ford use ranking for all their managers, but experts point out that ranking tends to be subjective and determined by factors unknown to the salesperson.[19]
- *Management by Objectives* (MBO) is a goal-setting and evaluative process between supervisor and employee that results in mutually acceptable performance measures and their assessment. Specifically, MBO is a three-step process: (1) setting mutually

**205**

agreed upon, well defined, and measurable goals within a specified time frame; (2) managing activities within the time period to achieve objectives; and (3) assessing performance against objectives.

■ *Behaviorally Anchored Rating Scale* (BARS) is a set of scaled statements that measures the level of performance on behaviors that are relevant to the job. The linking of behavior and results becomes the basis for evaluating salesperson performance. In BARS, salespersons identify critical behavior and performance required to achieve desired results. Since the scale describes job-related behavior for each firm, such an instrument is time-consuming and expensive to design.

Ratings vary across cultures, as seen in a study of Japanese and US managers. When US and Japanese sales managers utilized an identical scale, overall ratings differed. That is, most Japanese salespersons were placed in the middle with a few being ranked on the high and low ends of the scale. Conversely, US managers ranked a few salespersons high, but most were scored in the middle. No US salespersons were rated in the low categories. One explanation is that marginal salespersons in the United States either leave when they do not earn enough money or they are fired. Conversely, Japanese managers must contend with low sales performers.[20]

*Items*

The items adopted for an evaluation are dependent upon the objectives of the appraisal. For example, if the objective of the evaluation is to identify current salespersons for promotion to management, then items on organizing, planning, working with others, and acceptance of responsibility are important. Conversely, if the assessment's goal is to improve current performance, then the items employed should objectively rate a salesperson's duties and key responsibilities.

## Bias in performance appraisal

Sales managers must be careful to minimize the bias that can creep into evaluation efforts. That is, sales managers often rate salespersons they form a personal relationship with higher than more distance-based salespersons in the firm. Also, salespersons assigned to difficult sales territories are rated higher in ability and performance than those in less difficult territories.[21] Finally outcome bias, which means the results of an action influences the manager's assessment, can impact overall evaluations. In this case, when a salesperson makes the sale, their performance is rated higher than when the sales proposal is turned down – regardless of the quality of the decision made by the salesperson.

To minimize bias, it is important that the sales manager employ set standards wherever possible that directly relate to the job description. The appraisal system should be based upon behavior or results, rather than salesperson traits or characteristics. That is, if the sales force is instructed to complete four sales calls a day, this is the work standard regardless of the friendship, performance, or territory assigned the individual salesperson. Managers must be able to evaluate from as close to a point of neutrality as possible. Otherwise evaluation bias will harm the individual being rated and, in certain countries like the United States, may be illegal.

## Informal evaluations

Sales managers may claim that formal sales force evaluations are unnecessary because they informally evaluate the salesperson on a daily or "as needed" basis. While in passing this appears logical, such behavior is in fact of questionable value. For example, say that salesperson Jones wins a company sports tournament. One sales manager may view this as a positive achievement, while another manager may ask how Jones had time to work sixty-five hours a week and still excel in this sport? Second, informal evaluation results in differing amounts and quality of information about each salesperson reaching the sales manager. That is, a few salespersons will manipulate customers to write letters of appreciation and to provide positive feedback to the company. Conversely, other salespersons are reluctant to ask customers for such help. This means that when this happens the sales supervisor is unable to evaluate her sales force either consistently or comparatively. Finally, informal evaluation results in managers perceiving and retaining information differently. When this occurs, the manager may choose to believe only data that support a previous evaluation of the salesperson. Therefore, formal performance appraisals are necessary to insure the objectivity of salesperson evaluations.

## Evaluating sales team performance

In today's relationship marketing environment, and in collectivist cultures, it is important to set procedures for evaluating sales teams. This means sales managers must establish criteria and methods upon which team members are evaluated. It is important to establish links between team performance and outcomes in order to motivate both team and individual effort. Allowing team members to help develop goals and objectives enhances acceptance of the evaluation process. Also, team members are more willing to participate when individual and team goals are linked together.[22]

## Diagnosing salesperson performance

The sales manager next collects and organizes data, then interprets the findings. First, it is important to discern why one product has not met sales or profit expectations. Second, it is necessary for sales managers to monitor individual salesperson performance for a variety of reasons – counseling, promotion, bonus, termination, or transfer.

Typically, sales managers try to understand why organizational sales goals were not met – especially sales revenue goals. Too often, and without a systematic evaluation process, the simplistic answer is that the sales force did not work hard enough to reach the goal.[23] However, in addition to insufficient salesperson effort or an unrealistic sales forecast, there are other possible reasons for a sales revenue shortfall:

- Salespersons lack sales ability.
- Non-competitive pricing.
- Quality or delivery problems with the product.

Next, the sales manager lists the possible explanations for the missed performance objective and analyzes each reason. If lack of sales ability is suspected, then the manager should look at the salesperson's activities (number of calls made) to insure sufficient effort was extended. If effort was not a problem then the manager should examine past performance ratings for the sales force and "batting average" ratings per salesperson. Similarly if product quality and/or delivery are problematic, then several salespersons should exhibit low sales for that one product.

In those cases when initial analysis fails to pinpoint the problem, the sales manager should look at increased competitor effort in territories. Managers must also consider whether sales quotas were correctly set and if quotas should be set using different formulas. Some firms interview former customers, salespersons and sales managers to learn why the business was lost. Once apparent explanations are found, the sales manager should support the finding by examining call reports, salesperson activities and ratings, and available data to confirm the assumed hypothesis.

## EVALUATION AND ACTION

Once the sales manager evaluates the individual salesperson or entire sales force, it is time to recommend action. Evaluation uncovers weaknesses and reinforces the need to make changes to the current organization, production process, or sales force emphasis. For the sales force and salesperson this can entail the following alternatives.

### Personal development

If it is determined that the sales force or specific individuals need personal development, this must be clearly communicated. For example, if the analysis indicates the sales force is weak at making sales presentations, this must be communicated to the sales force and proper training must be provided to correct any deficiency. This is why MBO systems are employed to help salespersons set mutually agreed upon goals that they work to accomplish. However, without open communication between the manager and salesperson personal development will not succeed.

### Reallocation of effort

Should evaluation confirm that shifting priority from one activity to another will improve performance, the salesperson needs to be informed. For example, if it is apparent the salesperson has been devoting insufficient time to high margin products, management must redirect the salesperson. Firms can also reallocate the quota or bonus in certain cultures to refine performance and reward earned. Likewise, sales managers may be spending too much time selling instead of managing the sales force. In such circumstances the sales manager must be instructed to devote more field time to coaching the sales force.

## Modifying the performance setting

Evaluation may indicate that changes are needed in sales procedures or methods. Perhaps the sales training program is too costly or does not adequately prepare the sales force for success in the field. When this occurs, firms must consider modifying the training program or hiring more experienced and successful salespersons. Conversely, as new products are introduced or selling strategies change, firms may add high-tech training programs to prepare the sales force for marketplace changes.[24]

The diagnosis may confirm that new products need to be added, credit policy changes are necessary, the strategies employed are not working, or product quality is problematic. When sales managers uncover such problems, it is important to forward the findings and suggestions to upper management. Since these recommendations are outside the responsibility of sales management, it is imperative to submit a detailed and persuasive study to higher authority for consideration and further action.

## CHAPTER SUMMARY

Sales managers evaluate in order to know what is working, what is not and, most importantly, why. Sales managers make constant decisions about the sales force that must be based upon objective reasoning that emanates from evaluation efforts. Otherwise, decisions are likely to be haphazard and inconsistent. Global evaluations are more complex and, depending upon the culture, may focus on individual and group performance.

To increase the likelihood the sales force will reach set goals, sales managers analyze sales, cost, and profitability measures. Sales information provides managers with an understanding of performance, cost figures relate sales expense to sales goals, and profitability tells supervisors if the effort was worthwhile. Most analyses help managers identify potential problems, which are further investigated, to understand why deviations from plans occurred. Sales managers must determine if the plans were incorrectly set and/or if the sales force did not perform up to par. Finally, based upon evaluation, sales force changes may be necessary.

Individual salespersons are assessed regularly to understand their performance, potential for advancement, and qualifications for reward. Because the salesperson's role is complex, they are evaluated based upon activities, outcome, profits, and professional development criteria. By utilizing multiple measures, sales managers can gain a more comprehensive picture of the salesperson. Sales managers must also be aware of the potential for bias to enter the assessment process and must take steps to minimize this human weakness.

By performing regular, objective, and comprehensive evaluations, managers will be more cognizant of both their sales force and their markets. This situation will allow more informed decisions to be made that will lead to greater success for the individual salesperson, the sales force, and the firm.

## DISCUSSION QUESTIONS

1   What challenges are posed when firms evaluate sales force efforts globally?
2   Why is it important to differentiate between sales force effectiveness and salesperson performance?
3   Why is it necessary to assess sales, cost, and profitability data when evaluating sales force performance?
4   What is the relationship of activities and outcome measures?
5   What qualitative criteria do managers examine when assessing the salesperson?
6   Discuss the need to match assessment technique(s) to the goal(s) of the evaluation.
7   What pitfalls are inherent in informal evaluation systems?
8   Explain the evaluation problems caused by sales manager bias.

## REFERENCES

1   Donaldson, Bill (1998), *Sales Management*, New York: Palgrave.

2   Wotruba, Thomas R., and Edwin K. Simpson (1992), *Sales Management*, Boston MA: PWS-Kent.

3   Kotabe, Masaaki, and Kristiaan Helsen (1998), *Global Marketing Management*, New York: John Wiley & Sons.

4   Harzing, Anne-Wil, and Joris Van Ruysseveldt (1995), *International Human Resource Management*, London: Sage Publications.

5   Money, R. Bruce, and John L. Graham (1999), "Salesperson Performance, Pay, and Job Satisfaction: Tests of a Model using Data Collected in the US and Japan," *Journal of International Business Studies*, 30:1, 149–72.

6   Susumu, Ueno, and Uma Sekaran (1992), "The Influence of Culture on Budget Control Practices in the US and Japan," *Journal of International Business Studies*, 23:4, 659–74.

7   Hossain, S., and H.J. Davis (1989), "Some Thoughts on International Personnel Management as an Emerging Field," *Research in Personnel and Human Resource Management*, Supplement 1, 121–36.

8   "Up Front" (1995), *BusinessWeek*, May 15, 8.

9   Harzing and Van Ruysseveldt (1995).

10   Terpstra, Vern, and Ravi Sarathy (1997), *International Marketing*, Fort Worth TX: Dryden Press.

11   Donaldson (1998).

12   Jackson, Donald, Jr., John Schlacter, and William Wolfe (1995), "Examining the Bases utilized for Evaluating Salespeople's Performance," *Journal of Personal Selling and Sales Management*, 15 (fall), 57–65.

13   Jobber, David, and Geoff Lancaster (2000), *Selling and Sales Management*, Harlow: Prentice Hall.

14 Jobber, D., G. Hooley, and D. Shipley (1993), "Organizational Size and Salesforce Evaluation Practices," *Journal of Personal Selling and Sales Management*, 13:2, 37–48.

15 Wotruba and Simpson (1992).

16 Leong, Siew Meng, Donna M. Randall, and Joseph A. Cote (1994), "Exploring the Organizational Commitment – Performance Linkage in Marketing: A Study of Life Insurance Salespeople," *Journal of Business Research*, 29:1, 57–63.

17 Hill, John S., and Arthur W. Allaway (1993), "How US-based Companies Manage Sales in Foreign Countries," *Industrial Marketing Management*, 22, 7–16.

18 Wotruba and Simpson (1992).

19 Hymowitz, Carol (2001), "Ranking Systems Gain Popularity but Have Many Staffers Riled," *Wall Street Journal*, May 15, B1.

20 Cateora, Philip R., and John L. Graham (2002), *International Marketing*, New York: McGraw-Hill Irwin.

21 Marshall, Greg, John Mowen, and Keith Fabes (1992), "The Impact of Territory Difficulty and Self versus other Ratings on Managerial Evaluations of Sales Performance," *Journal of Personal Selling and Sales Management*, 12 (fall), 35–48.

22 Campion, Michael, and A. Catherine Higgs (1995), "Design Teams Work to Increase Productivity and Satisfaction," *HR Magazine*, 40 (October), 101–7.

23 Mowen, John C., Janet E. Keith, Stephen W. Brown, and Donald W. Jackson (1985), "Utilizing Effort and Task Difficulty Information in Evaluating Salespeople," *Journal of Marketing Research*, 22 (May), 185–91.

24 Jackson, Schlacter, and Wolfe (1995).

Part IV

# Global strategic management issues

## Chapter 13

# Identifying and forecasting global markets

This chapter presents a methodology for assessing market and sales potential in global markets.

---

### LEARNING OBJECTIVES

*After reading this chapter, you will be able to*:

- Understand how to effectively judge the attractiveness of potential cross-cultural markets for international sales purposes.
- Explain how economic conditions can affect sales success in different markets.
- Discuss the role of culture in new market assessment.
- Forecast sales for new markets in a cross-cultural setting using a variety of techniques.
- Understand how the political/legal conditions can affect sales potential.
- Assess the potential fit of a particular salesperson in a new cross-cultural market.
- Understand how the nature of competition can affect sales success in new global markets.

## KEY TERMS

- Urbanization.
- Gross national product (GNP).
- GNP per capita.
- GNP purchasing power parity.
- Subsistence, Industrializing, Industrialized, and Post-industrial Economies.
- Estimation by analogy.
- Trade audit.
- Maximum market potential.
- Chain ratio method.
- Extrapolation.
- Political risk assessment (PRA).

## INTRODUCTION

When sales managers evaluate the attractiveness of global markets, they must not simply employ the same selection criteria that are used in the home market. Even though sales managers are familiar with particular methods of forecasting and identifying home markets, they must not myopically assume these methods will work equally well in a cross-cultural context. To reiterate, sales management in a cross-cultural environment is governed by a different set of managerial decision rules. Therefore, much of what is done in the home market must be adapted and modified for different cultural settings. In this chapter, a series of estimation techniques are introduced that feed into a checklist that can be used to evaluate multicultural markets and determine which have the greatest chances for success based upon the type of sales force assigned and the cultural forces affecting the market(s). Illustrative examples that take the sales manager through the comparative process are also provided. Finally, market rankings are developed based upon relevant choice criteria.

### CASE VIGNETTE **ASSESSING OVERSEAS MARKETS**

Nigel West, European Sales Manager for a British manufacturer, must determine market potential for several areas of Eastern Europe. In his initial investigation of available data, West has found that data are missing or categorized differently than needed. West also wonders if he should rely upon official government data or utilize that of organizations like the United Nations and the World Bank. Finally, West has concluded that analyzing and forecasting in Eastern Europe differs greatly from the methods employed in Great Britain.

In order to evaluate market potential when assessing markets for a global sales force, there are a number of important criteria the sales manager can use to examine and rank alternatives. The criteria are shown in Figure 13.1 and discussed in detail below.

## ECONOMIC CONDITIONS

One of the most important factors affecting market potential is the economic condition in that marketplace. Economic conditions would include such measures as population, income, consumption, and economic development.

### Population

Success in sales necessitates an understanding of where customers can be found and how much they will spend. When entering new markets, it is important to realize that figures that are used at home may be unreliable or misleading when assessing an overseas market. Population figures are important indicators of where customers are located. The problem is that population figures, by themselves, can be very misleading because access to concentrated buyer pockets is far more cost-effective than reaching customers spread over a country. Thus population *distribution* is important. Target customers are most important to the company, since it is not feasible to sell products to all customers in the country; but

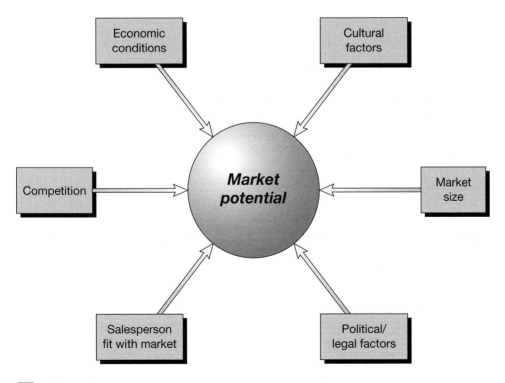

**Figure 13.1** *Criteria for cross-cultural market potential assessment*

population figures may not sufficiently categorize data into small enough subgroups for targeting purposes. It then becomes necessary to apportion out the figures from aggregated numbers to conduct reasonable comparisons.

It is also important to identify, as specifically as possible, how the target population is distributed in the potential market. Are there pockets of customers or are they spread evenly throughout the area or country? Population *density* is another important consideration. Are customers highly concentrated and more easily accessible as a result? Population density, as measured by population per square kilometer, can be found in the World Bank's annual *World Development Indicators*. When looking at population figures for 1999, Nepal had a population of 23 million while the Netherlands reported a population of 16 million. Yet, when population density is examined, 1999 figures indicate that 466 people per square kilometer live in the Netherlands, while there were 164 people per square kilometer in Nepal.[1] Certainly, the sales manager must make meaningful comparisons across potential markets that reflect a variety of views of population. What is desirable is to find densely populated areas that allow efficient sales force access.

Another way to understanding population density is the level of *urbanization* or the percentage of the population that is located in an urban (or city) setting as opposed to rural (or country) setting. Urbanization can be viewed as a measure of modernization or development, since people tend to move to the city to improve their economic and life prospects. High population densities in larger city centers offer logistical benefits when assessing sales potential. This applies to both consumer and industrial sales, since concentrations of buyers allow easier and more efficient access to buyers.

## Income

Income is an important component for assessing buying power; however, income can be distributed unevenly. When income is evenly distributed, then *per capita* income, or income measured on a per-person basis, is a more meaningful measure. But, in countries where there are uneven distributions (i.e., a large population of very poor offset by a small population of very rich individuals), *per capita* income may appear large and reasonable when real market potential is exceedingly small. However, additional information can assist in the accurate assessment of sales potential.

One of the most effective ways to make comparisons across countries is to examine *gross national product* (GNP) *per capita*. GNP consists of the total domestic and foreign value added by the residents of the country, and when this is calculated on a per-person basis, a more accurate measure of actual purchasing power is revealed. The data are available from the World Bank, and, using our previous example of Nepal and the Netherlands, one sees a widening gap between the two countries, with GNP *per capita* for 1999 of US$24,320 for the Netherlands (a rank of eighteenth in the world) and US$220 for Nepal (a rank of 194th in the world).[2]

Extending this example one step further, the best comparative measure of purchasing power involves an adjustment for international currencies. GNP *purchasing power parity* (PPP) adjusts GNP *per capita* to reflect real price levels across countries by placing different currencies and buying ability into a more comparable and meaningful framework. Adjusted PPP figures for the Netherlands for 1999 are $23,052 (US equivalent – a rank of seventeenth in the world) and $1,219 for Nepal (a rank of 177th in the world).[3] This narrows the gap a bit, for this example, but the results confirm significantly greater purchasing power in the Netherlands than in Nepal. When considering new markets for entry, it is more appropriate to compare regional countries that reflect greater similarity in PPP.

## Consumption

Another important aspect of sales potential involves the existing consumption of the product or service in question across the market(s) of interest. Numerous sources for this type of information exist, from World Bank data to UN sources to individual country statistical reports. Sales managers should remember that official government data are often biased, so, whenever possible, comparative reports from outside organizations like the World Bank, the United Nations, the International Monetary Fund, or Euromonitor are more objective sources of consumption information. High consumption levels of the products or services of interest are normally preferable to lower levels; however, high levels may reflect market saturation, which may signal difficult entry by a new competitor.

## Economic development

The level of economic development also significantly impacts the level of demand for particular goods and services in both industrial and consumer markets. It can be an effective selection mechanism, since different levels of economic development reflect disparate demand patterns for goods and services. Over time economies tend to become more sophisticated as demand patterns for goods and services change. Four different levels of economic development are discussed: (1) agricultural or subsistence economies, (2) industrializing economies, (3) industrialized economies and, (4) post-industrial economies.

*Agricultural or subsistence* economies are characterized by lack of an industrial base, heterogeneity of language, low levels of literacy, and farmers that bring their specialty goods to a central market. While there is limited demand for industrial products, subsistence-type goods (food, clothing, shelter) are in demand, along with goods and services that improve agricultural output. Nations that are represented in this category include smaller, agricultural countries of Africa like Cameroon.

*Industrializing countries* are those nations where an industrial base is developing (after first focusing on subsistence types of goods), with increasing income levels, improving educational systems, and growing opportunities for industrial products, like construction equipment and building supplies. There are also initial signs of a middle class that brings with it increasing demand for consumer durable and nondurable products. The problem is that large gaps can exist in both industrial and consumer market segments. Such nations are currently represented by Brazil and China.

*Industrialized countries* include those in which the industrial sector is far larger than the agricultural sector. Educational systems are well developed, language is standardized, literacy rates are high, and there is evidence of a thriving middle class, with a full range of goods and services available at both the industrial and the consumer level. Examples include such countries as Australia and Sweden.

**219**

The final group, *post-industrial countries*, are represented by nations that provide their own product and technology innovations. These countries have the most highly developed middle class, where gaps in income across different population groups are at their smallest levels. All goods and services are found in the marketplace, including the most complex and innovative. The United States and Japan belong to this group.

Products and services are needed in all four types of economies, but market potential is best understood when countries and target markets are categorized into comparable groupings. That is, a company selling gypsum and other building products might find tremendous potential when selling its products in *industrializing countries* where plant construction is rapidly expanding.

## CULTURAL FACTORS

Chapter 2 focused on cultural components that can be used to rank sales potential in new markets. Culture affects the success of the individual salesperson that calls upon cross-cultural customers with the goal of building a successful relationship over time. Certainly it is important that a cultural similarity exist between the salesperson and customers that are called upon in a new market. Culture also has an effect upon the potential use of a product or service in a new market, since tastes and habits are culturally driven. As a result, it is beneficial to include cultural components when evaluating market potential. Any checklist should contain a series of cultural components and an estimation of fit between the market, the product, and the potential salesperson.

## MARKET SIZE

A prime piece of information when assessing market potential is an estimation of market size. Market size can be estimated fairly easily; however, accuracy is often sacrificed when dealing with less developed country markets. If the sales manager can afford the expenditure, useful reports are available for many countries from research firms like A.C. Nielsen. These are quite expensive and they focus primarily on frequently purchased products or services. In most cases, when approaching a new overseas market for entry, it may not be possible to buy such a report. This is because no report may exist or the target market in question has yet to develop. For example, the company looking to enter the market may be the first firm to gauge the marketplace. When this is the case, the sales manager may have to compile his or her own estimation of market size.

A series of techniques that are useful in the global context to estimate market size include: (1) estimation by analogy, (2) the trade audit, (3) maximum market potential, (4) the chain ratio method, and (5) extrapolation. Each technique, along with an illustrative example, is presented below. While more sophisticated methods are available (e.g., advanced quantitative modeling based upon regression or cluster analysis), the illustrated mechanisms are far easier to understand and implement. Once industry experience is gained in different markets, it is possible to consider the development of a more sophisticated modeling approach to estimating market potential.

## Estimation by analogy

This technique involves finding a market size that is known in a similar country and extending from that information to the size of the market in question. The key is to identify a country at a similar stage of economic development as the country of interest and employ a surrogate measure for a parallel type of product that allows the two countries to be effectively compared. It is important that demand figures represent the same time period, wherever possible, for the three necessary quantitative inputs. The formula that is used for the estimation would be:

$$\frac{\text{Demand for product 1 in country A}}{\text{Demand for product 2 in country A}} = \frac{\text{Demand for product 1 in country B}}{\text{Demand for product 2 in country B}}$$

The figure that we want to estimate is the demand for product 1 in country A. The formula can be rewritten to solve for the missing information as:

$$\begin{array}{l}\text{Demand for product 1} \\ \text{in country A}\end{array} = \begin{array}{l}\text{Demand for product 2} \\ \text{in country A}\end{array} \times \frac{\begin{array}{c}\text{Demand for product 1} \\ \text{in country B}\end{array}}{\begin{array}{c}\text{Demand for product 2} \\ \text{in country B}\end{array}}$$

Central and Eastern European nations are useful for illustrative purposes. Suppose that you are interested in the market size for video camcorders for Poland. What is necessary is to find the figures for a country at approximately the same level of economic development. Hungary and the Czech Republic are countries that are viewed as being economically comparable. Suppose that the annual sales of video camcorders in the Czech Republic were 96,000 units in 2000. If we can obtain the sales figures for a related product, then we can mathematically estimate the market size.

Logically, it is reasonable to assume that those who own video recorders (VCRs) would be more likely to buy video camcorders. Now suppose that we know that 250,000 VCRs were purchased in the Czech Republic in 2000. The one additional piece of information that would make this method work is the VCR retail sales for 2000 for Poland. If 230,000 VCRs were sold in Poland in 2000, then the estimate for camcorder demand for Poland could be determined using the following equation:

$$\frac{\text{Demand for camcorders (Poland)}}{\text{Demand for VCRs (Poland)}} = \frac{\text{Demand for camcorders (Czech Republic)}}{\text{Demand for VCRs (Czech Republic)}}$$

This can be rewritten to solve for Demand for camcorders (Poland) as:

$$\begin{array}{l}\text{Demand for camcorders} \\ \text{(Poland)}\end{array} = \begin{array}{l}\text{Demand for VCRs} \\ \text{(Poland)}\end{array} \times \frac{\begin{array}{c}\text{Demand for camcorders} \\ \text{(Czech Republic)}\end{array}}{\begin{array}{c}\text{Demand for VCRs} \\ \text{(Czech Republic)}\end{array}}$$

Substituting the available numbers, the formula could be solved by:

$$\text{Demand for camcorders (Poland)} \quad = \quad 230{,}000 \quad \times \quad \frac{96{,}000}{250{,}000} = \quad 88{,}320 \text{ units}$$

We now have an estimate of the demand for camcorders in Poland using estimation by analogy. As long as you can access three of the necessary figures, the fourth can be mathematically estimated for either industrial or consumer markets. The key is to insure that the information gathered is accurate and timely. Sources for this type of information include such readily available publications as:

- *European Marketing Data and Statistics*, published annually by Euromonitor International, London, and covers only Europe.
- *International Marketing Data and Statistics*, published annually by Euromonitor International, London, and covers all areas of the world except Europe.
- *Economic Intelligence Unit (EIU) Country Indicators*, updated monthly, quarterly and annually and covering 117 countries.
- World Development Indicators, *published annually by the World Bank for 210 countries.*

## The trade audit

Another method for estimation of potential market size is the trade audit. This estimation examines the level of local manufacture for the product in question, along with imports and exports of that product. The formula is:

$$\text{Market size for country A} \quad = \quad \text{Local production} \quad + \quad \text{Imports} \quad \times \quad \text{Exports}$$

To provide another illustration, suppose that we need to determine the size of the market for tobacco products in Italy. This can be accomplished using the trade audit with information made available through the *OECD STAN Database for Industrial Analysis* that is published annually by the Organization for Economic Cooperation and Development. The 1996 figures for tobacco production for Italy were L4,909 billion.[4] The imports for the same period of time amounted to L1,982 billion.[5] Finally, exports for the same period were listed as L268 billion.[6] Applying these figures to the formula, the market size for tobacco products in Italy would be valued at L4,909 billion + L1,982 billion – L268 billion = L6,623 billion. This figure would need to be adjusted to a comparative currency valuation for cross-country comparisons. The exchange rate valuation for 1996 figures to convert to US dollars were L1,703.1 = $1.00; therefore the value in US dollars of the Italian tobacco market in 1996 would be approximately L6,623 billion/1703.1 = $388,879,100.[7]

This estimation approach can be utilized whenever appropriate production, import, and export figures are available. However, it is important to remember that when making comparisons across various target country markets, the data may be outdated, inaccurate, or noncomparable, since products may be combined into different categories for reporting purposes (e.g., the market for men's shirts may not be identifiable in a summary category of production, imports, and exports for men's clothing as the only relevant product category). It is normally helpful to use figures provided by an external, and hopefully objective, reporting agency like the OECD that applies standard estimation mechanisms to all data employed.

## Maximum market potential

This approach requires information about consumption in terms of average amount consumed per target customer, average price paid per unit, and the total number of consumers. The method can be tailored to the specific product and sales area that the sales manager is evaluating. This technique requires some information searching, and may even necessitate conducting primary research (e.g., asking potential consumers about their consumption habits for the product) to estimate the necessary pieces of the formula, but the result is worthwhile. The formula for this method is:

$$Q = n \times q \times p$$

where $Q$ = total market potential, $n$ = number of buyers in the specific market, $q$ = quantity purchased by the average buyer during the time period in question, and $p$ = price for an average unit of the product in question[8]

This type of information is more difficult to uncover – particularly in less developed countries – but, whenever available, produces a fairly accurate assessment of total market potential. For illustrative purposes, suppose that we need to know the potential market for office computers in a particular market. We know from chamber of commerce statistics that the total number of buying companies in the market in question is 1,245, and that on average these businesses buy twelve computers per year, and suppose that the average price per computer for the current year is US$1,200. Based upon this information, we can compute the total market potential by multiplying all of the individual numbers together. The calculation would be: $Q = 1,245 \times 12 \times 1,200 = \$17,928,000$ per year.

## Chain ratio method

This estimation technique begins with a general estimate of the entire population involved (e.g., total population figures) and applies to this base number a series of percentages that reduce the market size at each step. Presume that a company is interested in the potential market for a new infant care product in Malaysia. The starting point for the chain ratio method is to obtain the total population figure for Malaysia. The 1999 population was 23 million, according to World Bank data.[9] Since only the population in urban locations would be of interest, because reaching rural populations would be difficult and costly, the total population figure must be adjusted for the urbanization rate. The 1999 urbanization level for Malaysia was 57 percent; therefore the urban population is $23,000,000 \times 0.57 = 13,110,000$ people in urban locations.[10] This figure also needs to be modified to reflect the number of new births in the population, and, for Malaysia, the 1996 birth rate per 1,000 people was estimated by the World Bank at 27.[11] The total market potential would therefore be

**223**

13,110,000 × 0.027 = 353,970. This is an imprecise estimate, but one that serves as a reasonable and easily calculated starting point that is based upon readily available information.

## Extrapolation

One of the biggest problems with information gathering, as it relates to market potential estimation, is that data are often out of date. The sales manager may have access to data that is five to six or more years old, and the problem is how to estimate the present situation with old data. One way to accomplish this is to look for trends in past data that can reasonably be extended to the present time. Looking at the change from period to period in the most recent data available can identify a trend that could then be applied to the last known data. It may also be possible for the sales manager to locate published reports of market potential for the specific products/services that their company sells to an overseas market of interest; however, in most cases the information will not be for the current period. If the published data are available for several sequential years, then a trend can be calculated by averaging the percentage change from period to period over the years of available information. This trend percentage can then be applied to the last known data and carried forward to present and into future periods.

Suppose, for example, that our company sells window air conditioners, and the market of interest is Thailand. Presume also that the following estimates for window air conditioner sales were published by a consulting firm: US$16,600,000 in 1990, $19,350,000 in 1991, $22,608,000 in 1992, $25,260,000 in 1993, $27,540,000 in 1994, and $30,280,000 in 1995. Since no figures are available after 1995, extrapolation is necessary to estimate 2002 sales. This requires calculating the percentage change from one year to the next and averaging the percentage change figures over the available year of data reported and carrying this percentage change forward to the present time. From 1990 to 1991 the change was $2,750,000/16,600,000 = 16.6 percent, and the remaining percentage changes were:

- 1991–2 $3,258,000/19,350,000 = 16.8%
- 1992–3 $2,652,000/22,608,000 = 11.7%
- 1993–4 $2,280,000/25,260,000 = 9.0%
- 1994–5 $2,740,000/27,540,000 = 9.9%
- Average change (0.166 + 0.168 + 0.117 + 0.090 + 0.099)/5 = 0.128 or 12.8%

Using this information, it is possible to approximate sales for the missing periods, by calculating the 12.8 percent change estimation and bringing the sales forward to 2002:

> 1996 projected sales
> = 1995 sales ($30,280,000)
> + (1995 sales ($30,280,000)
> × 12.8 %)
> = $30,280,000
> + $3,875,840
> = $34,155,840

**224**

Taking this forward to 2002, the calculations are:

- 1997 $34,155,840 + $4,371,948 = $38,527,788
- 1998 $38,527,788 + $4,931,557 = $43,459,345
- 1999 $43,459,345 + $5,562,796 = $49,022,141
- 2000 $49,022,141 + $6,274,834 = $55,296,975
- 2001 $55,296,975 + $7,078,013 = $62,374,988
- 2002 $62,374,988 + $7,983,998 = $70,358,986

There are two points that need to be stated about the extrapolation method. First, the greater the number of years being projected forward, the less likelihood that the numbers will be accurate. Second, the larger the number of years of reported data and the greater the accuracy of the reporting source, the more accurate the extrapolation adjustments.

## Final suggestions for market size estimation

The global sales manager must be able to arrive at the most accurate estimation of the size of the potential markets under consideration, and the best way to accomplish this is to seek corroboration by using more than one method of estimating market size. It is reasonable to expect that gaps will exist in available information, and since educated guesswork becomes necessary, similarity in size estimation provides increased confidence. Each technique needs to be evaluated by the quality of the data provided, but when there is a wide discrepancy between two or more techniques, it is appropriate to average the results together, or at least discard the highest and lowest estimates. Acting conservatively is prudent in such a situation. If with conservative estimations the market size remains attractive, then the likelihood of achieving the projection is enhanced. *The point here is that no one technique is foolproof!*

Also, adjustments must be made in all estimation techniques to account for market conditions that impact total market potential. For example, an assessment of the number of competitors must be undertaken to determine the maximum share that could reasonably be attained by the company. If there are three competitors operating in the market, then it is unlikely that the entering company will gain more than 25 percent of that total market (being one of now four possible sellers in the market). The ability to achieve this level of sales also assumes that the new entrant will be able to gain its apportionment of the total market. This is less likely when the other three competitors have served that market for a long time. The key is to arrive at a reasonable estimate of the market size for your company based upon the total market potential and likely share of that potential. When performed correctly, this can be very effective and allows comparisons to be made across market segments in various countries that are both useful and accurate.

## POLITICAL/LEGAL FACTORS

Another important criterion for assessing market attractiveness, in a cross-cultural setting, is political/legal factors. Political factors involve examining the political climate in the target market to see if it is stable and supportive of the country your company represents and the products or services that you plan to offer to that market. In order to understand political stability, it is necessary to conduct a *political risk assessment* (PRA). This is an examination of the current government and its economic policies and relationships with other governments and its own citizens. The following are examples of aspects of a government which should be included in a political risk assessment:

- Type of government. (Is it a democracy or is it a dictatorship?)
- Stability of the government. (How long has it been in place?)
- Quality of the host government's economic management. (How healthy is the economy?)
- Changes in government policy. (Have policies been consistent or erratic?)
- Host country's attitude toward foreign investment. (Do they welcome outside investment?)
- Host country's relationship with the rest of the world. (Are they friendly with other nations?)
- Host country's relationship with the company's home government. (What are the relations like between the country most associated with your company and the country you are looking to enter?)
- Attitude toward assignment of foreign personnel. (Does the government have restrictions on your use of foreign nationals on their soil?)
- Extent of anti-private-sector influence or influence of state-controlled industries. (Do they really want outside businesses operating in certain industries?)
- Fairness and honesty of administrative procedures. (Does the government handle issues fairly and honestly?)
- Closeness between the government and the people. (Do they seem to get along?)[12]

The answers to such questions allow the global sales manager to better understand the government that controls the country in question and to see whether the risk associated with market entry is worth the potential rewards that could be achieved.

Legal issues are also important, since they can significantly affect the success of a salesperson operating in an overseas market. What the salesperson can say and do is governed by local laws, along with important issues like what constitutes a binding sales contract and what are the rights of both parties? A potential stumbling block in international sales expansion is the lack of any standardized worldwide legal system. This means that, all too often, company sales personnel operating in overseas markets must contend with the local legal system. When a contract is violated, the court system in the country in which the dispute occurs will hear the case and issue the decisions. Certain laws, like those below, can affect sales of products and business operations:

- Tariffs: government taxes placed on specific imports or exports.
- Antidumping laws: government restrictions on pricing of goods for sale in the country at too low a level.
- Import/export/business licenses: to engage in any kind of business for which a license may be necessary.

- Product standards regulations: what is being sold may have to meet certain government-set standards
- Inspections: imports may be subjected to special inspections mandated by the government, with accompanying fees and delays.
- Business operation laws: laws may regulate what you can pay people, the hours they work, the conditions under which they are working, etc. (Of course, this is particularly relevant if you are using host-country nationals as salespersons.)

The following list provides the web sites of a variety of organizations that may be helpful in providing information about political and legal conditions in most world countries:

- http://www.odci.gov/cia/publications/factbook/index.html This is the site for information gathered from a variety of American agencies and developed by the Central Intelligence Agency (statistics for many world countries).
- http://ciber.bus.msu.edu This site was developed by the CIBER at Michigan State University and provides a wealth of information regarding global markets.
- http://www.iccwbo.org This site is the home for the International Chamber of Commerce based in Paris.
- http://www.census.gov/ipc/www/idbprint.html This is a service of the US Census Bureau and provides a variety of country statistics.
- http://www.dbisna.com/newsview/menu.htm#global This is a service provided by Dun & Bradstreet and includes economic trends as well as country risk and industry overviews.
- http://www.countrydata.com This is a service which focuses on country risk forecasts.
- http://www.offshorebanking.barclays.com This is a site developed by Barclays Bank to provide profiles of a variety of countries.
- http://www.doingbusinessin.com This is a site developed by Ernst and Young with information on a variety of countries and industries.

## SALESPERSON AND MARKET FIT

Another consideration that impacts market potential is the fit of the salesperson with the market in which they operate. This is an important consideration because a salesperson may fit well with one market but not another. The global sales manager may have a particular salesperson in mind to use in the markets being considered or may be pondering the type of salesperson to use. Earlier we discussed the pros and cons of expatriates, host-country nationals and third-country nationals. If the sales manager is considering a particular person or group of individuals for use in a new global market expansion, then it is appropriate to consider the conditions within that market and whether there are potential concerns about the individual being assigned to that market.

Fit is normally influenced by culture, and the cultural components provided in Chapter 2 offer a basis for evaluation:

- *Communication*. Does the salesperson speak the proper language or languages?
- *Religion*. Would the religious beliefs of the salesperson affect dealings with potential customers?
- *Education*. Will the level of education play a role in dealings with potential customers?
- *Aesthetics*. Will the dress, appearance and grooming of the salesperson fit with the expectations of the potential buyer?
- *Social organizations*. Does the salesperson belong to the appropriate social organizations or have the proper relationships necessary to have credibility with the potential buyers?
- *Technology*. Will technological knowledge/sensitivity affect the dealings between the salesperson and potential buyers?
- *Time*. Does the salesperson have the appropriate sense of the relevance of time to allow effective interactions with potential buyers?
- *Values and norms*. Does the salesperson have the same or similar values as the potential buyers?

Salesperson fit may also require an evaluation of the following personal characteristics:

- *Gender*. Does the gender of the salesperson have a bearing on their dealings with potential buyers?
- *Age*. Is the salesperson old enough to be seen as credible by potential buyers?
- *Nationality/ethnicity*. Will the color of the salesperson's skin affect dealings with potential buyers?
- *Lifestyle/personality*. Will the individual's choice of lifestyle or their personality have an impact on dealings with potential buyers?

The important consideration for the sales manager is to understand the level of fit between the salesperson and the possible customers that he or she would be calling on.


## COMPETITION

The last of the criteria used to assess the attractiveness of new market opportunities involves the nature of the competition the company faces in the potential market. The competitive intensity that exists makes one potential market more attractive than another. Little or no competition may mean that the main competitor is the foreign government, which leaves little chance of success in that market. The number of competitors is also important. Many competitors signal a saturated market with little chance of success, while few competitors – if not the government or government-controlled – indicate an early stage of the life cycle with excellent potential for sales success. The types of questions that should be asked when assessing competition are as follows:

- How many competitors are there in the market?
- How well established are these competitors?
- Are any of the competitors connected with the government?

- How intense is the rivalry among the competitors?
- Do any of the competitors have significant competitive advantages?
- What stage of the industry life cycle is this market in presently?

The answers to these types of questions can provide valuable insight into the attractiveness of markets for sales force entry.

## THE MARKET POTENTIAL ASSESSMENT CHECKLIST

Now that the individual components of the assessment process have been covered, the final step is to provide a checklist that can be used to compare the various possibilities and to determine which markets have the greatest chance of success. In Figure 13.2 the columns represent the various markets under consideration and the rows represent selected evaluative criteria. A 1–10 rating system is suggested, with 1 signifying little attractiveness/poor fit and 10 representing high attractiveness/excellent fit. The sales manager can arrive at a

| Evaluative criteria | Country/market attractiveness/fit scores (based on 1 = poor and 10 = excellent) | | | | |
|---|---|---|---|---|---|
| | Country/market A | Country/market B | Country/market C | Country/market D | Country/market E |
| Economic conditions<br>Population<br>Income<br>Consumption<br>Development factor score | | | | | |
| Cultural factors<br>Communication<br>Religion<br>Education<br>Aesthetics<br>Social organizations<br>Technology<br>Time<br>Values/norms factor<br>  score | | | | | |
| Market size score | | | | | |
| Political conditions<br>  score | | | | | |
| Legal constraints score | | | | | |
| Salesperson fit<br>  with market | | | | | |
| Competition score | | | | | |
| Overall score | | | | | |

**Figure 13.2** Checklist of criteria for cross-cultural market potential assessment

score for each of the important criteria and then add the scores together to compute an overall score. Using this scoring system, the highest score would be the best choice. Other scoring systems can be used, however. If each potential market were ranked for each criterion, then 1 would indicate the best choice; therefore, when a final score is derived by adding the individual scores for the evaluative criteria, the lowest score would signify the best choice. Either method is acceptable as long as the evaluator is consistent in assigning measures.

Over time a multiplicative approach might make more sense than a simple additive process. That is, certain evaluative criteria may be more important than others, in which case some form of weighting is necessary. In this case, experience allows the sales manager to modify the checklist. A final caution is in order. The checklist is not a precise mechanism that provides guaranteed results; however, it does provide a useful overview of relevant information to assist the sales manager in finding attractive cross-cultural markets to enter.

## CHAPTER SUMMARY

While forecasting potential new market sales may be fairly precise when examining the situation in the home market, such accuracy can be lost when assessing overseas market potential. This is because the data available may be incomplete, outdated, or categorized in such a way that direct comparisons are difficult or impossible. This chapter provides a framework for assessment that allows the global sales manager to compensate for limitations and to enhance the chances of success in identifying and selecting new market opportunities. Finally, a checklist and scoring mechanism is provided to aid the sales manager in this important task.

## DISCUSSION QUESTIONS

1   Why is income problematic when trying to estimate buying power in an overseas market?
2   What is GNP purchasing power parity and how is it helpful in determining sales potential?
3   What are the four different levels of economic development, and what types of products/services would be appropriate for each?
4   What are the five different techniques that can be used for market size determination, and why would it be necessary to use more than one to get a reasonable estimate of sales potential?
5   What is a political risk assessment, and why would it be important when assessing market potential?
6   What are some of the laws that can affect overseas sales and business operations that are important for the sales manager?
7   How can the sales manager assess the fit of a particular salesperson for an overseas market?
8   Why is the level of competition important when assessing overseas market expansion, and how can the different market size estimation techniques be adjusted to reflect expected sales competition?

 **230**

# REFERENCES

1   World Bank (2001), *World Development Report 2000/2001* Washington, DC: World Bank, 275.

2   World Bank (2001), 275.

3   World Bank (2001), 275.

4   OECD (1978–97), *The OECD STAN Database for Industrial Analyses 1978–97*, Paris: OECD, 179.

5   OECD (1978–97), 179.

6   OECD (1978–97), 191.

7   OECD (1978–97) 189.

8   Kotler, Philip (2003), *Marketing Management*, eleventh edition, Upper Saddle River NJ: Prentice Hall.

9   World Bank (2001), 274.

10  World Bank (2001), 276.

11  World Bank (1998), *World Development Indicators 1998*, Washington DC: World Bank, 47.

12  Jain, Subhash C. (2001), *International Marketing*, sixth edition, Cincinnati OH: South Western, 245.

## Chapter 14

# Sales force strategies in the global marketplace

This chapter discusses planning and budgeting activities that impact the sales force and provides sales managers with strategic planning knowledge.

## LEARNING OBJECTIVES

*After reading this chapter, you will be able to*:

■ Understand the strategic planning process and its relationship to sales management.
■ Discuss the various methods for setting sales budgets.
■ Explain the important elements of an effective strategic sales plan.
■ Describe the environmental scanning process and its important components.
■ Understand how to control the strategic process by comparing actual to expected sales performance, and knowing when to take corrective action.

## KEY TERMS

■ Sales budgeting.
■ Goals and objectives.
■ Strategies and tactics.
■ Environmental scanning.
■ Strategic planning.
■ Mission and vision statements.
■ Balanced scorecard.
■ SWOT analysis.

## INTRODUCTION

Intense competition in home markets motivates firms to consider entering overseas markets that are at earlier or less competitive stages of product and industry life cycles. It is this competitive environment that demonstrates the value of strategic planning and the need for competitive advantage. Not only must firms survive in their markets, they must perform at ever higher levels. For this to happen, companies must match their skills and abilities to opportunities that exist in the global marketplace. Of extreme importance within the corporate hierarchy are the sales manager and the sales force. This is because sales figures and market share – relative to competitors – are measures by which firm performance is judged. Sales performance depends upon firm effectiveness, as implemented by the sales force, in meeting customer needs in relation to competitors. This requires a thorough knowledge of: (1) customers and their needs, (2) sales force capabilities, and (3) competitor strengths and weaknesses. The strategic planning process provides a mechanism through which the firm can address customer needs and fend off competitors, thereby improving its chances of survival and its performance. This chapter focuses on the strategic planning process and links this process from the corporate level to the sales department. An important sales force performance measure in an industrial setting is the retention of key customers. Known as customer relationship management (CRM), this area is presented in Chapter 15.

Businesses move through a series of evolutionary stages in terms of formalized planning, that include: (1) planning as a luxury, (2) budgeting, (3) annual planning, (4) long-range planning, and (5) strategic planning.

## PLANNING AS A LUXURY

Entrepreneurial firms begin with the assumption that day-to-day survival is all-important. As a result, there is little or no perceived need for formalized planning. Planning requires time, which is viewed as a luxury by company leaders.

CASE VIGNETTE **TO PLAN OR NOT?**

Peter Connery has been on board as sales manager of a British sales office for approximately two months. Connery has devoted significant time to learning his job, but he is stymied by a request that arrived in the post today. Headquarters has assigned the task of completing a five-year sales plan within a fortnight. Connery feels there is not sufficient time or information to complete the report and honestly believes such effort is a waste of his time. He must comply with the request, so Connery wonders whether he should devote significant time to the project or simply send in numbers that are rough estimates at best?

## BUDGETING

At some point, the entrepreneur realizes that s/he does not possess the necessary financial resources. The first need for formalization therefore focuses on the budgeting process, where the entrepreneur takes time to anticipate future financial needs and set aside proper amounts. Sooner or later, this minimal attempt at systematic planning falls short when the entrepreneur realizes that s/he has not paid attention to events outside the firm and is faced with a serious problem that requires an infusion of financial resources that exceeds the amount that has been budgeted. This forces the development of a marketing plan that takes not only the financial needs of the firm into consideration, but also the nature of the various markets being served, and the potential actions of competitors. The future time horizon that first makes sense is one year.

## ANNUAL PLANNING

This annual marketing plan is the first serious attempt at formalized planning that requires both internal and external assessments. The individual involved in planning must consider all possible events during the next twelve months of operation and think through what might occur in terms of the market and competitors and plan accordingly. By the time the firm looks to develop marketing plans, it has grown in size, which means the marketing plan contains components for different functional areas within marketing. A key component is the sales area. It is important to remember that plans are normally developed in a hierarchy that begins with the company and then flows to each of the separate functional areas operating within the firm. As the firm grows, and its markets become more competitive, the more sophisticated the hierarchy of plans. The primary focus of this chapter is the sales plan, which is a subset of the marketing plan, which is a subset of the overall business or corporate plan. The marketing plan, and the sales plan embedded within it, normally contain the following elements: (1) goals, (2) objectives, (3) strategies, (4) tactics, (5) budgeting, and (6) controls.

### Goals

Goals are the overall statements of where you want to be at a particular point in time in the future. Marketing goals are generally set in terms of one or more key performance criteria that are specific and quantifiable. If goals are not quantifiable, then there is no way to determine whether they are being accomplished. Think how useless a goal would be if it stated: "We will achieve the number one position in our market at the end of one year." How can you measure number one? Would it be measured by sales dollars, units sold, or market share? What increase in sales should there be, compared to competitors, to qualify as number one? These are questions that cannot be answered using such a nebulous measure as "number one." It is important to remember that goal statements are what is realistically expected to occur at the end of one year and, as a result, they serve as a benchmark against which actual performance is measured. The goal: "We want to increase sales by 20 percent over the same period as last year" can be measured and actual performance can be compared against expected performance. The one potential problem with this type of goal statement is that it is specified for the entire period involved, rather than setting performance expectations at several points in time during that entire year. This allows actual performance to be compared with expected performance at several points, so there is an opportunity to take corrective action when necessary. Otherwise, low sales may occur and there will not be time to get back on track.

## Objectives

Objectives are similar to goals in that they are statements of where and when; however, they are stated in terms of a variety of expectations that fall under the umbrella of the goal. When there is only one goal statement, there may be many individual objectives that are complementary in nature. Suppose that our overall goal for the sales force is to increase sales by 20 percent over the next year. (Even more appropriate would be a 5 percent increase by the end of each quarter during the coming year.) We might also have a series of supporting expectations like to: (1) increase customer satisfaction ratings by 10 percent, (2) reduce response time from thirty-six hours to thirty hours, and (3) increase time spent with A level customers by 5 percent while reducing time spent with C level customers by 5 percent. These are examples of objectives that support the overall sales goal.

## Sales strategies

Sales strategies are the action plans adopted by the sales force to reach the goals and objectives set at higher levels. That is, sales strategies describe how the sales force will accomplish the firm's objectives within a specified time period. This action plan includes things that must be done to get the firm where it plans to go. The strategies include such things as: (1) providing the entire sales force with laptops to increase efficiency, (2) improving customer service in European markets, (3) retraining North American sales personnel in customer relationship management to increase sales, and (4) introducing more efficient sales force call reporting mechanisms. It is necessary to develop strategies around a specific target market. Also, selected strategies impact the type of salesperson hired, how training is conducted, how duties are performed, motivational methods, and payment plans.

## Tactics

Tactics are day-to-day operational details that are part of the overall strategies and are each a separate piece of the action plan. The addition of three salespersons in Europe constitutes a tactic that supports the strategy of improved customer service.

## Budgeting

Budgeting involves the assessment of the financial/resource needs of the firm over a specific period of time. Sales managers must contemplate potential expenses for the sales force and present a budget to management. There are four regularly used methods for setting budgets: (1) "all you can afford," (2) percent of past sales, (3) percent of future sales, and (4) objective and task.

## All you can afford

A common scenario for setting the sales budget is the "all you can afford" method. It involves firm management informing the sales manager exactly how much money is available for sales activities. This occurs in centralized, top-down structured enterprises where budgets are determined and apportioned by senior management. It is a less than optimum way to set sales budgets because it does not consider the particular needs and expectations set for the sales function.

## Percentage of past sales

The percentage of past sales method is based upon historical evidence that a particular percentage of total sales is appropriate. Some firms annually allocate the sales area the same percentage of the previous year's sales revenue. For example, there may be an unwritten rule that 10 percent is a reasonable amount to allocate the sales department for the upcoming period based upon the revenue achieved last year. The rationale used for this action is that these were actual sales as opposed to projected sales, and projected sales may not be achieved. The flaw in the logic is that sales do not produce sales budgets – but sales budgets do lead to the achievement of sales.

## Percent of future sales

The percent of future sales method is based upon different logic and is a popular method for budget allocation. The allocated percentage is based upon industry standards, and a series of examples from the United States is shown in Table 14.1 as compiled from the *Sales Force Compensation Survey* developed by Dartnell Corporation.[1] A large disparity is evident between the 1.7 percent of sales for the business services industry and the 47.9 percent of sales for the educational services industry. It is interesting to note the proportionally large amount used by small companies as opposed to the small amounts for the larger companies. Firms may believe that if they budget an amount equal to competitors, then they will be on equal footing. Conversely, using industry averages to set budgets does not necessarily lead to accurate resource allocations. The percentages represent the collective wisdom of the industry and serve as an effective starting point for sales managers when computing expenses for the upcoming period.

## Objective and task

The objective and task method focuses more appropriately on what the sales manager is trying to accomplish and what the tasks will realistically cost. First the sales manager must consider the objectives that have been set for the sales function, and then s/he examines each task or tactical action that will be completed to achieve the objectives that comprise the sales strategies. Finally the costs related to each activity are assessed in developing the overall sales budget. Unlike other budgeting methods discussed, the objective and task method is a realistic approach that lists specific actions that will be undertaken and predicts what those actions will cost. Firms may be reluctant to adopt the objective and task

**237**

**Table 14.1** *Sales force expenditures as a percent of sales*

| Category | % of sales |
|---|---|
| *Company by sales (US$)* | |
| Less than 5 million | 14.7 |
| $5 million – 25 million | 10.5 |
| $25 million – 100 million | 7.9 |
| $100 million – 250 million | 3.5 |
| Greater than 250 million | 6.8 |
| *Company by product/service* | |
| Consumer products | 5.4 |
| Consumer services | 7.9 |
| Industrial products | 4.1 |
| Industrial services | 6.4 |
| Office products | 9.4 |
| Office services | 8.1 |
| *Company by industry category* | |
| Business services | 1.7 |
| Chemicals | 2.9 |
| Communications | 9.8 |
| Educational services | 47.9 |
| Electronics | 4.2 |
| Fabricated metals | 10.8 |
| Health services | 19.9 |
| Hotels and other lodging | 21.4 |
| Instruments | 2.3 |
| Insurance | 2.5 |
| Machinery | 10.1 |
| Manufacturing | 13.6 |
| Office equipment | 9.0 |
| Paper products | 6.8 |
| Printing/publishing | 12.0 |
| Retailing | 6.1 |
| Trucking/warehousing | 12.2 |
| Wholesale (consumer) | 3.7 |
| Wholesale (industrial) | 9.5 |

budgeting approach because financial resources are scarce and management are concerned that proposed numbers will be inflated.

When approaching the subject of budget allocation, it is important for the sales manager to examine all possible types of sales function expenditures. The following list of common sales expense categories should be considered when developing a sales budget:[2]

- Sales force salaries, commissions, and bonuses.
- Sales manager salaries, commissions, and bonuses.
- Social security.
- Retirement plans.
- Hospitalization.
- Life insurance.
- Automobile.
- Travel, meals, lodging, and entertainment.
- Cellular phone, long-distance, and Internet communications.
- Samples and other sales aids.
- Recruiting and training.
- Clerical and secretarial services.
- Office rent and utilities.
- Office supplies.

## Controls

Controls deal with the need for mechanisms the sales manager can utilize to monitor ongoing performance and take corrective action when necessary. The issue is to have a way in which actual performance is monitored during the implementation of the plan to see whether the firm is on target. When goals and objectives are specific and quantifiable, they serve as effective performance benchmarks. At various points in time, the sales manager compares actual sales performance against expected sales performance (established in the goals/objectives) to see if things are progressing as planned. If there is a deviation, then corrective action can be taken. If things are not going well, there are three possible considerations: (1) the goals/objectives were inappropriately set, (2) the strategies for achieving the goals/objectives are inappropriate, or (3) both the goals/objectives and the strategies may be flawed. The point is to ensure that a mechanism is in place to oversee progress. If evaluation is postponed until the end of the year, it will be too late to take corrective action and the shortfall cannot be repaired. What mechanisms can be effectively used for monitoring and control purposes? This depends upon the goals/objectives that have been set. Using examples of previously discussed objectives (increase customer satisfaction ratings by 10 percent, reduce response time from thirty-six hours to thirty hours, and increase time with A level customers by 5 percent while reducing time with C level customers by 5 percent), customer surveys can be employed to assess satisfaction levels and call reports and other information fed into CRM systems can evaluate response times and time spent with various classes of customers.

## LONG-RANGE PLANNING

The next evolutionary step involves the expansion of the planning time horizon. No longer is a one-year horizon sufficient for assuring firm success. Annual planning is maintained while a longer-term perspective is achieved through a long-range plan. Such plans are written in more general terms, but while a new annual plan is set forth for the upcoming year, the five-year plan is adjusted and rewritten, based upon changes that have occurred during the past year, to project five years into the future. It is necessary to look at trends that occur outside the firm, so the company will not be surprised by changes that significantly affect firm performance. The time horizon should extend out at least to a five-year window. Some firms, like IBM, scan fifty years into the future, looking for important potential changes. While this appears impossible in a time of exponential technological change, many innovations are developed in attempts to envision life in the future. A major component included in this type of analysis is *environmental scanning*. Environmental scanning involves careful examination of changes that occur outside the firm that can significantly impact company performance, and includes the following external assessments: (1) political changes, (2) legal changes, (3) economic changes, (4) technological changes, (5) societal changes, and (6) cultural changes.

### Political changes

Political changes involve assessing possible shifts in the political structure of the countries or markets in which you are already operating or are considering entering. If political stability becomes questionable, it may be best to pull salespeople out of the country and move them to a nearby nation to avoid potential harm or impediment. This scenario has been utilized by many global firms post 9/11 world events.

### Legal changes

Legal changes include modifications in the legal structure in the markets being served or under consideration. New laws, in a particular global market, can affect important sales aspects like: (1) who can serve as a salesperson, (2) what hours they can effectively operate, (3) what types of sales tactics they can use, (4) what constitutes an agreement between the salesperson and the customer, and (5) what paperwork/licensing is required for the sales force to operate in that country or locale. Careful scrutiny of existing and pending local and national laws is always a sound planning strategy.

### Economic changes

Economic changes involve potential variations in earning and purchasing power, the cost of capital, and the rate of inflation. Also changes in economic development permit new infrastructure changes that can significantly affect sales and distribution efforts in a particular country. The advent of a recession would significantly affect incomes and purchasing power, and increasing inflationary pressures can affect spending behavior. Why should customers wait to make large purchases if they believe their money will be worth less in the future? If interest rates drop, customers may make big-ticket purchases that they would not make when rates were higher.

## Technological changes

Technological changes have a staggering potential impact on sales and firm performance. Take, for instance, the advent of the Internet and e-commerce. Technology has a significant effect on how customers are reached and serviced. The staggering growth of mobile telephones in Europe has coincided with an ever-increasing shift to data transmission via telephone. This growth has not been seen concurrently in the United States, and how the salesperson interacts with customers may differ when addressing the needs of American and European customers. Will customers buy big-ticket items over the Internet? The success of Dell Computers in many countries suggests that they will. The nature of the sales force, and the types of accounts handled, will likely be impacted by technological changes. Other aspects of sales potentially affected by technology include: (1) Will customers demand personal visits or will e-mail messages suffice in certain situations? (2) Will training the salesperson to use new laptop-based activity tracking software make them more efficient? (3) Will video teleconferencing allow the salesperson to make "team" presentations to customers instead of personal visits?

## Societal changes

Societal changes also have a significant impact on sales and firm performance. Changing lifestyles and work habits can affect customer expectations. Increasing concern for eating healthy foods, better use of leisure time activities, increasing sensitivity to ethical issues and social responsibility (particularly in light of the Enron crisis in the United States), and increasing concerns over safety and security (e.g., the United States after the terrorist attacks of September 11, 2001) are all examples of issues which will change the habits and expectations of both consumer and industrial customers. Awareness of these kinds of changes offers astute firms profitable opportunities.

## Cultural changes

Cultural changes become particularly relevant when the sales manager looks at an increasingly global marketplace. Most environmental scanning models exclude cultural changes as a key component; however, imagine the importance of language shifts, educational changes, and modifications in religious teachings and preferences in the era of global sales. Chapter 2 provided a detailed discussion of culture in a global setting, and research indicates that cultures are changing due to technological advances in communications and increasing exposure to outside cultures (e.g., McDonald's, Starbuck's, and the influence exerted by the US and European movie and music industries). Being culturally sensitive and aware can only help sales managers view changes as they happen and adjust sales practices to permit the sales force to address customers' needs and wants.

If the fundamental tenet of sales is to be in the right place, at the right time, with the right product, it is not clear how the sales firm can enhance its survival without using environmental scanning. The extension of the time horizon in long-range planning from that of annual planning is a necessity to give the firm a greater chance of success in an ever-intensifying competitive global marketplace.

## STRATEGIC PLANNING

The most advanced of all evolutionary planning stages is strategic planning, in which the previous components are all retained within the strategic plan (budgeting, annual planning, and long-range planning). However, the strategic plan adds significant amounts of information based upon an additional set of perspective-enhancing tools and techniques, which greatly increase the chances of seizing and maintaining competitive advantage. Strategic planning enhances the likelihood of gaining a competitive advantage by systematically matching the firm's skills and abilities with marketplace opportunities. More intelligence gathering is involved, and the increased information allows the planner to make more informed decisions. The company that gathers this information, in theory, is better able to find mechanisms for differentiation and distinction than those not collecting such information. In essence, the goal is to maximize the firm's strengths while minimizing its weaknesses. The only way for this to happen is by thoroughly analyzing not only the firm and its resources, but also customers and competitors. Each of the tools and techniques utilized enhances the sales manager's perspective and provides a forum for making strategic decisions that capitalize on competitor weaknesses. Larger and more sophisticated firms recognize the need for strategic planning, but even a small entrepreneurial operation can benefit from strategic planning.

Intense competition faces any firm that sells its products in maturing markets and, as competition intensifies, it becomes obvious that when products and services move towards standardization (as they will inevitably in mature markets[3]) the only way for the firm to survive is by differentiating itself from direct competitors. Strategies need focus and direction, and when a firm arrives at this point, a better system is needed for developing marketing and sales plans. As a result two new corporate mechanisms provide this strategic focus: the mission statement and the vision statement.

- *The mission statement* communicates what the company is in business for and is employed in the drive for distinctiveness. The mission statement provides a description of the firm's purpose and serves an important strategic application because it sets limits on the company. Through the mission statement, management and personnel understand what the firm *does not do*. Ries and Trout talk about firms that continually lose sight of what they are and extend their brands to the point that they become sellers of all things to all types of customers.[4] The mission statement helps the firm maintain consistency in its offerings so that it avoids the tendency to confuse its customers by being something that it is not. Annual and long-range plans are therefore written under the umbrella of the mission statement to maintain consistency and focus.
- *The vision statement* is a more recent addition to the strategic planning literature. The vision statement communicates where management would like to see the firm move in the future. This is written, needless to say, under the limitations of scope established by the mission statement. Because the vision statement appears in both internal and external corporate communications, inconsistencies with the mission statement will confuse important constituencies.

With these two statements in place, the entire company must adhere to the constraints these statements impose when developing functional strategic plans. It is necessary at this evolutionary stage for performance needs to be viewed in a slightly different format. No longer are financial performance measures (e.g., return on sales, return on investment, sales, market share) sufficient. In intensely competitive markets the firm also must be concerned with softer measures (e.g., customer satisfaction levels, community opinion, employee morale). As a result, Kaplan and Norton developed a new approach to measuring performance known as the *balanced scorecard*.[5] This measure integrates financial performance with three other perspectives: customer, operational, and innovation and learning. The firm's goal is to succeed in a more holistic way, by incorporating customer satisfaction, operational efficiency, and innovativeness with profitability, sales, and market share measures.

This holistic approach fits effectively with the ever-increasing focus on customer relationship management and stresses the need for improved cross-functional communications in organizations. What is key is that the sales manager should approach the strategic planning process with the realization that sales, along with other functional components, can benefit from such a broad performance measurement. Why should only sales, profits or market share be monitored? Should we not be concerned with customer satisfaction or the way that s/he has been dealt with by company salespeople? A negative incident might not immediately result in a loss of sales, but without an indication that the customer is dissatisfied, the sales manager might not foresee the potential for lost sales. We also need to know if sales force members are satisfied and whether the mechanism for communication between sales, advertising, and operations is in sync so as to avoid making customer promises that cannot be kept. What tools and techniques should be employed to develop effective strategic sales plans? Figure 14.1 provides an overview of important tools and techniques.

## Decision support system

This tool involves the intelligence gathering and storing mechanism used in the strategic planning process. For the sales function this includes systematic input from field sales personnel about what is happening in their territories, internally generated data that are useful for planning (e.g., sales to quota reports, new account generation reports), pertinent outside secondary data studies (e.g., Arbitron reports, A.C. Nielsen reports, European Monitor reports), and relevant primary data studies (e.g., consumer satisfaction surveys, perceptual mapping studies). The sales manager needs relevant data for strategic planning purposes, and the key to facilitation is a well developed data generation, storage, and dissemination system that is easily accessible. Such a system is developed in conjunction with key individuals from the firm's information technology area. At a minimum, a formalized method should exist for data input, storage, and retrieval. One way this can be facilitated is to have salespersons complete activity reports (beyond the normal, who was called upon, how much time was spent, and did a sale take place?) and note customer comments on appropriate forms or enter that information into a laptop. This is all valuable information, and the sales force must be trained to gather intelligence for use in the planning process. Information that resides in the head of the salesperson is of little value in strategic planning.

**243**

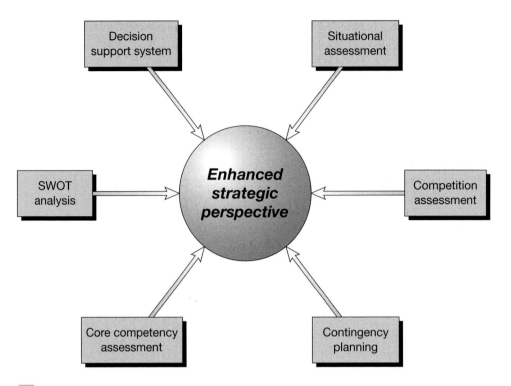

**Figure 14.1** *Important strategic perspective enhancement tools*

## Situational assessment

Another important tool for effective strategic planning is situational assessment, which is a detailed report of what is happening in the various markets served by the company and why. This report examines customers served, competitors, marketplace dynamics, environmental factors that affect the market, company sales, profits, and costs. Situation assessment requires answering the following types of questions:[6]

What
- benefits does the customer seek?
- factors influence customer demand?
- functions does the product/service perform for the customer?
- are important buying criteria?
- is the basis for comparison with other products/services?
- risks does the customer perceive?
- services do customers expect?

How
- do customers buy?
- long does the buying process last?

- do various elements of the marketing program influence customers at each stage of the process?
- do customers use the product/service?
- does the product/service fit into their lifestyle or operation?
- much are buyers willing to spend?
- much do they buy?

Where
- is the decision made to buy?
- do customers seek information about the product/service?
- do customers buy the product/service?

When
- do customers buy?
- do customers choose one brand as opposed to another?

Who
- are the occupants of segments identified by any previous questions?
- buys our product/service, and why?
- buys our competitors' products/services, and why?

The answers to such questions not only allow the sales manager to perform effective situational assessments, but they permit the identification of potentially new customer segments. Once this process is completed, the sales manager should have a clearer picture of what is happening in the various markets being served, as well as the forces driving the events. This analysis is valuable to the planner because s/he is now in a better position to think about the future.

## Competitor assessment

A synergistic tool that helps to improve the situational assessment is a competitor assessment. The most noteworthy model for this type of assessment is the Five Forces model developed by Michael Porter at Harvard University.[7] The five components for the model include:

- The intensity of the various rivals.
- The bargaining power of the buyers.
- The bargaining power of the suppliers.
- The threat of potential new entrants.
- The threat of substitute products or services.

The model, as adapted for the sales function, is shown in Figure 14.2. Each component must be assessed separately for the model to provide the necessary insight. The most important component is the central box: intensity of the rivals. The key is to determine just how intense salesperson rivalry is for each market segment in which the company operates. Intensity of rivals is determined by evaluating the following types of market segment characteristics:

**245**

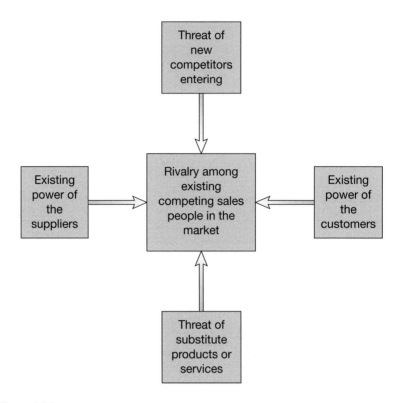

**Figure 14.2** Porter's Five Forces model of a sales context

- *Barriers to entry or exit*. The smaller the barriers to entry to the segment, the greater the number of rivals, thus greater intensity of rivalry exists. The greater the barriers to exit, the greater the commitment to the segment, thus greater intensity of rivalry.
- *Number of competitors*. The greater the number of competitors, the greater the intensity of rivalry.
- *Sales growth patterns*. Slow sales growth intensifies rivalry.
- *Product/service differentiation*. The less differentiable products and services are, the greater the intensity of rivalry.
- *High fixed costs*. If fixed costs are high, intensity of rivals is high.

The right-hand box represents the power of existing customers. The concern is how much power is actually in the hands of customers. Customers have power when: (1) there are few customers that make large purchases, (2) the products/services involved are a large proportion of the customer's purchases, (3) the products or services involved are not easily differentiated, and (4) the costs to switch to a new supplier are low.

The left-hand box focuses on the power of the suppliers of the product for sale by the salesperson. This is a less important component to analyze unless products are purchased from a range of distinct suppliers for sale to different segments. In this case, the suppliers have power when: (1) there are only a few suppliers of the product, (2) the number of readily available substitutes is low, (3) the salesperson does not sell large amounts of the product, and (4) the products offered can be differentiated from competitors.

The last two components are the threat of new entrants into the market and the threat of substitutes. For new entrants, the important considerations are: how high are entry barriers? Is it expensive for new competitors to access the market? Are the relationships that have been built between the salesperson and his or her customers deep and meaningful? If a global competitor is looking to enter the market, is there a chance that its sales force can offer the product at a lower price? These are the kinds of questions that must be asked. In terms of substitutes, the concern is whether alternative products/services would be seen as comparable to what you offer. This type of analysis is helpful because it sets the stage for understanding how competitors might retaliate to strategic moves by the firm's sales force, and vice versa.

## Core competency assessment

A valuable tool for strategic planning is the assessment of core competencies. What this involves is the identification of what you do that is not possible, or is at least extremely difficult, for others to provide. That is, what do you have or do that no one else can have or do? When examining the sales function in particular, the sales manager must look at the entire area to see where distinctive competencies may lie. One way to achieve a competency is by providing the highest value for the customer. Here are other examples of potential distinctive competencies that may be extremely valuable:

- A brand name that is highly valued by the customer.
- A delivery system that outperforms competitors.
- Long-term relationships that provide exceptional customer value.

If the company does not possess any core competency, then strategically it is valuable to develop a competency that can serve as the basis for customer value enhancement.

## Contingency planning

Contingency planning involves the development of a series of alternative responses to particular market occurrences. What is potentially deadly for a company is when something unanticipated happens. When this occurs, the firm must stop, step back, and assess the situation, and then develop a strategic response to the event. If history teaches companies anything, it is that a delay of this kind can be disastrous. In order to avoid such a possibility, the sales manager must look, at a minimum, at three scenarios: best case, worst case, and *status quo*. In other words, what if the best possible situation occurred, what if the worst possible situation happened, and finally what if things continue as they are now (*status quo*)? It is always important to consider variations from one extreme to the other, and as a result, there is less chance that something unforeseen will happen. Having a terrific result can be just as potentially problematic as having a sales slump. If orders go through the roof, will the customers receive the products they have ordered if we have not manufactured enough or do not have inventory on hand? Most managers find it useful to contingency plan with spreadsheet software like Lotus,© Quattro,© or Excel© so that they can change various important inputs and outputs in planning models and, thereby, consider a range of possible outcomes.

## SWOT analysis

SWOT analysis attempts to assess the company's Strengths, Weaknesses, Opportunities, and Threats. The previously discussed tools and techniques all add valuable information that is effectively used in this type of analysis. Company strengths and weaknesses are internal elements, while opportunities and threats are external elements. Assessing sales force strengths and weaknesses can be accomplished by analyzing the sales force and all available support mechanisms. For example, are any salespeople experiencing personal problems? Have any expatriate sales personnel had trouble adjusting to their new territories? Are customers receiving purchased goods and services in a timely manner? When assessing opportunities and threats, the sales manager has to consider what might happen. Looking at the information generated by the situational analysis and the future assessment in contingency planning provide an excellent basis for estimating the probabilities of future occurrences. What is the likelihood of new competitors entering our overseas sales territories? What is the probability that the upcoming election in one of our global markets will negatively affect sales revenues? The sales manager must also carefully consider both the short- and the long-term effects of possible changes in policies and practices. Once a thorough SWOT analysis is completed, then the sales manager is in a much stronger position to develop meaningful annual and long-range plans that are strategically focused.

## CHAPTER SUMMARY

The highest level of planning evolution today is strategic planning. This chapter focused on how planning has evolved over the years and presented specific applications for the sales function. The use of various strategic perspective enhancing tools and techniques allows the sales manager to develop both effective annual strategic sales plans and long-range plans that improve sales performance in competitive global markets. All tools discussed are easily adapted for sales so that the chances of achieving competitive advantage are greatly enhanced. In conclusion, the better-prepared strategic planner is the one who will win the battle in the marketplace.

## DISCUSSION QUESTIONS

1   What is the goal of strategic planning and how is it achieved?
2   What are the five evolutionary stages that most companies pass through in regard to planning, and what distinguishes each new stage?
3   What are the four different methods that were discussed for developing sales budgets? Which is the most appropriate, and why?

4   Why is environmental scanning important? What are the different types of changes that should be monitored?

5   What differences exist between mission and vision statements?

6   Why is a decision support system so valuable in strategic planning, and what would the sales manager want to include in this system?

7   What is the Porter Five Forces model, and how can it assist the sales manager in developing a strategic sales plan?

8   What is a core competency? Can there be any core competencies in sales?

## REFERENCES

1   Staff (1992), *Sales Force Compensation Survey*, Chicago: Dartnell Corporation, 109.

2   Dalrymple, Douglas J., and William L. Cron (1995), *Sales Management: Concepts and Cases*, fifth edition, New York: John Wiley & Sons, 65–6.

3   Porter, Michael E. (1980), *Competitive Strategy*, New York: Free Press, 159–61.

4   Ries, Al, and Jack Trout (1986), *Positioning: The Battle for your Mind*, New York: Warner Business Books, 101–13.

5   Kaplan, Robert S., and David P. Norton (1992), "The Balanced Scorecard: Measures that Drive Performance," *Harvard Business Review*, January–February, 71–9.

6   Abell, Derek F., and John S. Hammond (1979), *Strategic Market Planning*, Englewood Cliffs NJ: Prentice Hall, 49–50.

7   Porter, Michael E. (1980), *Competitive Strategy*, New York: Free Press, 1–33.

## Chapter 15

# Customer relationship management

This chapter presents concepts and theories pertaining to customer relationship management (CRM) and discusses implementation issues when applied to culturally diverse customers.

## LEARNING OBJECTIVES

*After reading this chapter, you will be able to*:

- Understand the importance of CRM.
- Define CRM and describe its evolution.
- List the determinants of CRM and key stages in its development
- Explain the main functions and various models of CRM.
- Discuss the role of salespeople as relationship developers.
- Explain issues pertaining to the management of customer relationships.

## KEY TERMS

- Customer relationship management.
- Trust and value.
- Relationship promoters.

With the globalization of business, competition has intensified. Companies have become more customer-driven and salespeople increasingly focus on customer retention. The notion of having a customer "for life" has become the prevailing business philosophy. Salespeople are repeatedly reminded of the need to build strong and lasting relationships with customers and measure their success by the "share" of their customers. In order to establish and maintain strong relationships, salespeople need to focus on lifetime customer value and invest a significant proportion of their time understanding customers' needs. Salespeople must work together with customers to promote growth opportunities in the same way they would for their own company.

Today, the challenges facing sales managers in the global marketplace are how to develop a strategic approach to customer relationship management and provide adequate support that enables the company to build profitable relationships. To make the most of customers, salespeople need to know not only how to attract, but also how to retain, profitable customers by creating opportunities for delivering incremental value. Customer relationship management rests heavily upon the shoulders of salespeople and their ability to embrace customer needs, increase customer satisfaction by identifying what creates value, and delivering that value to each customer.

## CUSTOMER RELATIONSHIP MANAGEMENT DEFINED

Customer relationship management can be defined in many different ways. For example, Buttle (2000) defines CRM as "the development and maintenance of mutually beneficial long-term relationships with strategically significant customers."[1] Furthermore, Plakoyiannaki and Tzokas (2001), state that "CRM is an IT enhanced value process, which identifies, develops, integrates and focuses the various competencies of the firm to the 'voice' of the customer in order to deliver long-term superior customer value, at a profit to well identified existing and potential customers."[2]

CASE VIGNETTE **THE "VALUE PROPOSITION"**

Philip, a key account manager for a computer software company, was confronted with an unusual situation. His customers were not purchasing like before, despite the fact that he had intensified his selling efforts. To find out what was wrong, Philip used a vacation week to socialize with key customers and uncover the root of the problem. In these discussions the customers said that competitors offered tailor-made software, provided twenty-four-hour service support, offered free training, and charged less for their products. Philip talked to his manager about his dilemma and two months later the company embraced a CRM philosophy. The new approach gave Philip the flexibility to move away from the old "arm's length" practice of dealing with customers and eventually he won every account back.

Customer relationship management, therefore, focuses on strengthening the bond between customers and the firm by maximizing the value of the relationship for the benefit of both the customer and the sales firm. Although CRM is an IT enhanced value process, it is more than automating the sales function. Technology is necessary to obtain customer information, but what is most important is how that information is used within an organization for value creation and for the enhancement of customer relationships.

As a business philosophy, customer relationship management is based upon individual customers and customized products and services supported by open lines of communication and feedback from the participating firms that mutually benefits both buying and selling organizations. The buying and the selling firms enter into a "learning relationship," with the customer being willing to collaborate with the seller and grow as a loyal customer. In return, the seller works to maximize the value of the relationship for the customer's benefit. It is this business philosophy that is CRM. With the objective of most businesses today being to create and maintain loyal customers at a profit, CRM provides the platform for seeking competitive advantage by embracing customer needs and building value-driven long-term relationships.

Developing strong and lasting customer relationships offers several advantages. Notably, the sales organization can increase its profitability by increasing customer loyalty and decrease threats from competition. As the case vignette indicates, Philip's company stopped offering value to its customers at the cost of losing them. By developing a customer relationship that was based upon mutual benefits and trust, the company regained the customers.

## EVOLUTION OF CUSTOMER RELATIONSHIP MANAGEMENT

Customer relationship management has evolved from the marketing concept. CRM represents a refocusing of marketing with greater emphasis on the creation of customer value. More specifically, the main emphasis has shifted from satisfying customer needs to building relationships through a long-term value creation process.

As discussed in Chapter 3, the focus and status of the sales force have evolved over time. Also, different firms utilize the sales force in distinct ways. For example, the selling approach prevalent in the 1970s was based on persuading customers to buy, whereas in the 1980s persuasion lost much of its effectiveness and transformed to transacting with individual buyers. In the 1990s more lifetime bonds were developed between selling organizations and customers, and this marked the genesis of the CRM philosophy. Nowadays, sales organizations and customers are active players that cocreate value through long-term business relationships.

The introduction and wide use of information technology in the marketplace has empowered customers with broader knowledge and facilitated the constant exchange of information between sellers and buyers. By moving closer to customers, understanding their needs, and allowing customers to actively shape their own expectations by cocreating value, sales organizations obtain a strategic customer focus.

## DETERMINANTS OF CUSTOMER RELATIONSHIP MANAGEMENT

In customer relationship management the two most essential ingredients are trust and value. Trust is the willingness to rely on the ability, integrity, and motivation of one company to

**253**

serve the needs of the other company as agreed upon implicitly or explicitly.[3] Trust, according to the definition, implies that: (1) companies should have confidence in each other; (2) each company's judgment reinforces the belief that the other is able to deliver value and has the integrity and the required level of motivation to deliver; and (3) each company will comply and honor the implicit and explicit parts of the reached agreement.

Value refers to the ability of a selling organization to satisfy the needs of the customer at a comparatively lower cost or higher benefit than that offered by competitors and measured in monetary, temporal, functional, and psychological terms. When companies trust each other and have the ability to offer superior value, then the foundations for developing and sustaining a customer relationship are indeed strong.

In addition to trust and value being essential ingredients in building customer relationships, other key factors that influence the creation and effective management of a customer relationship management program are: (1) long-term perspective, (2) honesty, (3) post-sales support, (4) understanding customer needs, and (5) meeting commitments.[4]

*Long-term perspective.* The success of any customer relationship program depends upon the salesperson's passionate interest in the relationship and constant efforts to establish and retain a long-term relationship. The salesperson should adopt a long-term approach rather than aim for short-term results. Global firms can benefit considerably from establishing lasting relationships with global customers because the expense of retaining existing customers for life is less than the cost of gaining new customers.

*Honesty.* Honesty and sincerity are important ingredients in a business relationship. The salesperson must make sure that the customer is always told the truth in order to retain both the business and the trust of the customer. Honesty also improves a salesperson's communication effectiveness and leads to a better understanding of customer needs. Honesty crosses cultural borders and, as a value, is appreciated by customers worldwide.

*Providing after-sales support.* It is very important that salespeople provide thorough follow-up services with positive responsiveness to customer concerns. Outstanding aftersales service prompts attention to disagreements and helps resolve problems. It is almost certain that, from a buyer's point of view, a purchase signals the beginning of a relationship rather than the end. Adequate aftersales support enhances the relationship and allows it to survive and strengthen as time evolves.

*Understanding customer needs and problems.* Any CRM program relies on the understanding of customers' needs. For example, once a customer realizes that a salesperson can be trusted and is a valuable resource for new ideas and solutions, the buyer will share appropriate information regarding business and needs and make an effort to strengthen the relationship. It is through understanding customer needs that an international salesperson is equipped to provide added value to his/her customers.

*Meeting commitments.* It is important that the trust-building effort of a salesperson gains the buyer's positive evaluation. When this is coupled with the salesperson's commitment to serve the account in the best possible way, and more competently than other competitors, then the foundations for establishing a strong relationship are in place. Undoubtedly, the skills and competencies of salespeople in delivering value and meeting commitments not only contribute to maintaining the relationship, but they also drive the customer relationship to a partnership level.

## STAGES IN THE DEVELOPMENT OF A CUSTOMER RELATIONSHIP

The key factors that drive the development of an effective customer relationship are inter-dependence, cooperation and mutual trust.[5] Perceived interdependence is the catalyst that gives both sellers and buyers a reason to cooperate and the motivation to reciprocate the necessary trust and commitment to build a successful relationship. The stages that companies pass through in building a relationship, according to the Industrial Marketing and Purchasing Group,[6] are:

- *Complementary needs*. At this stage two companies recognize that they depend on each other for resources that each company is lacking.
- *Interactions*. Repeated personal contacts and exchanges that help build the relationship.
- *Outcomes and satisfaction*. Repeated personal contacts and exchanges lead eventually to mutually beneficial outcomes and satisfaction.
- *Investments*. Companies become dedicated to each other and their willingness to invest is a reciprocal act of both companies.
- *Commitment*. Reciprocal investments perpetuate the trust-based relationship-building process.

The starting point of a business relationship is transactional in nature and the level of initial commitment is rather limited and short-term in nature. As the relationship grows, the level of commitment becomes more complex and the nature of the relationship progresses from short-term transactional to long-term collaborative.

The developmental stages are the pre-key account management (KAM) stage (where product need is established), the early stage (where transactions take place), the middle

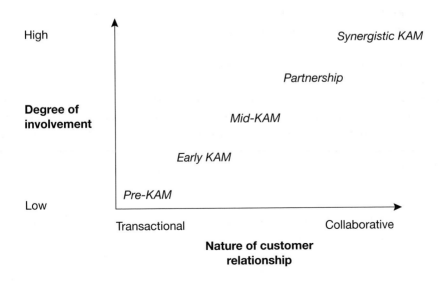

**Figure 15.1** *The stages in the development of a customer relationship*
*Source: adapted with some modification from Millman and Wilson (1995)*

**255**

stage (where the selling company becomes a preferred supplier), the partnership stage (where supplier and buyer form a partnership) and the synergistic stage (where supplier and buyer integrate activities to deliver value to customers). From a global salesperson's perspective, the key issue is to effectively manage the progression from one stage to the next within a well defined time framework that meets the approval of culturally diverse customers.

The global salesperson guides the development process by first focusing on establishing the relationship (pre-KAM), second, increasing the volume of business (early KAM), third, establishing distinct competitive advantages (mid-KAM), fourth, identifying opportunities for process integration (partnership KAM) and fifth, coordinating large matrix teams (synergistic KAM). Successful management of the development process leads to superior long-term performance of the selling organization through improved customer retention.

In a similar vein, Ford (1980)[7] put forward a relationship development model that consists of five stages:

- The *pre-relationship stage* – or the event that triggers a buyer/supplier to seek a new business partner.
- The *early stage* – where experience is accumulated between the two parties although a great degree of uncertainty and distance exists.
- The *development stage* – where increased levels of transactions lead to a higher degree of commitment and the distance is reduced to a social exchange.
- The *long-term stage* – that is characterized by the companies' mutual importance to each other.
- The *final stage* – where the interaction between the companies becomes institutionalized.

An example of a company that has moved towards a greater degree of collaboration is United Parcel Services (UPS), which integrated the Internet into its business processes to offer superior customer services, like parcel tracking and online customer interface. This service has been integrated with its customers' business processes, by offering increased service quality, leading to greater customer commitment and loyalty.

With the recognition that customer relationships evolve and change over time, the notion of the relationship life cycle is an important tool that explains not only the development of a relationship but also its dissolution. For instance, according to the development models, during the early development stages the companies are distant from one another. In later phases the relationship is characterized by increased commitment and cooperation, whereas in the final stages the relationship declines as patterns of interaction are institutionalized.

As with any life cycle model, the duration of each stage is variable. It is difficult to predict how long two firms will remain in one phase before moving to the next. It is also possible that one or both parties may decide not to allow the relationship to progress through the life cycle. However, as long as this decision satisfies both firms, it should not be seen as a "negative sign" in the relationship. When a relationship enters the decline phase of its life cycle, the level of commitment and cooperation drops significantly. The relationship life cycle model is shown diagrammatically in Figure 15.2.

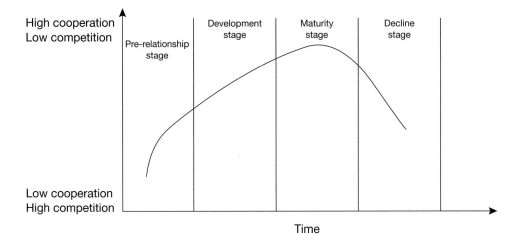

**Figure 15.2** *A relationship life cycle model*
*Source: adapted with some modification from I.F. Wilkinson and L.C. Young, "Business Dancing: the Nature and Role of Interfirm Relations in Business Strategy," in D. Ford (ed.),* Understanding Business Markets, *London: Dryden Press, 1997*

The life cycle depicts the development and potential decline of a customer–supplier relationship. In establishing long-term relationships, the most important task of the salesperson is to initiate the relationship and move it to the maturity phase, with each phase strengthening the company's relationship with the customer. It is also important that salespeople prevent the relationship from entering the decline stage.

## FUNCTIONS OF CUSTOMER RELATIONSHIP MANAGEMENT

In the process of creating and nurturing a customer relationship, the value component is of utmost importance. Delivering superior value to global customers should be an ongoing concern of international salespersons that base their selling strategies around the value creation process. Consequently, knowing and understanding how value is created, perceived, and measured by customers can help salespeople move toward a process model that links several organizational functions in creating value for customers. Modern sales organizations should combat value migration and capture it for their customers by investing in technology, adapting their product offerings, and focusing on enhancing the distribution process to customers. Integration creates value, and the role of salespeople in this new business philosophy is to become relationship promoters and to communicate value-based strategies to their customers.

The key to designing an effective value-driven strategy is to move away from traditional functional job roles to a process model that links the functions in creating value for customers. The technology, product, and customer delivery process as depicted by Sharma[8] *et al.*'s (2001) model are interconnected processes. By investing in technology, adapting product offerings, and focusing on enhancing the distribution process, a company creates and delivers value to its customers.

**257**

**Value creation process**

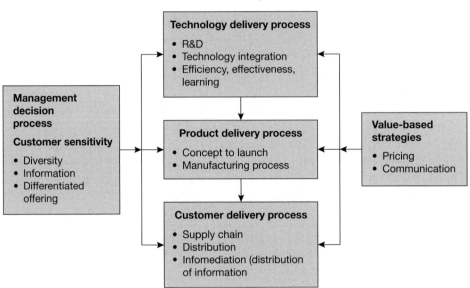

**Figure 15.3** *Value-based strategies*
Source: adapted with some modification from A. Sharma, R. Krishnan, and D. Grewal,
"Value Creation in Markets: a Critical Area of Focus for Business to Business Markets,"
Industrial Marketing Management, 26, 4 (2001), 391–402

The functions of a customer relationship management program can be direct and indirect. Direct functions are profit, volume, and safeguard, whereas indirect functions include innovation, market, scout, and access. The direct functions are the basic requirements of a company that are necessary to survive in the competitive marketplace. The indirect functions, however, can be achieved only through a customer relationship program that convinces the customer to participate in these marketing activities.[9]

The direct function of profitability distinguishes between the profitable customer (who provides the supplier with a positive cash flow) and a high volume customer (who helps the supplier achieve economies of scale). The volume function secures the necessary break-even position of a supplier and enables him/her to operate on a profit-making basis. Finally, the safeguard function improves the cost efficiency of a supplier and helps in obtaining stability and control in sales terms within a dynamic marketplace.

The relationship-based indirect function of innovation allows products and processes to be developed together so that, in turn, the value of the offering to the customer is improved. The market function wins customer support through referrals/recommendations when entering new markets and establishing new commercial relationships. The scout function results in market information gathered by customers and communicated to the supplier earlier than would have been known. Finally, the access function refers to help received from customers' experience and networking when the supplier interacts with authorities and trade associations.

## THE ROLE OF SALESPEOPLE AS RELATIONSHIP BUILDERS AND PROMOTERS

Customer relationship management normally involves a team effort and a multiplicity of tasks in both supplier and customer companies. Research indicates that an effective team in terms of composition, group processes, and organizational context significantly enhances the maximization of the potential of a customer relationship.[10]

Salespeople have always occupied a boundary role position. Nowadays, with the change in business philosophy, salespeople are best positioned to contribute to the exploitation of sales, innovation development, and access market potentials in relationship management. Salespeople can act as relationship promoters by identifying appropriate key decision makers in the buying company, bringing these significant people together, and advancing dialogue and mutual trust. In addition, salespeople can coordinate the cooperation between the customers and their company, encourage the interorganizational learning process, and contribute to constructive resolution of existing conflicts.[11]

Although teams manage customer relationships, and all team members must be to a certain extent relationship promoters, clearly this role belongs to salespeople in the organizations. Salespeople can contribute to the effectiveness of the customer relationship by identifying, negotiating with, and bringing together key decision makers in both companies while at the same time nurturing the relationship by working together with the customer's relationship promoters.

Sharland (2001)[12] proposes that negotiation and relationship building are integral to successful long-term business relationships. Also, the task of negotiating is an integral part of a salesperson's job. After all, it is through negotiations that buyers and sellers achieve improved results and build strong and lasting relationships. However, CRM requires persons other than the salesperson to be involved in the management of a customer relationship; usually it is a team. Customer relationship teams must have a leader in order to maximize the opportunities of a customer relationship.

Since negotiation is important to firms that embark on long-term relationships[13] the salesperson must be the first line individual to be *aligned with the relationship paradigm* (ARP).[14] ARP is defined as an individual's attitude toward a cooperative buyer–seller relationship as a preferred business model. The dimensions of ARP are attitudes toward: (1) cooperation, (2) trust, and (3) interdependence in business relationships. The global salesperson is expected to possess the attitudes that facilitate the conditions for successful management of customer relationships and help instill these values and attitudes in both the company's team and that of the customer.

## MODELS OF CUSTOMER RELATIONSHIP MANAGEMENT

From a global perspective, it can be argued that companies may have a different perspective on customer relationship management. For example, some may be driven by the competitive environment and view CRM as a means of gaining a competitive advantage. Others may perceive CRM to be an opportunity to integrate a stand-alone management information system into one application that manages all data. Still other companies may

**259**

see CRM as an opportunity to interlock themselves in a relationship and interact with another company to minimize the effects of market volatility. Whatever the objectives of companies introducing a CRM strategy, the question is whether CRM models are capable of providing a functional framework that salespeople can use to build strong and lasting relationships.

There is little doubt that the manner in which international salespeople establish and maintain relationships is a sophisticated part of their job. The salesperson who is honest, accountable, and cares about the customer's business adds value to the relationship. Salespeople should recognize that the quality of the partnership they create is at least as important as the product they sell, and to this end, they must adapt to the buying needs of customers whenever possible. A model of relationship selling, which was developed by Evans and Laskin (1994), is illustrated in Figure 15.4. The model clearly distinguishes between three fundamental components: relationship inputs, relationship outcomes, and assessment.

Effective relationship marketing, according to the model, is achieved by implementing strategies aimed at:

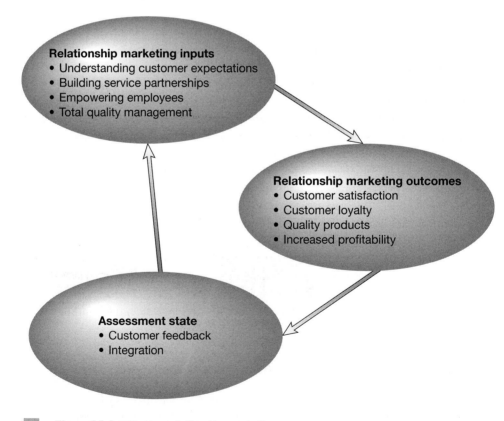

**Figure 15.4** *Effective relationship marketing*
*Source: adapted with some modification from J.R. Evans and R.L. Laskin, "Relationship Marketing can help a Firm escape Commodity-like Status,"* Industrial Marketing Management, *23, 5 (1994), 440–1*

- Understanding customer expectations.
- Building service partnerships with customers.
- Empowering employees to satisfy customer needs by taking initiatives beyond the norms of the company.
- Providing customers with the best overall quality relative to individual need.

These inputs result in a multidimensional output that includes improved customer satisfaction, loyalty, perceptions of firms' product/service quality, and profits. The assessment state incorporates two additional inputs. First, the solicitation of customer feedback by the firm to ensure customer needs are being addressed and, second, the integration of relationship marketing processes into a strategic planning framework.

Smith and Barclay (1999) advanced a more generic model for building effective customer relationships that is based on the following key factors:

- Interdependence.
- Cooperation.
- Mutual trust.

Perceived interdependence is the catalyst that provides both parties with a reason to cooperate and the motivation to reciprocate trust and commitment. Interdependence influences cooperation and relative influence affects mutual trust. Mutual trust, in turn, influences further cooperative attitudes, and cooperation and mutual trust both contribute to the effectiveness of the relationship.

The interplay of the above factors creates *relationship dynamics*. As the relationship develops into a partnership, effectiveness is maximized because both parties share agreed upon objectives and a vision for the future.

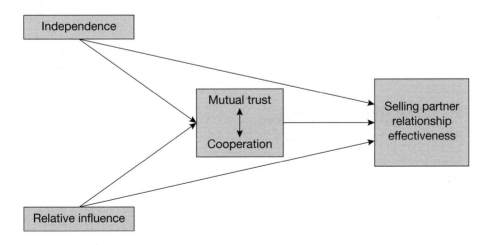

**Figure 15.5** *A model of selling partner relationship effectiveness*
*Source: adapted with some modification from J. Smith Brock and D.W. Barclay, "Selling Partnership: Role of Interdependence and Relative Influence,"* Journal of Personal Selling and Sales Management, *19, 4 (1999), 21–40*

## MANAGING CUSTOMER RELATIONSHIPS

Although the models of customer relationship management delineate the major requirements for effective implementation of a customer relationship management approach, managing a relationship is far more complex and requires exceptional skills on the part of global salespeople. The means by which value is created for customers is through *processes*. Processes, or the way we do things, are dynamic in nature and linked with sets of activities that cut across conventional functions and need to be managed on a cross-functional basis. These processes are the means by which customer value is generated and determined.[15]

For any customer relationship there is an initiating point and a constant effort thereafter to develop and enhance it. The salesperson during the initial and development stages must be involved in the following activities in order to manage the process that is aimed at building trust and commitment with the customer.

Initiating the relationship:

- Engage in strategic prospecting and qualifying.
- Gather and study precall information.
- Identify buying influences.
- Plan the initial sales call.
- Demonstrate an understanding of the customer's needs.
- Identify opportunities to build a relationship.
- Illustrate the value of a relationship with the customer.

Developing the relationship:

- Select an appropriate offering.
- Customize the relationship.
- Link the solutions with the customer's needs.
- Discuss customer concerns.
- Summarize the solution to confirm benefits.
- Secure commitment.

Enhancing the relationship:

- Assess customer satisfaction.
- Take action to ensure satisfaction.
- Maintain open, two-way communication.
- Work to add value and enhance mutual opportunities.[16]

With regard to initiating the relationship, the salesperson has to decide the type of customers to target. The well known "Pareto law" postulates that 80 percent of total sales revenue of a company is generated by 20 percent of its customers. Similarly, 80 percent of the total cost of servicing customers is caused by 20 percent of the customers, but not necessarily the same 20 percent. Therefore, targeting the correct group of potential customers is crucial. In addition, opportunities that exist for creating additional value for potential customers and customer profitability are two key determinants.

Customer profitability requires a change in focus from the profitability of products to the profitability of the customer. After all, it is the customer that generates profits, not the product, and this is what salespersons should focus their attention on at this stage of the sales process. The opportunity for adding value is a critical factor, as it allows the customer and the supplier to recognize the advantages to be gained through a closer relationship and provides an opportunity for the salesperson to develop and enhance the relationship further. When these two critical factors are combined, they result in a 2 × 2 matrix, illustrated in Figure 15.6.

The matrix illustrates that it is appropriate to have disparate types of relationship strategies for different types of customers. Based on a careful assessment of the potential profitability and opportunities for adding value for each customer, the salesperson should have a "healthy" portfolio of customers and expend appropriate efforts depending on the type of customer that s/he is targeting.

Following the identification of opportunities for relationship building with various prospective customers, the salesperson has to work toward developing the relationship. Customizing the relationship by linking the solutions with the customer's needs, and

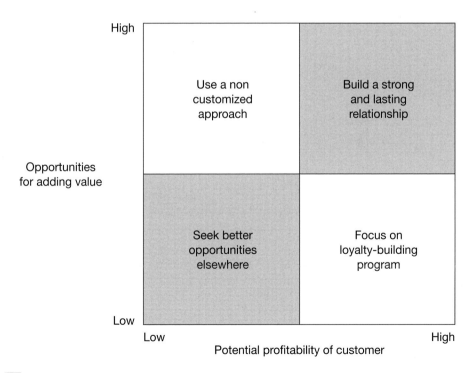

**Figure 15.6** Qualifying prospects for relationship building
Source: adapted with some modification from H. Peck, A. Payne, M. Christopher, and M. Clark, Relationship Marketing: Strategy and Implementation, London: Butterworth Heinemann, 1999, 414

securing commitment, are vitally important tasks. By actively working to create a win–win situation, and opportunities for mutual gain, a cooperative spirit is achieved and the relationship is firmly established.

When an international salesperson manages the relationship s/he should always try to further enhance the relationship. Assessing customer satisfaction, and taking any actions to insure that the customer is satisfied, is of the utmost importance. Satisfaction is the extent to which the benefits received actually meet or exceed the perceived equitable levels of benefits.[17] It has been shown that trust in a business relationship increases with growing satisfaction with the business partner.[18] Maintaining open, two-way communications with the customer provides the salesperson with the opportunity to add value and enhance mutual gain.

In order to effectively implement a CRM strategy, companies must pursue compatible goals and expectations that will not jeopardize the relationship in the long term. To this end, companies need to exchange potentially valuable information about their long-term goals and strategies and make the commitment to invest resources that will benefit both companies.

## THE WAY FORWARD

Wilson, as early as 1990,[19] argued that the way forward is to develop and nurture a long-term and mutually beneficial partnership based on the following three key factors:

- The relationship is built upon shared values. If your client feels that you both share the same ideas and values, it goes a long way toward creating a powerful relationship.
- Everyone needs to clearly understand the purpose of the partnership, and be committed to the vision. Both the salesperson and the customer must agree on what they are trying to accomplish.
- The role of the salesperson must move from selling to supporting. The salesperson in a partnership is actively concerned with the growth, health, and satisfaction of the company to which he or she is selling.

Since then, customer relationship management has reached new heights through the widespread use of the Internet. The Internet offers companies opportunities to gain easier and less expensive access to new customers and new markets, while communicating more effectively with existing customers. For example, sellers and buyers can communicate, on a twenty-four-hour basis, different types of information (e.g., pricing, product specifications, financial arrangements) with different people in the organizations during the selling/buying process and beyond. The Internet provides customers with an opportunity to access various personnel in the selling organization, thus making the relationship richer and more integrated.[20] This type of access function adds to the value creation process.

The Internet, according to Rheault and Sheridan (2002),[21] has intensified the need for change. Customers now have greater control and expect easy online access to information about the company's offerings. This ready access, however, means that customers can bypass the salesperson who once pulled solutions together from a, sometimes, disjointed set of products and services. The salesperson's responsibility is to manage the interface between the company and the customer. The role of the salesperson is critical and requires many skills and competencies to work effectively with a wide range of people within the company and the customer. After all, one of the most fundamental jobs of the salesperson is to create value for both the company and customers.

The current shift of marketing from understanding and satisfying customer needs and wants to understanding and managing customer relationships in a dynamic environment where customers are co-planners and co-creators of value marks the importance of selling as the primary mechanism for relationship building. Building a customer relationship is by definition a future-oriented process and, as a result, customer expectations of future benefits should be a primary focus. Companies need to consider how such expectations can be managed and monitor both current levels of customer satisfaction and customers' anticipated future benefits.[22]

Customer relationship management results in strong economic and social ties between buyer and supplier. The ultimate outcome of a successful CRM strategy is the creation of a unique company asset known as a *relationship network*. A company's relationship network consists of the company and its major customers with whom the company has established long and enduring business relationships. Nowadays, competition is no longer between companies, but between networks. The company with the superior network will be the clear winner and the rationale is rather simple: build an effective network of relationships and profits will follow.[23]

In this new hypercompetitive global business environment the international salesperson focuses on facilitating conditions for a long-term satisfying relationship between the customer and the company. In simple terms, during the last decade global sales positions have been transformed. Some specific aspects of this new transformed position are that salespersons:

- Become the managers of customer value.
- Act as customer advocates, communicating what customers need and value to those inside their company.
- Are an important resource to the policy and strategy makers inside their own company.[24]

The benefits of CRM, which are now firmly established as an effective new business philosophy, are that both customers and suppliers can operate together to identify and capitalize on market opportunities that span national borders. At the individual salesperson level, CRM offers the opportunity to enhance customer loyalty and build a "healthy" and profitable network of relationships.

## CHAPTER SUMMARY

This chapter introduced concepts and issues related to customer relationship management. CRM, as a new business philosophy, offers many advantages. For example, when a firm establishes long-term relationships, the cost of servicing its customers is reduced, customers become loyal, and are more satisfied.

From a supplier's point of view, establishing effective customer relationships requires an understanding of customer needs and wants, commitment and the ability to offer superior value. In addition, suppliers that are honest and trustworthy in their business dealings and adopt a long-term perspective are best qualified to succeed in creating an effective network of relationships with their customers.

The development of a customer relationship follows five steps: the pre-relationship stage, the early stage, the development stage, the long-term stage and the final stage. Each stage is linked with the stages proceding and following it, and a range of functions need to be performed if the relationship is to fully develop. The role of global salespeople in the process is that of both relationship builders and relationship promoters charged with the responsibility to initiate, develop, and enhance the relationship.

Several models of CRM have been developed that capture the dynamics of the process. CRM is a dynamic process and, with the advancement in information technology, parameters may change in the foreseeable future. However, the basic premise of CRM will remain the same. That is, trustworthy, honest, and committed salespeople that are able to offer superior value to their customers in the long-term will turn prospects into customers, customers into loyal customers, and loyal customers into partners. In other words salespersons will find themselves in a win–win situation.

## DISCUSSION QUESTIONS

1   Define CRM and identify and discuss each factor contributing to the development of a business relationship.
2   What does the *dissolution stage* of a relationship refer to and why do companies reach this stage? What can salespeople do, if anything, to prevent a relationship from arriving at this stage?
3   Identify the main activities in the management of the customer relationship process and explain how salespeople acting as relationship promoters can contribute to this process.

## REFERENCES

1   Buttle, F. (2000), "The S.C.O.P.E. of Customer Relationship Management," Manchester Business School, www.crm-forum.com/library/aca/aca-007/aca-007.htm, pp. 1–9.

2   Plakoyiannaki, E., and N. Tzokas (2001), "Customer Relationship Management: A Capabilities Portfolio Perspective," Working Paper, Norwich: School of Management, University of East Anglia.

3   Mittal, B. (1996), "Trust and Relationship Quality: A Conceptual Excursion," in A. Parvatiyar, and J.N. Sheth (eds), *The Contemporary Knowledge of Relationship Marketing*, Atlanta GA: Centre for Relationship Marketing, Emory University.

4   Boles, J. S., H.C. Barksdale, Jr., and J.T. Johnson (1996), "What National Account Decision Makers would tell Salespeople about Building Relationship," *Business and Industrial Marketing*, 11:2, 6–19.

5   Smith Brock, J., and D.W. Barclay (1999), "Selling Partnership: Role of Interdependence and Relative Influence," *Journal of Personal Selling and Sales Management*, 19:4, (fall), 21–40.

6   IMP Group (1982), "An Interaction Approach," in H. Hakansson (ed.) *International Marketing and Purchasing of Industrial Goods*. Chichester: John Wiley & Sons.

7   Ford, D. (1980), *Managing Business Relationships*, London: John Wiley & Sons.

8   Sharma, A., R. Krishnan, and D. Grewal (2001), "Value Creation in Markets: A Critical Area of Focus for Business to Business Markets," *Industrial Marketing Management*, 26:4 (May), 391–402.

9   Walter, A., T. Ritter, and H.G. Gemunden (2001), "Value Creation in Buyer–Seller Relationships: Theoretical Considerations and Empirical Results from a Supplier's Perspective," *Industrial Marketing Management*, special issue: *Customer Value in Business Markets*, 30:4 (May), 365–77.

10  Helfert, G., and K. Vith (1999), "Relationship Marketing Teams: Improving the Utilisation of Customer Relationship Potentials through a High Team Design Quality," *Industrial Marketing Management*, 28, 553–64.

11  Walter, A. (1999), "Relationship Promoters: Driving Forces for Successful Customer Relationships," *Industrial Marketing Management*, 28, 537–51.

12  Sharland, A. (2001), "The Negotiation Process as a Predictor of Relationship Outcomes in International Buyer–Supplier Arrangements," *Industrial Marketing Management*, 30, 551–9.

13  Dwyer, R.F., P.H. Schurr, and S. Oh (1987), "Developing Buyer–Seller Relationships," *Journal of Marketing*, 51 (April), 11–27.

14  Kothandaraman, P., and D. Wilson (2000), "Implementing Relationship Strategy," *Industrial Marketing Management*, 29, 339–49.

15  Peck, H., A. Payne, M. Christopher, and M. Clark (1999), *Relationship Marketing: Strategy and Implementation*, Oxford: Butterworth Heinemann.

16  Ingram, T. (1996), "Relationship Selling: Moving from Rhetoric to Reality," *Mid-American Journal of Business*, 11, 6.

17  Gruen, T. (1995), "The Outcome set of Relationship Marketing in Consumer Market," *International Business Review*, 4:4, 447–69.

18  Ganesan, S. (1994), "Determinants of Long-term Orientation in Buyer–Seller Relationships," *Journal of Marketing*, 58:2, 1–19.

19  Wilson, L. (1990), "Selling in the 90s," audio-cassette, Niles IL: Nightingale Conant, p. 35.

20  Rheault, D., and S. Sheridan (2002), "Reconstruct your Business around Customers," *Journal of Business Strategy*, 23:2 (March/April), 38–43.

21  Rheault and Sheridan (2002).

22  Lemon, K.N., T.B. White, and R.S. Winner (2002), "Dynamic Customer Relationship Management: Incorporating Future Considerations into the Service Retention Decision," *Journal of Marketing*, 66:1 (January), 1–14.

23  Anderson, J.C., H. Hakansson, and J. Johanson (1994), "Dyadic Business Relationships within a Business Network Context," *Journal of Marketing*, 15 (October), 1–15.

24  Wotruba, T.R. (1994), "The Transformation of Industrial Selling: Causes and Consequences," *Industrial Marketing Management*, 25, 327–38.

# Appendix
# Selected Cases

## 1 ASIAN HOTEL GROUP

David Jones, Ph.D., Assistant Professor, William F. Harrah College of Hotel Administration, University of Nevada, Las Vegas. Reprinted with permission.

Arthur Hildebrand was hired as the first vice-president of sales for Asian Hotel Group. Hildebrand and his family moved to Hong Kong and settled in for an extended tour of duty.

*Hotel group background.* Asian Hotel Group, a Malaysian-Chinese corporation registered in Hong Kong, owns twenty-five four and five-star hotels located at various locations in China and Southeast Asia. The group's four regional sales offices are located in Hong Kong, Singapore, Kuala Lumpur, and Tokyo. At each of the twenty-five hotel locations the sales staff numbers approximately ten salespeople, while each regional office is comprised of four sales personnel. The total number of salespersons employed by Asian Hotel Group is about 300. The sales directors are a mixture of local hires and expatriates, while the sales staffs are primarily local hires of Chinese ancestry.

*Issues faced.* Shortly after coming on board, Hildebrand began making plans to implement a standardized sales training program that could be used at each hotel location. However, he soon learned that differences existed among hotel locations. First, in China only local hires were provided with sales training although expatriates needed the training and would sit in the back of the room during training sessions. Second, property locations were autonomous in their decisions to use sales training. As a result, the corporate office was placed in the position of "selling" each location on what they needed to do to behave like a group of hotels. Third, some hotel locations utilized British training companies and trainers, while other hotels preferred North American firms. Fourth, sales training was conducted Western-style, although most trainees were of Asian-Chinese ancestry. The customer in the sales situation might be from a variety of nationalities, since most people

**269**

using the hotel were managers of multinational companies based in the region. A few hotel properties used British trainers located in Asia who understood the market; others employed British or American trainers based in their home countries who traveled to Asia once a year. Fifth, the attitude of the hotel's local management was often "Let's do training, just for training's sake," rather than conducting results-oriented human resource development. This suggested that local sales directors were more concerned about completing a requirement than actually benefiting from sales training. Sixth, in Asia, one concern with utilizing Western trainers is that the Asian salespersons don't want to be perceived as making mistakes in front of their peers (loss of face). So when programs included participative techniques like role playing, they were often ineffective. Finally the sales director, or the person who heads the property level sales force in a hotel, often would not participate in the training. Many times they were expatriates and felt the training was just for the staff. The result was that the sales directors did not know what principles they should enforce and measure after the training was completed. In fact, as far as Hildebrand could ascertain, no hotel location measured the success of their sales training.

After several months of surveying the conditions that existed within the Asian Hotel Group, Hildebrand still wants to formulate a training plan that will provide the sales force with the desired skills, knowledge, and attitudes to perform their jobs. Based upon your knowledge of sales training, what advice would you offer Mr. Hildebrand?

## Questions

1   What type of training program would you design? Should the training be standardized? Why or why not? What type of trainer should be employed?
2   Where should the pilot program be held? Why?
3   What actions might headquarters adopt to gain more control over training at distant hotel locations?
4   Eventually, the hotel group wants to implement a standardized sales training program. What forces might conflict with this corporate sales force goal?

*Note.* In many Southeast Asian countries, citizens of Chinese ancestry control the majority of commerce. For example, in Indonesia, Malaysia, and the Philippines small percentages of citizens with Chinese backgrounds control more than 50 percent of the business enterprises within the country's borders.

# 2 BP FUJIAN: MARKETING LPG IN FUZHOU

Willem Burgers, Philips Electronics Chair Professor of Marketing, and Ms. Maggie Zhu. Copyright © 2001 CEIBS, Shanghai, PRC. Used by permission.

On April 1, 1997, BP Fujian, a joint venture between BP Oil and the Fuzhou Municipal Coal Gas Company, finished construction of its liquid petroleum gas (LPG) filling plant and formally started operations. BP had been successful in Malaysia, where BP owned a very profitable LPG company that generated annual sales volume of 137,000 metric tons and recent profits of around $11.9 million. BP wished the new operation in Fujian to mirror the experience in Malaysia. A senior manager in the BP operation in Malaysia was assigned to China to assume the position of general manager. The GM was able to contribute to the planning and organization – from factory design to daily management – of the new company.

*Product*. LPG is sold in bulk and in different bottle sizes according to customer requirements. Big tanks are used for bulk sales of LPG to the largest customers. All other customers use bottles that come in 4.5 kg, 11.5 kg, 14.5 kg, and 50 kg sizes. The 14.5 kg bottles are the largest seller. BP Fujian's sales volume in 1997 was 90,100 tons for bulk sales and 21,100 tons for bottle sales. Sales volume in 1998 was 110,000 tons in bulk and 16,400 tons in bottles. However, after nearly two years in operation, the plant was running at only about 60 percent capacity.

Although bottle sales represented only a small percentage of total sales, they were considered very important. This is because, according to BP, retailing offers more opportunity to create added value for customers and higher profit margins for the firm. For example, in 1998, bottle sales represented 19 percent of metric ton volume, but 47 percent of gross profit contribution in Fuzhou. In addition, bottle sales offered better growth opportunities, especially considering the low percentage of total sales now.

Still, bottle sales were more difficult to control, since BP relied on dealer distributors. The company's major job in bottle sales involved developing, educating, and managing the dealers, rather than interacting directly with customers. The building of long-term relationships with large and small dealers was perceived as an important cornerstone of selling bottled gas.

*Distribution*. Like in Malaysia, BP Fujian provided free iron bottles for dealers when they paid a deposit of RMB 150. This effort attracted dealers into BP Fujian's distribution system. To achieve results quickly, 50,000 iron bottles were offered to the dealers in 1997. Another 140,000 bottles were provided in 1998.

Besides supplying free bottles, the company tried to ensure superior operating results for the dealers under the philosophy that the dealers were its customers as well as partners, and that BP Fujian could hardly become prosperous with unsuccessful dealers. In mid-1998, for each 14.5 kg bottle of gas sold, BP Fujian allowed the dealer a fixed gross

**271**

profit of RMB 6. This margin added up to a gross profit of around $50 per ton for the dealers, while the company made a gross profit of $49 per ton in 1998.

These policies were successful in attracting new dealers. The company decided to judge applicant dealers on whether they: (1) possessed a business certificate for selling LPG; (2) possessed minimum assets; and (3) were honest in making payments. In reality this policy was seldom followed closely and the number of dealers grew quickly and steadily. Five dealers were recruited in April 1997, increasing to thirteen dealers by the end of 1997, and seventeen by the end of 1998.

These dealers varied in size. Small dealers might serve several dozens of customers and larger dealers supplied over 1,000 families and small businesses. By the end of 1998, the six largest dealers sold about 75 percent of total bottle sales. In addition to sales to end users, a dealer would also supply "subdealers." These subdealers might own a convenient place to sell bottled gas, such as a grocery store or a cooking equipment shop. But the subdealers would lack the business certificate needed to engage in such commerce. The number of subdealers was estimated to be 143 at the end of 1998. However, BP Fujian lost US$4.3 million and US$3.69 million in 1997 and 1998, respectively.

*Problems.* One explanation for poor financial results was the dishonest behavior of dealers, who took advantage of the free BP bottles but sold LPG from other sources. The gas used was a lower quality but cheaper LPG, obtained from unlicensed filling plants. Also dealers underfilled and evaded taxes to obtain higher profits. According to estimates, a dishonest distributor could earn RMB 9 for each bottle of LPG sold, versus RMB 6 for an honest distributor. Therefore it was not surprising that, out of the seventeen dealers recruited by BP Fujian, only two still conducted regular business. The remainder brought much less business than they should and several dealers disappeared completely. As a result, the damage to BP Fujian's reputation was considerable.

*Internal debate.* It is an understatement to say that the management of BP Fujian was not pleased with these developments. Several managers challenged the function of dealers and argued that dealers did more harm than good. As one manager said: "We consider the dealers our customer, but see how treacherous and tricky they are! What can we do to motivate them and bring them back to us? Or what can we do to control them? Almost nothing! The only thing we can do, and definitely we should do, is to get rid of them and sell by ourselves."

But this point of view was not widely accepted in the company. There was a fear that harsh action might do worse damage. Bottles still did bring in sales, even if these sales were far behind what they should have been. As another manager argued: "It's too late to give up the dealers now. It took us more than a year to develop them, and in total they hold 190,000 bottles of ours! If we start to sell by ourselves, they will know that we are going to dump them soon and they will dump us first! If that happens, we will have no bottle sales at all until our own sales system works! Who knows how long that will take and how well the system will go? Attempting direct sales alone is simply too dangerous for us."

Still other managers pointed out: "Dealers allowed us to expand quickly. Without them, there was no way for us to sell over 1.4 million bottles of gas in the first year! As a new business, we needed dealers because they enabled us to expand quickly. We should fix the way we work with them, rather than give up on them."

There were significant difficulties, like the business certificate issue, with setting up a direct selling system. Currently the dealers possessed certificates from counties where they operated, but if the company started direct selling on its own, it would need business certificates for the different counties, where it wished to operate. It would be difficult to obtain certificates in some counties since the local governments there would want to protect the local filling plants which are a source of taxes for them.

## Questions

1    BP had been successful in Malaysia. Should the same system work in China that succeeded in Malaysia? Why or why not?
2    How wise was it to provide free bottles in order to "expand quickly"?
3    BP managers saw dealer actions as being dishonest; what explanation might the Chinese dealers offer in defense?
4    What would happen if BP were to dump the existing distributor dealers?
5    What other alternatives does BP have? What should BP do?

*Note.* This case was prepared to provide material for class discussion and is not intended to illustrate either effective or ineffective handling of a managerial situation. Certain names and key data were changed to protect confidentiality.

## 3 DELL COMPUTER CORPORATION

Antonis Simintiras, University of Wales, Swansea

Michael Dell started his business by custom-building PCs and selling direct to customers via telephone and mail. He priced his PCs lower than comparable computers sold in stores because he built only as needed and ordered, and he did not have to factor in profits for wholesalers and retailers. This strategy enabled Dell to successfully challenge larger, more established rivals like IBM and Compaq. When Dell began selling PCs via the Internet, it was able to reduce costs even more and let customers configure their own PCs by choosing among dozens of features and options. Now Dell Computer Corporation is the leading PC company in the world and it sells as much as $50 million worth of PCs and related products via the web every day.

Dell has been successful in enhancing automated customer relationships by highlighting the importance of customer identification and interaction in a cost-effective manner. For example, the company provides service for its computer equipment at different levels. Larger and more complex installations that must be operational at all times qualify for round-the-clock support and personal service visit, whereas installations that are less

*Case 3 Table*

| Account management phase | Status | Goals | Type of salesperson |
|---|---|---|---|
| Acquisition | Dell has done little or no business with the firm/an identified prospect | ? | Hunter |
| Development | Dell is on client's approved vendor list; client buys at least one Dell product line | ? | Developer |
| Retention | Client buys frequently; uses premier Dell.com to compile reports, track history on online purchases | ? | Developer |

*Sources.* "Web Smart: Michael Dell," *Business Week*, May 14, 2001, p. 52; "Bleak Earnings News Depresses Techs," Reuters, January 18, 2002, news.com.com/2100–1017–818387.html.; "Dell's Support Services Split into Four Tiers", *Computer Weekly*, April 12, 2001, p. 6; Peppers & Rogers Group (2001), "A CRM Blueprint: Maximizing ROI from your Customer-based Strategy', Insight Report, pp. 1–14.

complex or time-sensitive receive telephone service support. Dell has also developed a web-based facility that assists its customers in business information management in addition to a web-based cost-efficient purchasing function. While offering an easier life for employees of their larger customers, such a facility enables the company to have direct communication with its customers.

Dell also differentiates customers depending upon where they are positioned in the account process. The company understands different "vintages" of customers who have different needs and require different approaches. It is also understood by the company that there are those salespeople who are better at obtaining new customers than managing existing ones. On that basis salespeople are either "hunters" or "developers." Using the table, provide a description of the goals that each type of salesperson has to accomplish.

## 4 THE EUROPEAN TRAIN(ING) WRECK!

Lew Kurtzman, President, Growth Resources Associates, Wilmington NC. Printed by permission.

Two successful laboratory equipment companies merged, creating the need for reorganization and a new corporate culture. Senior management of the newly merged divisions convened frequently to decide how to transition from two mid-size companies into a united corporate worldwide powerhouse.

One plan was to bring people from both divisions together for training sessions that stressed teamwork and corporate citizenship. Since each division had its own sales force, it was the decision of senior management to begin the sessions in the United States with training workshops that emphasized how each sales team could complement the other: sharing mail lists, making joint sales calls, and providing account information to each other. Twenty-five sales reps from different areas were selected to participate in each respective session. Eleven sessions were conducted in the United States with rave reviews from the attendees. For the most part the workshops were upbeat and reported to be effective.

The next mission was training the European subsidiaries to become a united force against the mounting competition in each country. The European director of human resources was assigned to organize the training sessions along with the newly appointed corporate director of worldwide sales training. The directive from senior management was to conduct the workshops *exactly* as they had been done in the United States.

This presented an extraordinary challenge. The European subsidiaries of both divisions had been autonomous, each headed by a managing director. They were accustomed to doing business their own way. Many of the subsidiary offices were located in distant cities within a single country. Little or no contact had been made among managing directors or sales reps of the two companies prior to the merger.

The European HR director selected Barcelona as the venue for all four workshops. All were to be conducted within a two-week time period as sales reps from different countries and different divisions would be brought together for two and one half days for their respective doses of corporate "sales education."

Representatives from France, the United Kingdom, the Netherlands, Germany, Belgium, Switzerland, Italy, and Sweden were in attendance for the first session. It began with introductions of all attendees. There was light-hearted cultural stereotyping and humorous comments were made by many of the reps as they followed one another in a prearranged seating order at a horseshoe-shaped table. Name tents were carefully placed so that no two countrymen sat together. For the most part, all attendees spoke English reasonably well.

Following the introductions, the HR director handed the meeting over to the director of worldwide sales training. He was a veteran sales trainer in the United States, highly respected by senior management of both divisions for his enthusiasm and his leadership during the US training sessions.

Following the morning break the three French reps returned to the training room earlier than the others and sat down together. They had even moved their name tents, two of them trading places with a German and a Dutch representative. As the others took their seats, there was some confusion as to where some should sit. The training director returned to the room to find many of the name tents switched and the seating arrangement organized more or less according to language orientation. Not risking discord, he let the matter rest. Upon her return, the HR director sternly ordered everyone back to their original seats, causing a chaotic few moments of name tent exchanges and chattering in as many as four or five languages.

When organization was restored, the training director tried to stimulate discussion about the benefits of shared resources. Much to his dismay, the group seemed annoyed by the parental treatment they had just received. One of the Dutch reps uttered, "Dat is stom" (This is silly). Participation became limited to a few reps who spoke perfect English; those from the United Kingdom, two Swedes and a German. As the session continued, even their participation waned. By lunchtime, several of the attendees were drawing doodles. One of the French reps had been drawing clever cartoons depicting an American car salesman with a rat's head. The salesman was named "Billy Jones, le vendeur raton." Every so often he would hold up a new cartoon for the group's entertainment.

Lunchtime in Spain is later than in most countries. By 1:30 p.m. most of the members of the group were suffering from hunger pangs. The two-hour lunch break didn't help, as most of the reps dozed off in their seats during the afternoon session. The lack of attention and participation caused a struggle for the American facilitator, who tried gallantly to interject some humor. American humor is not always funny to people of other cultures, and in this case drew little more than polite chuckles.

Late night dinners in Barcelona resulted in an hour delay on day two due to oversleeping and severe hangovers. When the session finally began, shortly after 10:00 a.m., the training director was so frustrated that he could hardly perform. His attempts to control the group were frequently interrupted by wisecracks whispered in several languages.

During the morning break, the American training director phoned back to the president of the company to explain the situation and ask for a dignified way out of his tortuous situation. The president expressed little understanding and ordered that the session be completed, and that the program continue with three more workshops. Earlier the HR director had reported that the session was progressing well.

Upon hearing about the first workshop, several of the European managing directors refused to send their sales personnel to the remaining sessions.

## Questions

1   What assumptions did senior management make about the European sales organizations?
2   What was the primary objective of the training as viewed by: (1) upper management, (2) the European HR director, and (3) the training director?
3   When planning an international sales training session, list three key factors to consider prior to implementation.
4   What were some of the likely consequences of the European sales training sessions?

# 5 MOTIVATION AND TURNOVER: THE CASE OF A SOUTHERN EUROPEAN SALESPERSON

Antonis Simintiras, University of Wales, Swansea

The company had been experiencing two decades of success by selling a range of well-branded alcoholic drinks in the southern European Union. The sales force consisted of thirty-five salespeople. Every day, each salesperson, accompanied by a driver and helper in a truck, was visiting several customers. Salespeople were responsible for checking the stock of their customers, selling the entire range of products, opening new accounts and clearing "accounts receivable". After the placement of an order by a customer, the salesperson asked the helper to unload the requested quantities from the truck. All customers were benefiting from a one-month credit term. The competitors were offering the minimum of three and up to six months' credit.

One customer had accumulated a debt to the company of around €25,000 and was refusing to clear it in the last twelve months. This customer was allocated to a newly hired salesperson. Prior to visiting this customer, the sales manager informed the new salesperson to try to collect some money from him but not leave any products unless the customer was prepared to pay cash. The salesperson heard very carefully the words of his manager. When he visited this customer the following conversation took place.

*Salesperson*. Good morning. My name is Jose and I am the new sales rep for this area. I do visit all our customers and make myself known. Is there anything I can do for you? Do you need anything from us today?

*Customer*. Thanks for calling in. Yes, I do need some products [and he went on listing the products and specifying the quantities he wanted].

*Salesperson*. [ordering his helper to unload the products that the customer had requested]. How do you want to pay?

*Customer*. By credit. You come and collect the money after a month.

*Salesperson*. That's fine.

The salesperson agreed to leave the products on credit terms despite the different instructions he had received from his sales manager. When the salesperson, driver, and helper were ready to leave the customer asked the salesperson a question.

*Customer*. Did you not receive any instruction from your company as to how to handle this account?

*Salesperson*. Yes, I did.

[really puzzled]

*Customer*. Why did you not then follow your manager's instructions?

*Salesperson*. Don't worry. I think I did the right thing. Even if I lose my job it will be for a good reason. I trust all my customers. So I trust you, and I am one hundred percent sure that you will not let me down. Bye for now. I'll see you later.

When Jose arrived back in the office and told his manager what he had done, the manager was furious. The manager told him that he was not prepared to work with him and reported this to the general manager. The salesperson was totally disappointed, not so much at his manager's reaction as that he had not wanted to hear the reasons for his actions. Ten minutes later he was asked to go and see the general manager. Apparently the general manager was interested in hearing the reasons.

*Salesperson*. All my predecessors were allowed to build such debt in the hope of changing this customer. I thought I should take my chance as well. I'll never do it again but I bet this one will soon be one of our most valuable customers.

*General manager*. That's a good approach. Well done. Let's see what happens.

The sales manager never approved Jose's action, even when the customer went the way Jose had predicted. The antagonism between sales manager and salesperson following this forced Jose to eventually leave the company.

## Questions

1  What did the sales manager do wrong? Why?
2  How should the manager have handled this case after it happened?
3  What theories of motivation can be used to explain the behavior of the salesperson and his manager?

# 6 SELLING A LUXURY DESTINATION IN TURBULENT TIMES: THE MOUNT JULIET ESTATE

Susi Geiger, Smurfit Business School, University College Dublin. Reprinted by permission.

Mount Juliet is one of Ireland's premier golf and sporting estate hotels. An award-winning five-star property, it caters both to the leisure as well as to the conference and incentive markets, boasting diverse luxury accommodation, conference facilities, 1,500 acres of woodland, a championship golf course, a recently developed spa, fishing, horse riding, tennis, clay shooting and archery. The task of the nine-person sales and marketing team is to sell the property and its facilities to the local Irish market as well as to European and overseas business and leisure travelers. Sales team responsibilities are mainly structured in terms of sales territories: the local Irish market, the UK market, the European market, and the North American market.

*The issues.* The sales team at Mount Juliet has been working hard to overcome the crisis that befell the Irish tourism industry in 2001 with the foot-and-mouth crisis in the United Kingdom and the attacks of September 11 later that year. The national tourism board and industry representatives report that tourism figures for the whole of Ireland are down approximately 7 per cent from 2000 to 2001 and could decrease further by as much as 20 per cent in 2002. The number of US travellers in particular has dropped to its lowest level since 1996. As international companies postponed or canceled conferences and incentive travel estates like Mount Juliet, which draws up to 70 per cent of its clientele from this market sector during the winter season, have faced declining occupancy rates in both corporate and leisure markets. Industry experts predict that it will take up to three years for the Irish tourism industry as a whole to recover from the 2001 events. Many luxury hotels in Ireland and the United Kingdom reacted to the decline in occupancy rates with price discounts; however, the management at Mount Juliet decided to uphold their premium pricing strategy. Instead, they determined to intensify sales efforts, particularly with existing corporate clients, realizing that just as in so many other operations, 80 per cent of their turnover was provided by 20 per cent of their clients.

While struggling to fill the hotel's accommodation and conference facilities, the sales team at Mount Juliet received unexpected help from the outside. In March 2002 the estate signed a management agreement with the Conrad Hotel Group. The Conrad group represents the luxury end of the Hilton family of brands and with Mount Juliet added its fourteenth property to its portfolio of city and resort hotels. Through the Hilton reservation system this management agreement opens up a worldwide network of sales offices, Internet, and telesales facilities to the sales team at Mount Juliet Conrad.

## Questions

1 As the sales director of Mount Juliet estate, how would you employ the principles of relationship selling to boost sales among existing clients in the face of a tourism and conference travel crisis?

2 Until now the sales team at Mount Juliet has mostly relied on personal selling approaches to sell the hotel into the corporate market. With the new Hilton reservation facilities, it now also has the possibility to be marketed as one of more than 2,000 properties under the Hilton brand umbrella. How would you incorporate this new facility into your existing sales strategy?

3 Given the new worldwide sales resources available to the team, would you suggest a restructuring of responsibilities within the sales team to take account of the new reality?

*Sources.* www.mountjuliet.com, www.ireland.com, www.conradhotels.com.

# 7 RELATIONSHIP MARKETING IN THE NEW ZEALAND WINE INDUSTRY

Michael Beverland, Monash University. Printed by permission.

The New Zealand wine industry has become increasingly complex and competitive in the last fifteen years. In 1991 large supermarkets began legally selling wine and over the past decade competition has also increased. That is, in 1990 there were 100 wineries but by 2002 there were 390. Babich Wines, an old established medium-size family firm, had just hired some new sales staff and was putting them through an induction program, run by its sales manager, Joe Babich.

"Welcome to Babich wines," stated Joe. "As many of you are new to the wine industry, let me describe the changes that have occurred in the last decade. Ten years ago we faced fewer competitors, and enjoyed a period of increasing demand for our wines. During that time, a sales force was unnecessary – we simply sat by the phone and took orders. This success encouraged more entrants into the market, and now we face a highly competitive marketplace, with large local and overseas competitors and powerful buyers. In response to increasing competition, Babich Wines focused on price discounting and sales promotions to larger stores. With our smaller customers we had more leverage, and gained higher margins at less cost."

"Why not deal with them, then? Large chains and supermarkets sound too much like hard work," remarked John (a new employee).

"It is not that simple," said Joe. "Firstly, the market is smaller. Remember that supermarkets control over 50 percent of total sales. Secondly, in small store, we compete against highly focused niche players, and customers have enormous choice. Lastly, small stores have got smart and formed themselves into larger purchasing groups in order to gain greater discounts and counter the power of sellers. For a firm of our size, we cannot afford to give these discounts, nor undertake the level of promotion that large buyers demand."

"Well what do we do then?" asked Caroline (another new employee). "It seems that we either get bigger as a company, which you have stated is not an option, or we have to do something different. I'm not sure how the sales force fits into all this, as many of our traditional tools obviously will not work."

"That's not quite true, Caroline. Tried and true sales tactics have a place in today's market, but you're right, you will need to sell differently. You need to focus on building long-term relationships at many levels."

"That is quite easy: as a salesperson I'm used to building relationships with the people I sell to. They know me by name, we have often had a few beers after hours, and I count some of my customers as personal friends," said Richard.

"Yes," said Joe, "that's true, but again, building relationships in this market is a little different. You have to deal with customers at many levels. For example, most purchase decisions are made at the head office by a very knowledgeable liquor buyer. They won't be impressed by traditional sales talk, and have to consider what is best for the group overall. They are unlikely to be interested in being friends, and they will want to see how you will support your product, and help them sell it. You need to sell to them, and form a professional relationship. We can support you in that, and form teams when dealing with these buyers. Peter, the CEO, will usually initiate a relationship, as it shows the buyer how seriously we take the relationship. But then you need to deal with the local store managers, as they are the ones who make decisions about shelf space, pricing, and promotions. If we don't form relationships at that level, we will lose shelf space to our competitors, and have our wines used as loss leaders. So we need to get into the stores, stack shelves, do tastings, and work closely with the managers. We also need to train the sales staff in the stores, as they are very influential on customers."

"But how do we build relationships?" asked Amelia. "It's not an easy thing to do, and not all customers want a relationship, and some customers may say they want greater intimacy, but when it comes to the crunch, price is still the issue."

"The customer's personality is the key to whether they will want a closer relationship," said Joe.

"That's true," said Caroline, "and also, your biggest customer may require little by way of communication, while your smallest customer is often the one who rings once a week. Not all customers deserve a relationship!"

"That's where we can help," said Joe. "First, you need to act professionally, and find out how relationship-oriented each customer is. In my experience, some just want the wine, nothing more. Others are more open, and are happy when you turn up and discuss things with them, while others demand that you make an appointment. None of this is new to you. However, there are many subtle ways of forming, and maintaining relationships. Then, if a customer wants a relationship, you will have to see yourself as a partner in their business. Often, the customer needs help on how to sell your product, how to put it on the market, how to generate sales. This helps build a relationship, as well as loyalty, as the buyer views you as an asset."

"But why would customers want a relationship?" said John. "I am still having difficulty with this idea, as, in my experience, performance is key. People may not like you, but they will buy your product if it is good."

"That's true in New Zealand," stated Joe. "But, remember, it is a competitive market out there, and there are many cowboys. Basically, intimacy is a security thing. You build a strong relationship with somebody and that builds trust and certainty. The customer knows that you're not going to put one over him. He knows he can rely on you to supply the product to him at a good price. You actually have to become his friend."

"We're back to being friends again," stated Richard.

"That's right," said Joe, "and we'll get to what you can do to support that friendship later. Also, remember, many of the buyers are not wine experts, and some are very young. Technical wine talk and a strong sales pitch may put them off. Building a relationship will require you to listen, and therefore drop a lot of the traditional sales pitch and just make people feel welcome. This will enable you to understand where the customer is coming from. I remember a few years ago we had a problem with a new customer and one of our young sales reps. We sent the CEO in to meet the customer. The customer was a new wine buyer for a large supermarket chain. This was when supermarkets had just started selling wine. The customer always seemed very defensive, and it turned out that he didn't know much about the wine trade. We invited him out for lunch at our premises and just talked to him. We found out that he liked Rugby League, so we talked to him about that. After that there was no problem, he relaxed and we understood that he was nervous about a new position. It enabled us to move from a $20,000 per year account to a $150,000 account."

"That's great!" exclaimed Caroline, "but what else do we have to do, and how will you support us?"

"That's a good question," said Joe, "and it is why we do things a little differently. You need to build multiple relationships, between the company and the buyer. An account involves many aspects of the company, beyond what you can do for the buyer. I often entertain our clients in here; introduce them to everybody, as it's all the people in the company that will keep his business, not just me. People will always move on, so you need to build the commitment between the companies. Finally, you must constantly and regularly visit your customers. I know it sounds complicated, but remember: listen to your customers, and meet their needs. We will support you with all the material you need, as you are the people who will sell the company, its philosophy and message. You will also help us create new opportunities."

## Questions

1   What evolution had Babich Wineries taken regarding its marketing strategy over the past decade? Why is it now advocating relationship marketing?

2   In this case, large chains and supermarkets were more difficult to please. What might explain this perception? Then why pursue business with such organizations?

3   Salespersons have traditionally formed relations with their customers. Is this the same as relationship marketing? How are the situations similar and different?

4    How are relationships formed with customers? Do all customers warrant a
     relationship? Why or why not?
5    What type of role does the selling organization play in relationship marketing? What
     is the salesperson's role?

# 8 PACIFICO SOFTWARE

Earl D. Honeycutt, Elon University, Elon NC

John Aquino recently accepted the sales management position at Pacifico Software, and he began traveling with his sales force to learn about their performance and relationships with customers. In general, Aquino was satisfied with the quality of his six-person sales force, but during sales calls, he observed some behavior that concerned him:

- While traveling with Lawrence, a sales veteran of twenty years, Aquino observed Lawrence on two separate occasions overpromising customers. One customer told Lawrence that he would order a new software system if it could be installed and training completed within three weeks. When Aquino asked why he had agreed to this customer request when it would take a minimum of thirty to forty-five days, Lawrence said he would simply call the customer and explain that an unavoidable delay had occurred.
- A second salesperson, Adriana, had been with the firm for less than a year. On numerous visits it was obvious that Adriana did not possess adequate product knowledge. That is, she did not understand which product to recommend for specific situations. Worse, she gave incorrect or incomplete answers to client questions.
- When auditing travel expense reports, Aquino saw examples of questionable expenditures charged by sales representatives. It was Pacifico's policy to reimburse all "legitimate" expenses.

Based upon his observations, Aquino decided he must either establish and/or clarify certain sales policies. However, he knew that his actions would have to be logical and fair so that sales force morale would not be adversely impacted.

## Questions

1   How should Aquino correct Lawrence's behavior? How does such behavior impact the firm's relationship approach to customers?
2   What type of action will help Adriana improve her product knowledge? What other options are available to Pacifico?
3   Why are sales expenses important to monitor and control? What is the best way to communicate with the sales force about sales expenses?
4   Combined, do these three areas of concern point to serious sales force problems?

# 9 SMITH AND NEPHEW AND INNOVEX

Lluis G. Renart, University of Navarra, Barcelona. Copyright IESE and reprinted by permission.

At the beginning of March 2000, James Brown, CEO of Smith and Nephew (S&N), met with Joseph Serra, director of the medical division. Six months earlier they had signed an agency contract with Innovex whereby Innovex employees would promote S&N's moist wound healing (MWH) products in Galicia and Asturias. It was the first time S&N had used the services of a contract sales force in Spain.

As soon as the contract was signed, and with S&N's approval, Innovex selected two sales representatives:

- Isabel, the person selected for Galicia, already had experience of medical sales visits. The S&N products she would promote were known and used in the region, thanks to the hospital work done by Arturo, the local representative. This meant that Isabel would have local support.
- The person chosen for Asturias, Federico, had little experience but the right profile and plenty of enthusiasm. Asturias had been neglected during the previous two years following the death of S&N's sales representative, who had not been replaced. The products Federico would have to promote were practically unknown in the region.

Both Innovex sales representatives were given two weeks' training. In the first week they had three days' instruction on the products they would promote (given by S&N), and one day on sales techniques (given by Innovex). The second week was devoted to on-the-job training, supervised by an S&N regional sales manager. Both the sales representatives took about three months to adapt to the normal pace of work.

*Evaluation of the results.* At the end of February 2000 the director, sales manager, and marketing manager of S&N's medical division analyzed the data available at the time. The average amount billed by Innovex to S&N had been pta 810,000 per sales representative per month. Everyone agreed that the results were significantly different in the two areas.

- *In Galicia (Isabel).* According to the October–December report, the market share of MWH product sold for Galicia had increased from 3.3 percent to 6.4 percent of the total value. In Orense and Pontevedra, where the products were heavily promoted, the increase had gone from 5.5 percent to 12 percent.
- The additional sales revenue, on top of the revenue obtained previously in the region, amounted to pta (pasettas) 5,133,000 in four months (October 1999–January 2000 inclusive) and the gross margin had been pta 1,540,000, i.e. 30 percent on average.

■ *In Asturias (Federico)*. The market share of the products in the last quarter of 1999 had increased from 0.9 percent to 2.36 percent of total sales for all MWH products sold in Asturias. The additional sales revenue amounted to about pta 1,484,000 in four months (October 1999–January 2000), with a gross margin of pta 371,000 (25 percent).

The explanations for the difference in gross margin were mixed. First, Federico had sold more products at lower gross margins. S&N's sales representatives were unaware of the gross margin of the products they sold, and only through marketing action were they encouraged to sell higher gross margin products. Second, the difference in gross margin between Galicia and Asturias could be attributed to chance factors. Finally, the regional sales manager felt that Federico would have to improve his sales techniques, in particular his closing abilities.

*Sales projection.* In view of these results, the medical division's marketing manager estimated that, if new Innovex sales representatives were introduced in other geographical areas, each could generate roughly the following sales:

| Month | Pta/month |
|---|---|
| 1 | 450,000 |
| 2 | 900,000 |
| 3 | 1,650,000 |
| 4 | 2,250,000 |
| 5 | 2,700,000 |
| 6 onward | 3,000,000 |

Assuming a gross margin of 30 percent, with average costs remaining at pta 810,000 per representative per month, breakeven for the representative would occur in the fifth month (2,700,000 × 30% = pta 810,000 of gross margin). If sales and margin forecasts are accurate, after month 6 the company would generate new gross income of pta 90,000 per month (gross margin less the amount billed by Innovex).

*The decision.* Given the results of the trial, Brown and Serra considered a set of alternatives deriving from combinations of three variables:

■ To use salaried representatives or contract sales representatives employed by Innovex.
■ Level of geographical coverage.
■ Timing: when would be the best moment to do one thing or another?

Without being exhaustive, the three variables were combined to generate the following potential courses of action:

- Terminate the contract with Innovex and leave Galicia and Asturias as before, i.e. with a single representative, Arturo, visiting hospitals.
- Renew the contract with Innovex for another six months for Galicia and Asturias, in order to extend the trial, obtain more reliable data on sales trends, and verify whether sales and financial performance could be consolidated.
- Terminate the contract with Innovex and immediately hire: (1) one salaried sales representative for Galicia, (2) two salaried sales representatives for Galicia and Asturias, (3) two or three salaried sales representatives for Galicia and one for Asturias.
- Sign a new agreement with Innovex to establish contract sales representatives in all or some regions currently lacking coverage: Valencia (two or three representatives) and Andalusia (two or three representatives). The contract could be for six months or one year. Following that, introduce own salaried sales representatives in all or some regions, depending upon the level of sales and profitability attained.
- Hire a specific number of direct salaried sales representatives for those same underserved regions.

Finally, if new salaried sales representatives were hired, it would have to be decided whether the representatives would work in tandem, as Isabel and Arturo had in Galicia, or whether it would be better to divide up the territory and have each representative visit both hospitals and primary care centers in the assigned territory. Obviously, for each option the costs and benefits, both financial and in terms of sales and marketing strategy, would have to be weighed.

CEO James Brown was beginning to get excited at the strategic possibilities that would open up if a sales team was fully deployed throughout Spain. However, he needed to insure that the S&N group's Spanish subsidiary earned a profit, as he personally desired and as the company's year 2000 budget demanded.

## Questions

1  Were the two territories equal in their potential? Why or why not?
2  What are the advantages and disadvantages of allowing Innovex to represent S&N's MWH products?
3  What might be one reason Isabel appeared to perform at a higher level?
4  Was the training program adequate? Why or why not?

5   Should sales representatives know the profit margin of each product line?

6   Do you agree with the projected sales levels presented by the marketing manager?

7   What course of action would you recommend S&N to take?

*Note.* The case is a condensed version of a longer case and is written as a basis for class discussion and is not intended to illustrate either effective or ineffective handling of administrative situations.

# 10 WRT

Earl D. Honeycutt, Elon University, Elon NC

---

Fred Johnson is the Asian sales manager for WRT, a large US conglomerate that manufactures electronic components for the worldwide marketplace. In his capacity, he travels to Asia approximately one month each three months. Normally the trips rotate between East Asia – Japan, Korea, and China – and Southeast Asia: Malaysia, Vietnam, and the Philippines. Although Johnson enjoys his job, three situations are seriously distracting his efforts:

- *Sales support*. While he is away, the sales support staff continues to respond to customer requests and problems. Fred Johnson is highly satisfied with the level of service provided, but several customer support representatives make inappropriate remarks after his return. A few imply that a month-long sales trip is a vacation from the "real work" conducted at the office. Likewise, sales support appears to perceive that Johnson's expense account and entertainment of clients are benefits of the job.
- *His wife*. Andrea Johnson, Fred's wife of ten years, is not pleased with his month-long sales trips. Andrea works as an attorney and also cares for their two small children. Fred's absence places a strain on their relationship that is felt just before, and for several weeks after, business trips.
- *Customers*. A number of Asian customers are very important to WRT and this necessitates spending long evenings entertaining and being entertained. Although he knows that entertaining helps build relationships, Fred has encountered several ethical dilemmas. First, in East Asia, women are normally present at events to serve and entertain. On several occasions, his hosts have stated that these women are available for "private entertainment." Second, in certain Southeast Asian locations, customers appear to expect the services of "hospitality" women at the end of the evening. To date, Fred Johnson has politely refused all customer offers and requests. However, he wonders how his behavior has influenced his relationships with customers.

Fred Johnson has just returned from a four-week trip, and a five-week business excursion is scheduled in about sixty days. What actions would you recommend that Fred take in the interim to address these three areas?

## Questions

1 Why might customer support personnel make such comments? How informed or knowledgeable is customer support of sales manager duties? Of overseas markets and cultures?

2 Does Andrea Johnson have a legitimate right to her feelings? How might this situation be minimized? Will it ever be eliminated?

3 How should Fred respond to entertainment requests and offers? Is this behavior culturally influenced?

4 Are these three areas direct or indirect job stressors? How important are they?

# Index